British Battlecruisers
1905-1920

BRITISH BATTLECRUISERS
1905–1920

JOHN ROBERTS

Frontispiece: *Inflexible* sails from Malta on 27 March 1913. (R Ellis)

Acknowledgements

The author's thanks are due to D K Brown RCNC, Ray Burt, John Brooks, Guy Robbins and the staffs of the National Maritime Museum, London and the Public Record Office for their invaluable assistance. My gratitude is also due to my wife Jean for her infinite patience, encouragement and very real help during the preparation of this work.

Copyright © John Roberts 1997 & 2016

First published in Great Britain in 1997 by Chatham Publishing.

This revised edition first published in Great Britain in 2016 by
Seaforth Publishing,
An imprint of Pen & Sword Books Ltd,
47 Church Street,
Barnsley
South Yorkshire S70 2AS

www.seaforthpublishing.com
Email: info@seaforthpublishing.com

British Library Cataloguing in Publication Data
A catalogue record for this book is available from the British Library

ISBN 978 1 4738 8235 5

All rights reserved. No part of this publication may be reproduced or transmitted in any form or by any means, electronic or mechanical, including photocopying, recording, or any information storage and retrieval system, without either prior permission in writing from the publisher or a licence permitting restricted copying. The right of John Roberts to be identified as the author of this work has been asserted by him in accordance with the Copyright, Designs and Patents Act 1988.

Designed by typeset by Neil Sayer

Printed and bound by 1010 Printing International Ltd

Contents

Preface to New Edition	6
Abbreviations	6
Introduction	7
Origins	10
Design and Construction 1905–14	24
Battlecruiser Revival	46
ORIGINAL PLANS IN COLOUR *between 64 and 65*	
Machinery	65
Perspective drawings	80
Armament	82
Armour	100
Conclusion	114
Summary of Service	122
Sources	124
Notes	125
Index	127
Folding plans of HMS Queen Mary 1913	Inside back cover

Preface to New Edition

The reprint of this book has provided the opportunity to update some of its content and correct a few errors in the original. The updates are primarily the result of further research that serves to expand and alter parts of the original text. Much of this has caused me to modify my opinion on some aspects of battlecruiser development, especially in relation to the German influence on the post-Jutland evolution of fire control in the Royal Navy. The more important changes are contained in the Armament and Armour chapters, especially those relating to fire control and APC shell. I have also expanded my views on the Battlecruiser concept at the end of the Conclusion chapter, which I hope will clarify the point I was originally trying to make in regard to the quality of design as opposed to the value of a concept.

John Roberts, March 2016.

Abbreviations

AA. Anti-aircraft
ADNC. Assistant Director of Naval Construction (this was not a singular post)
AEW. Admiralty Experiment Works
AP. Armour piercing (shell)
APC. Armour piercing capped (shell)
ATB. Anti-torpedo-boat (guns)

BCS. Battlecruiser Squadron
BL. Breech loading
BM. Board Margin

c. circa
cal. calibre
C-in-C. Commander-in-Chief
C and M. Care and Maintenance
CP. Common pointed (shell)
CPC. Common pointed capped (shell)
crh. calibre radius head
CS. Cruiser Squadron
CT. Conning tower

DNC. Director of Naval Construction
DNI. Director of Naval Intelligence

DNO. Director of Naval Ordnance

efc. equivalent full charge
E-in-C. Engineer-in-Chief

fps. feet per second

GCT. Gun control tower

HA. High angle
HE. High explosive
HP. High pressure
HT. High tensile (steel)

ihp. indicated horse power

KC. Krupp Cemented (armour)
KNC. Krupp Non-Cemented (armour)

LCS. Light Cruiser Squadron
LP. Low pressure

LWL. Load water line

MPI. Mean Point of Impact.

MS. Mild Steel

NS. Nickel steel

pdr. pounder (gun)

QF. quick-firing

RMA. Royal Marine Artillery
RMLI. Royal Marine Light Infantry
rpg. rounds per gun
rpm. revolutions per minute

shp. shaft horse power
SW. Steel wire (hawsers)

TS. Transmitting station
TT. Torpedo tube(s)

WO. Warrant Officer
W/T. Wireless transmitter

Introduction

Between 1900 and 1914 the Royal Navy underwent a rapid revolutionary change as a result of a combination of major technical developments and the arrival at a senior level of officers who were ready and willing to use these developments to maintain Britain's position as the world's leading naval power. These changes effectively resulted in the total replacement of the frontline ships of the fleet with vessels that were larger, more powerful and, in what was expected to be the conditions of a modern naval war, more capable. This was, however, undertaken without direct experience of such a war and to a large extent the success or otherwise of the fleet depended on the accuracy of the decisions and assumptions made by these officers. Foremost among their number was Admiral Sir John Fisher, First Sea Lord 1904–11, who initiated what was to become known as the Dreadnought Revolution – the introduction of the fast, all-big-gun battleship, driven by turbine machinery. On the material side this should have been Fisher's greatest achievement but he was inclined to believe that the day of the battleship was over because they were too vulnerable to the torpedo and mine. He saw the future in the development of torpedo craft, particularly the submarine, and the armoured cruiser, but his writings on this subject are confused. The obvious conclusion to draw from Fisher's statements is that he considered that torpedo craft and mines would take care of naval operations in European waters while the armoured cruiser would secure the deep ocean against commerce raiders. He did not, however, make as clear a statement as this and also indicated that the armoured cruiser could replace the battleship in fleet operations, without explaining why such a vessel was not equally at risk from the mine and torpedo. The Royal Navy's attachment to the battleship was, however, too strong for even Fisher to break and he accepted, sometimes with little grace, that the construction of these vessels would have to continue. The armoured cruiser, with the provision of the same all-big-gun armament of the battleship, became the battlecruiser and was integrated with the dreadnought fleet to serve as a scouting force and as a fast wing for the battle squadrons. However, Fisher continued to maintain that the battlecruiser was the capital ship of the future because he considered its high speed would be the key to success in a naval war.

The construction of the battlecruisers was somewhat patchy, for reasons that will become clear later, and they fall into a number of basic sub-groups. The pre-war ships divide neatly between those armed with 12in guns and those armed with 13.5in guns, the former representing the direct armoured cruiser derivatives while the latter moved closer to the designation of fast battleships. The first group consisted of two classes – the *Invincible* class *(Invincible, Inflexible* and *Indomitable)* and the *Indefatigable* class *(Indefatigable, Australia* and *New Zealand)*. The second group of four ships – *Lion, Princess Royal, Queen Mary* and *Tiger* – were of clearly related design but only the first two were direct sisters. The design of the last two ships of the first group overlapped that of the first ships of the second group and

The first battlecruiser, *Indomitable*, shortly after completion in 1908. (MoD)

this parallel construction of both the new and old types is one of the peculiarities of the pre-war construction programmes. The battlecruisers constructed during the war show a much more diverse pattern and are actually distinguished entirely by the class they belonged to. The first two, *Renown* and *Repulse*, were effectively a repetition of the original battlecruiser concept of 1905, while the next three, the large light cruisers of the *Courageous* type, are so unusual as to defy attempts at classification. The last battlecruiser of this era, *Hood*, moved the entire concept forward into the fast battleship class and, being the only vessel of the type entirely free of Fisher's influence, gives a good indication of the expectations of the other officers involved in the final development of the type – in particular Admiral Jellicoe.

The battlecruiser type was the subject of considerable controversy prior to the First World War when many saw them as very expensive vessels which could carry out no obvious function that a more conventional cruiser type could not fulfil. Nevertheless, they caught the public imagination and gained a reputation as the 'glamour' ships of the fleet – a reputation enhanced during the war by their being under the command of the charismatic Rear Admiral David Beatty.

The battlecruisers were involved in a number of minor skirmishes during the war but only three major battles. The first of these, the Battle of the Falkland Islands, took place on 8 December 1914 and was remarkable for being an almost perfect example of the type of action originally envisaged by Fisher for his new ships. The main battle was, moreover, fought between two ships of the first group of British battlecruisers, the *Invincible* and *Inflexible,* and two of the most modern of Germany's armoured cruisers, the *Scharnhorst* and *Gneisenau.* Both German ships were sunk with heavy loss of life, but this was by no means easily accomplished. The *Scharnhorst* did not sink until three hours after the commencement of action and the *Gneisenau* lasted two hours longer, the British ships expending the majority of their ammunition in the process (*Invincible* 513 and *Inflexible* 661 12in shells). There were reasons for this apparently poor performance in that the British were seriously hampered by their own funnel smoke, the action involved a considerable amount of manoeuvring and the battlecruisers were deliberately kept at long range in the hope of avoiding as much damage as possible by keeping to the extreme range of the German guns. All this worked against the accuracy of the ships' fire control systems and limited the percentage of hits to rounds fired to a very low figure. However, it is worth bearing in mind that in 1904 Fisher was anticipating a marked advantage in long-range fire for British ships and this was in part used as a basis to justify the battlecruiser type.

The battlecruisers' second major battle was the Dogger Bank, fought in the southern North Sea on 24 January 1915 and for the first time this saw them in action against their opposite numbers of the German 1st Scouting Group. The fight consisted entirely of a long stern chase in which the British ships, in the order *Lion* (flagship), *Tiger, Princess Royal, New Zealand* and *Indomitable* pursued the German ships in the order *Seydlitz* (flagship), *Moltke, Derfflinger* and *Blücher* towards the latter's base. The action was largely fought at high speed with the fastest of the British ships gradually overhauling the German squadron which was held back in support of the *Blücher,* a hybrid armoured cruiser which was considerably slower than her companions. Fire was opened at very long range and with both sides hampered by problems of visibility it was some time before any hits were scored by either side. Most damage was suffered by the ships closest to the enemy – the *Blücher* at the stern of the German line and the *Lion* at the head of the British line. The *Blücher* suffered steadily mounting damage as she was engaged by each British ship in turn and eventually began to lose speed and drop astern. The *Lion,* although better able to absorb damage, eventually suffered a hit which required her to stop her port engine and she had to retire from action. Unfortunately, confusion resulting from the flagship's signals as she dropped astern led to a misinterpretation of Beatty's intentions and the remaining British ships turned on, and eventually sank, the unfortunate *Blücher* while the rest of the German squadron escaped at high speed. Apart from the obvious recriminations with regard to the escape of the German squadron, the British were comparatively pleased with their performance, believing that they had caused major damage to the enemy ships. In fact, *Blücher* excepted, they scored only three hits

The German armoured cruiser *Blücher* was the only uniform main armament ship of the type and the obvious logical development for heavy cruisers, but was totally outclassed by the battlecruiser. (Author's collection)

Tiger following *Lion*, with *Princess Royal* in the distance, 1917. (Author's collection)

each on *Seydlitz* and *Derfflinger* and of these only one, a shell that put both of *Seydlitz*'s after turrets out of action, was serious. In contrast six hits were made on *Tiger* and no less than seventeen on *Lion*. Several lessons that could have been learnt from this battle appear to have received scant attention, particularly the quality of German gunnery and the dangers from long-range fire in which shells fell at steep angles of descent. Both Captain Chatfield of the *Lion* and Rear Admiral Moore (second-in-command of the Battlecruiser Force with his flag in *New Zealand*) commented on the dangers posed by the latter and Moore recommended the thickening of protection to turret roofs, but their words went unheeded.

The last and most important of the battlecruiser actions was the Battle of Jutland, fought in the eastern part of the North Sea during 31 May–1 June 1916. The battle opened with the meeting of the opposing battlecruiser squadrons, both scouting ahead of their main fleets. The opening moves followed the pattern of the Dogger Bank except that in this case the German Admiral, Hipper, was attempting to draw Beatty south into the arms of the German battlefleet rather than trying to escape. The British ships consisted of *Lion* (flag), *Princess Royal, Queen Mary, Tiger, New Zealand* and *Indefatigable*. They were supported by four of the fast battleships of the 5th Battle Squadron which had been temporarily attached to the Battlecruiser Fleet while Admiral Hood's 3rd Battlecruiser Squadron (*Invincible* [flag], *Indomitable* and *Inflexible*) went north to Scapa Flow for gunnery practice. However, due to a signals failure the battleships took some time to get into action and initially the opposing battlecruisers had only each other to contend with. The German force consisted of *Lützow, Derfflinger, Seydlitz, Moltke* and *Von der Tann*.

During the run southward the light and visibility favoured the German squadron and the British suffered accordingly. They also received a substantial shock when first *Indefatigable* and then *Queen Mary* suffered magazine explosions resulting in them sinking very rapidly and with heavy loss of life. On the appearance of the main German fleet Beatty turned his ships northward, in order both to escape and to reverse the previous situation and draw the enemy fleet onto the guns of the Grand Fleet. By this time the light was less favourable to the Germans, and the British battlecruisers (but not the 5th Battle Squadron which came under heavy fire from the German main fleet) fared better while Hipper's ships began to suffer more severely.

In the meantime the 3rd Battlecruiser Squadron had proceeded ahead of the Grand Fleet with the intention of rejoining Beatty and arrived to the north east of the scene of action. Hipper thus found himself between Beatty on the port bow and the 3rd Battlecruiser Squadron on his starboard bow. Correctly assuming that this new enemy was the vanguard of the British fleet, he hauled round to starboard to retire on his own main fleet and, soon found himself in action with Hood's battlecruisers. Initially the British ships were very effective but after only twelve minutes in action the *Invincible* also blew up and sank. This effectively ended the major part of the battlecruisers' involvement in Jutland although they continued in intermittent action for the remainder of the day. The loss of three of their number under such appalling circumstances produced a strong reaction against the type, or at least against the type as conceived by Admiral Fisher. In the interim report of the Battlecruiser Fleet's post-Jutland Committee on Construction the following passage appears:

> The Committee consider that British battle cruisers, whether in service or about to be commissioned, are unequal to the duties assigned to them, as their protection is insufficient to enable them to encounter the capital ships of the enemy without incurring undue risk of destruction.
>
> For these duties the Committee are of opinion that vessels of very great protection, offensive power and speed are requisite; and that having regard to the existing naval situation and to the latest known foreign construction, the vessel required must be of fast battleship type, rather than on the lines of a battle cruiser. The 'Queen Elizabeth' type appears more nearly to fulfil the conditions required than does any other; but higher speed, greater protection and greater offensive power should be attempted, in conjunction, perhaps, with draught diminished to reduce under water target.

This sums up the opinion of the time and much of the opinion expressed since but, regardless of the value of the battlecruiser as a type, their failings were not simply a question of insufficient protection as, hopefully, this book will serve to make clear.

Origins

The *Invincible* had a totally different genesis from the *Dreadnought*. She was designed in order to meet a want that had long been felt but never supplied, namely, a ship fast enough to hunt down any armed merchant ship afloat, and at the same time to be able to fight any cruiser afloat. The word 'fight' with Fisher meant 'to crush'. With him there was no question of designing a cruiser *equal* in strength or speed to that of the enemy; for then the result of an action might be uncertain. His contention was that we should be superior to the enemy in numbers, in guns, in hitting power, in speed, and in personnel; and then, and only then, could the people of this country sleep peacefully in their beds.

Admiral Sir R Bacon, *The Life of Lord Fisher of Kilverstone*, 1929

Fisher's introduction of the battlecruiser type was open to more severe criticism [than the dreadnought battleship], because it fulfilled no real strategic nor tactical need. The statement that it was required to hunt down German liners is absurd. Trade has never been protected by hunting down raiders in the great ocean spaces, but if it were, the task could be performed more effectively by smaller cruisers costing less than half the price of a battlecruiser.

Vice Admiral K G B Dewar, *The Navy From Within*, 1939

On 20 October 1904 Admiral Sir John Fisher became First Sea Lord of the Admiralty. He came to his new post armed with radical plans to modernise and reform the Royal Navy's organisation, training and material with the intention of improving its efficiency both in terms of readiness for war and financial economy. Although our primary concern here is with the most controversial of his material reforms – the introduction of the battlecruiser – it is necessary to have some understanding of Fisher himself and of contemporary battleship development before the evolution of the type can be fully understood.

Admiral Bacon, commenting on Fisher's practices, wrote that 'Every officer with ideas was consulted and their views assimilated, till Sir John became the embodiment of the advanced ideas of all classes of officers of the Fleet.'[1] In essence Fisher gathered together the ideas of others, combined them with his own and then campaigned for the adoption of the result. This process was developed and refined over a number of years, his plans being modified as necessary to accommodate changing circumstances, new developments in technology and, occasionally, adverse comment on their feasibility. Whilst C-in-C Mediterranean Fleet, during 1899–1902, Fisher made a practice of giving lectures to its officers and it was from his notes on these that he began to organise a collection of papers which detailed his intended reforms. These were printed late in 1904 as the first iteration of *Naval Necessities*. In these papers, and in many of his letters of the period, it is possible to trace the above-mentioned process although never with absolute clarity. Fisher promoted his ideas with great passion and communicated these with a mixture of logical thought and simplistic dogma. It is difficult to tell how much of this was a true reflection of Fisher's thoughts and how much was intended as propaganda to persuade his reader or listener that his ideas were the obvious and logical answer to the Navy's future development. Large sections of these papers were written or inspired by others, principally those officers whom he regarded highly and upon whose advice he relied – particularly with regard to technical and tactical matters in which areas Fisher was less than fully competent, despite his background as a gunnery officer and fleet commander. Among his closest advisers were Captains John Jellicoe, Reginald Bacon, Henry Jackson and Charles Madden (all technical officers of considerable talent destined for high office – with or without Fisher's patronage), Constructor W H Gard of the DNC's department and the marine engineer Alexander Gracie of the Fairfield Shipbuilding Co. He also counted amongst his close friends Sir Philip Watts (DNC 1902–12) and Sir Andrew Noble (head of the Armstrong Whitworth shipbuilding and armaments company), which gave him direct access to the latest thinking in warship design and weapon development.

For the majority of the time Fisher was absolutely convinced that he was right and one of his greatest talents was his ability to convince others to the same view. At a time when the Navy was conservatively approaching momentous changes in naval technology, he provided the focus and the inspiration required to move the Navy forward and to get things done efficiently and quickly. History has judged him a great leader because he was more often right than wrong. In part this was due to the fact that he never had absolute power – even as First Sea Lord he needed the support of his fellow officers and was answerable to his political masters – and this prevented many of his wilder schemes being put into effect. It should be added, however, that this also slowed the introduction of some of his more worthwhile ideas.

Fisher was quick to see the advantages of new developments in technology but slow to appreciate the disadvantages and limitations that usually accompanied them. He has often been described as a visionary because of his early and enthusiastic promotion of such innovations as the steam turbine, diesel engines, water tube and oil-fired boilers and submarines, but he tended to do this with *all* new developments and more often than not his predictions were somewhat less than accurate. The turbine did revolutionise warship propulsion but the diesel engine (submarines excepted) did not; oil-fired boilers were an immediate success but water tube boilers took some time to fulfil their initial promise; the submarine eventually became a very potent weapon but did not render the battleship obsolete. It is worth noting also that Fisher was far from alone in the promotion of new technologies, although the majority of those who were most enthusiastic were younger officers (who had limited ability to influence Admiralty policy) and it was from the brightest of these

The very large protected cruiser Terrible in 1899. She and her sister, Powerful, displaced 14,200 tons which was only slightly less than that of the contemporary battleships of the Majestic class and considerably greater than other British cruiser then in existence. The increased size was necessary to accommodate a large machinery installation for a speed of 22kts, at a time when the standard maximum speed for British First Class cruisers was 20kts. Both vessels were designed and built during the time of Fisher's period as Controller (1892–7). (Author's collection)

that Fisher formed his group of close advisers.

In his proposals for improved warship designs Fisher had an unwavering, almost obsessive, desire for high speed or, more exactly, a substantial excess of speed over foreign warships of equivalent type. In simple terms this was a perfectly logical requirement for which he argued in the following terms:

> The Battleships must be large because they must be fast; they must be fast because we want to take the offensive, and also because speed is both the principal tactical as well as the principal strategical factor. Superiority of speed corresponds to the 'weather gage' of the old sailing days. It permits you to decline or to bring on an action. It enables you to anticipate the strategic dispositions of the enemy. It affords the necessary scope for endless schemes for enticing and entrapping the enemy. It makes your economic speed of a higher ratio.[2]

Fisher was, however, overestimating the tactical advantages of speed and made the critical mistake of assuming the enemy would not possess ships of equivalent speed. As any country embarking on challenging Britain's naval power would have to design ships capable of representing a serious threat, it followed that any escalation in the power of warships could ultimately lead to a technological naval race. There is the possible alternative, although not to my knowledge ever expressed by Fisher, of a deliberate escalating of naval development as a means of dissuading any challenge to Britain's naval supremacy. At the turn of the century most of Britain's potential rivals were military powers with large standing armies and limited desires to become involved in an escalating and expensive naval race with Britain and, like many others in the service, Fisher saw few problems in Britain continuing to maintain her supposed technological lead provided the country continued to see Britain's primary defence as on the sea. This view was reinforced by Britain's long naval tradition and the efficiency of her warship construction organisation. Unfortunately, it also tended to produce an arrogant belief in the superiority of British material which limited (along with financial restraints) critical appraisal of ships and their equipment prior to the First World War.

As acknowledged above, speed could be bought with increased size but this was limited by docking facilities and financial restraints. Britain's battleships already tended to be larger than their foreign contemporaries and there was strong political resistance to increases in the size, and therefore cost, of these vessels. Ultimately Fisher did, in instigating the dreadnought type, obtain sanction for larger ships but they were still required to be within certain limits and were only accepted on the understanding that there would be a compensatory overall saving in the Naval Estimates. However, Fisher also understood that speed could be obtained by modifying the balance of a design. In January 1901 he gave his requirements as firstly speed and secondly gunpower while *'the obligatory limit entailed by docking capabilities must curtail the other features in the design,* such as protection, amount of stores and provisions, etc … So in the internal arrangements, sacrifices must now be made to get our requirements within docking dimensions (not before this time compulsory), and there must be ruthless pruning of all accessories.'[3]

The first records of Fisher's development of a new approach in warship design date from early 1900 and by the summer of 1901 at the latest, he was communicating these ideas to the Admiralty. In December 1900 he suggested that new battleships should be larger than proposed French ships of 14,865 tons and should have a speed of 19kts if the French went to 18.5kts.[4] This is hardly a vast margin of speed (particularly as the French vessels in question proved to be 19kt vessels), but this requirement was soon to increase to 21kts. In his 'Rough Headings of 6th Lecture' (to the Mediterranean Fleet) dated 30 December 1901 he stated:

> The question of armament is all important! If we have the advantage of speed, *which is the first desideratum in every class of fighting vessel (Battleships included), then, and then only,* can we choose our distance for fighting. If we can choose our distance for fighting, then we can choose our armament for fighting! But how in the past has the armament been chosen? Do we arrange the armament to meet [the] proposed mode of fighting? Doesn't it sometimes look like so many of each sort as if you were peopling the Ark, and wanted representatives of all calibres?
>
> Now the armament we require is the greatest number of the largest quick-firing guns in *protected positions*. They call it the *secondary* armament; it is really the *primary* armament!
>
> In these days of very rapid movement the huge gun firing (comparatively) *slowly* is as obsolete as the foot soldier in the Boer War!
>
> **Whoever hits soonest and oftenest will win!**
>
> By many, a 10-inch gun (of the newest type and, say, 3300 feet [per second] initial velocity) is preferred to those of larger calibre. Why? Because it admits of so much more rapid firing; there is said to be a 10-inch gun now feasible which would be practically a quick-firer, and all the weights involved admit of hand working if the mechanism or

The battleship *Swiftsure* and her sister *Triumph*, under construction for Chile by Armstrong's and Vickers respectively, were purchased by the British Government in 1903 to prevent their purchase by Russia. They closely approximated to Fisher's ideal, being armed with four 10in and fourteen 7.5in guns, lightly protected and of comparatively high speed (20kts). (Author's collection)

electro-motors fail, where in these respects the heavier calibre would offer great difficulties.

... So the problem is to fix the smallest large gun to put at each end of the ship, and the largest small quick-firing gun to put elsewhere with the largest arc of fire and the best view.[5]

Fisher's requirement for a reduction of the main armament calibre from 12in to 10in was based on the fact that the 12in guns of the 1890s were slow, ponderous weapons. Although their projectiles were heavier and potentially more damaging, the number of hits they might achieve, particularly at long range, compared badly with a lighter, faster-firing weapon that was easier to control.[6] His proposal for the 'largest small quick-firing gun' was the 7.5in, the increase from the standard 6in weapon being (a) to achieve improved accuracy at long range, (b) to compensate for a general increase in the thickness of medium armour in foreign ships, and (c) to increase hitting power. His great attachment to quick-firing guns resulted from their ability to smother a target in shells in a short space of time and thereby seriously reduce the enemy's secondary and minor armament, command and control positions, and signalling abilities.

These requirements were evolved in part from a series of interwoven developments and ideas related to progress in long-range gunnery and fire control. The French had begun serious work on the latter in the early 1890s and by 1897, when the generally accepted fighting range was about 1000yds to 2000yds, had carried out successful long-range firing trials at up to 4000yds.[7] In 1901 Fisher mentioned that 'Two Italian Admirals informed us last year that, following French practice, it was their intention to open fire at 7000 yards, as excellent results had been obtained by themselves and the French at that range, and though some ammunition would be wasted, yet the chance of a lucky shot ... and the moral effect of commencing the action together with avoiding the demoralising effect of being fired at without firing back, all united to extend the practice of long-range firing, especially as the increased rapidity of firing in recent quick-firing systems enables the range to be quickly obtained.'[8] The latter remark refers to a method, initiated by the French, of using a QF gun to find the range by deliberately firing short and then progressively increasing the elevation of the gun until the target was crossed (a method which could not be employed with slow-firing weapons like the 12in gun). The British had begun experiments with long-range fire in the Mediterranean shortly before Fisher became C-in-C and by 1902 6000yds was generally accepted as the range for opening fire. Initially this was seen as a means of (a) inflicting damage on an enemy during the early stages of an action before closing to the fighting range of 3000 to 4000yds, and (b) to allow ships at long range to support other vessels more closely engaged with the enemy. However, as early as 1901 Fisher was predicting a fighting range of 6000yds and planned to use the gunnery exercises of the following year to establish what percentage of hits could be expected at different ranges. Within a few years practices were being carried out at 8000yds, and 5000yds to 6000yds was the expected fighting range. At this range, however, more sophisticated fire control techniques were necessary and during the period from 1902 to 1905 a great deal of effort was put into improving the method of controlling guns by both improving the gun mountings and in providing rangefinding, control and communication instruments.

One of the principal driving forces behind the need to extend the fighting range was a substantial improvement in the accuracy of the torpedo. Until the mid-1890s torpedoes were limited to short-range attack largely because they could not maintain a reasonably straight course for any distance. By 1898 this had been corrected by providing the torpedo with gyroscopic stabilisation, which gave a remarkable reduction in 'deviation' (drift away from the line of fire) and made the development of longer-range torpedoes worthy of consideration. It was also a relatively cheap innovation and could be applied without difficulty to existing torpedoes. In 1898 the longest standard range settings for the most recent British 18in torpedo was 800yds. By 1902 this had increased to 2000yds and there were prospects of even greater increases in the near future. Under these circumstances increased gun range was essential but even here Fisher managed to get in his requirement for speed: 'Thus the employment of the gyroscope makes it imperative [that] we should never close the enemy within 2000 yards *or 3000 yards if pursuing! This, however, infers superiority of speed, especially for the Battleships.'*[9]

Early in 1900 Bacon submitted a paper to Fisher pointing out that the advent of long-range gunnery favoured single line formation for the tactical employment of the battlefleet. Up to this time naval tacticians had favoured the use of semi-independent squadrons to break up an enemy fleet by 'concentration of force', a method which lent itself to short ranges and the mobility provided by steam propulsion but which also led to some very complex systems of fleet manoeuvre and control. Bacon argued that line-ahead maximised available gunfire, ensured clear arcs of fire and gave 'the greatest flexibility and simplicity of manoeuvre'. He added that as the gun was the primary weapon 'the best tactics were those that gave the gun the fullest possible scope. Gyrations which upset gun pointing were obviously bad, and therefore the advantages of the single line became even more apparent.' He added that under these conditions a faster fleet would have advantages and outlined much the same tactical arguments for speed in battle as those subsequently used by Fisher (see above).[10]

Fisher seems to have accepted the line-ahead formation with some reluctance for although he advocated its use – and employed Bacon's arguments often – he also recorded the comment that 'The British Navy is armed at present for broadside fighting; it may be a matter for regret but there is the fact that it is so.'[11] He thus accepted it as a *fait accompli* resulting from the design of ships rather than a matter of choice resulting from tactical thought. It seems probable that this prompted his advocacy of ships designed to give 'equal fire all-round' in order to restore mobility of action, concentration of force, etc. Unfortunately, ships do not lend themselves to a suitable distribution of armament to achieve this end and most of the capital ships of the early dreadnought period were compromised to some extent by an excessive emphasis on end-on fire. It is worth noting that fire-control is also much more difficult end-on than on the broadside particularly if a ship is rolling. One interesting point made by Bacon was that 'Mobility was useless without considerable excess of speed' and it

Table 1: White's armoured cruisers

Class	Design year	Completion	No of ships	Displacement (tons)	Armament	Speed (kts)	Belt armour KC(ins)
Cressy	1897	1901–2	6	12,000	2 x 9.2in, 12 x 6in	21	6
Drake	1898	1902–3	4	14,150	2 x 9.2in, 16 x 6in	23	6
Monmouth	1899	1903–4	10	9800	14 x 6in	23	4
Devonshire	1901	1905	6	10,850	4 x 7.5in, 6 x 6in	22	6

is hardly likely that Fisher did not take note of what he would certainly consider a statement of great significance.

The armoured cruiser

During the 1890s the armoured cruiser became a very popular type among the world's navies. These were large vessels – usually approaching the size of contemporary battleships – of high speed and armed with QF guns. They came close to supplanting the construction of other, smaller, cruiser types but had the disadvantage of being exceedingly costly and could not therefore be built in the numbers required by a colonial power like Britain. They were 'armoured' as opposed to 'protected' because their primary passive defence was vertical side armour as opposed to an arched steel deck and were consequently much more capable of withstanding attack from QF guns. Britain began to build vessels of this type somewhat later than other countries. Between 1897 and 1901 four classes (totalling twenty-six ships) were designed under the direction of the DNC, Sir William White (see Table 1), the first entering service in 1901. They all had turret mountings fore and aft – single 9.2in in the Cressy and Drake, twin 6in in the Monmouth and single 7.5in in the Devonshire. The latter class also had a single 7.5in turret on each side abreast the bridge. The remaining 6in guns in all these ships were mounted in broadside casemates.

Fisher was much impressed by large cruisers in general and the armoured cruiser in particular, although not necessarily with White's interpretation. In particular he would have regarded the two 'County' classes as too small and did not care for casemate-mounted guns. He much preferred an all-turret armament, each turret being a well-protected, self-contained unit with its own ammunition supply. This was intended to provide for the improved survivability of the guns and reduce the dangers inherent in

A typical armoured cruiser of the White era, *Essex* of the *Monmouth* class, seen here in 1913. Note the 6in casemate guns on the broadside. (Author's collection)

Table 2: Watts' armoured cruisers

Class	Design year	Completion	No of ships	Displacement (tons)	Armament	Speed (kts)	Belt armour KC(ins)
Duke of Edinburgh	1902	1906	2	13,550	6 x 9.2in, 10 x 6in	23	6
Warrior	1903	1906–7	4	13,550	6 x 9.2in, 4 x 7.5in	23	6
Minotaur	1904	1908–9	3	14,600	4 x 9.2in, 10 x 7.5in	23	6

extended ammunition supply routes via ammunition passages, which were particularly vulnerable to torpedo attack (and, as it turned out, long-range gunfire). It also served to reduce the number of personnel involved in passing ammunition. In addition Fisher was much against unnecessary superstructure that might serve to detonate shells and White's ships carried substantial superfluous (for fighting purposes) structure above the upper deck. There was a marked change in approach when Philip Watts succeeded White as DNC in 1902. Under

One of the armoured cruisers designed under the direction of Sir Philip Watts, *Cochrane* of the *Warrior* class. Note that all the main armament is mounted in single turrets: two 9.2in on the centreline forward and aft, and two 9.2in and two 7.5in on each broadside. (Author's collection)

Watts' direction three further armoured cruiser classes were designed (see Table 2), all of substantial size, with considerably reduced superstructure and, with the exception of the first two ships, which had ten 6in guns in casemates, an all-turret mounted armament. They could, however, still be criticised for poor ammunition supply arrangements and by the time they were under construction Fisher had concluded that their speed of 23kts was insufficient.

There was another class of vessel to which Fisher was very much attached. This was the Second Class battleship, of which there were several examples in the British and other navies. Generally these were more lightly armed and protected than First Class battleships and slightly faster. Fisher's particular favourite was *Renown,* which had been designed and built during his term at the Admiralty as Controller (1891–7) and had served as his flagship when C-in-C of the North America and West Indies Station (1897–9) and in the Mediterranean (1899 – 1902). The particulars of this ship are given in Table 3; her light armament and relatively light armour are worthy of note. She was not only faster than the contemporary First Class battleships of the *Majestic* class but in heavy weather she was, because of her size, capable of overhauling a cruiser.

In 1901 Fisher was proposing much the same armament for his ideal armoured cruiser as he was for battleships and was indicating that the armour in the latter should be reduced to improve speed. This effectively blurred the distinction between the two types and seems to have caused Fisher to develop the notion that the armoured cruiser could replace the battleship; or more correctly that the two types should be merged since the new type would automatically have become

Fisher's favourite flagship, the Second Class battleship *Renown*. (Author's collection)

the prime unit of the fleet. In December 1900 he described the latest French armoured cruisers as 'battleships in disguise', a phrase he was to use often during the next few years in describing his armoured cruiser proposals. He also often referred to his fast battleship designs (and to *Renown*) as 'glorified armoured cruisers'. At times he seems to have become somewhat confused as to which type, battleship or armoured cruiser, should be developed and occasionally made incompatible statements on the subject within the same document. One suspects that, given subsequent events, he always had a strong personal preference for the armoured cruiser as the capital ship of the future but could find little support for this view among his contemporaries and was therefore forced to accept the battleship as a necessary part of any future programme. Initially his view was not entirely unsupportable given the proposed armament of QF guns and the expectation that actions would be fought at long range (both of which allowed for thinner armour) but with the subsequent readoption of the heavy calibre gun it is difficult to understand why he continued to advocate high speed at the expense of protection.

At the beginning of 1902 Fisher enlisted the help of W H Gard, then Chief Constructor at Malta, to produce an outline design to meet his requirements for a 25kt armoured cruiser. The result, which Fisher christened HMS *Perfection,* had the following outline particulars:

Displacement: 15,000 tons (14,000 tons with oil-fired boilers)
Dimensions: 500ft (min) x 70ft (min) x 26ft 6in (mean)

Table 3: HMS *Renown*

LAID DOWN:	1893
LAUNCHED:	1895
COMPLETED:	1897
DISPLACEMENT:	12,350 tons
SPEED	18kts
ARMAMENT:	4 x 10in/40cal (2 x 2)
	10 x 6in (10 x 1)
	12 x 12pdr (12 x 1)
ARMOUR:	Main belt 8in; upper belt 6in; bulkheads 10in and 6in; casemates 6in–4in; CT 10in; deck 2in–3in

Armament: 4 x 9.2in (2 x 2); 12 x 7.5in QF (6 x 2) Machinery: 35,000ihp (max) = 25kts
Protection: 6in–5in side; 6in bulkheads; 6in on 9.2in mountings; 4in on 7.5in mountings; 10in CT; 2in upper deck; 2.5in (forw), 2.5–3in (aft) lower deck.

Table 4 Particulars of ships employed in Senior Officers' War Course, January 1902

	Type A *Heavily armed battleship*	Type B *Lightly armed battleship*
DEEP DISPLACEMENT:	17,604 tons	15,959 tons
SPEED AT LOAD DRAUGHT:	18kts	22kts
ARMAMENT:	4 x 12in (2 x 2); 8 x 8in (4 x 2); 12 x 7in (7 x 1)	4 x 10in (2 x 2); 16 x 6in (16 x 1)
ARMOUR:	10in–8in belt; 6in upper belt; 11in main armament; 8in intermediate armament; 7in secondary armament; 1.5in deck	6in belt; 5in upper belt; 9.5in main armament; 5in secondary armament

He wrote to the First Lord, Selborne, in March 1902 stating that he had this design 'ready for May [Rear Admiral W H May, Controller 1901–4] and Watts' and outlined its general features including the facts that she would be able to fire ten guns ahead and astern; had an all-turret armament, each turret being a self-contained unit; no masts, derricks, anchor gear or bridges; linoleum-covered decks instead of wood planking; and telescopic funnels. The last item, one of Fisher's constant favourites, was intended (a) to reduce the target in action, and (b) limit the observability of the ship when scouting – how it was intended to cope with the smoke is not recorded. This proposal had little effect on Admiralty construction policy. The only similarities between this vessel and the armoured cruisers designed in the following two years was an increase in the calibre of the secondary armament, a reduction in top hamper and an all-turret armament – all items which resulted from decisions emanating primarily from Watts and May.

In June 1902 Fisher left the Mediterranean to take up the post of Second Sea Lord at the Admiralty where, if he was not aware of it already, he would soon have discovered that battleship design was moving in a quite different direction to that proposed by him from the Mediterranean. Rear Admiral May had begun a detailed study of the requirements for future armoured ships in light of recent developments in naval construction abroad (particularly in the USA[12]) and in naval gunnery. The conclusions ultimately reached were that the heavy-calibre gun was of primary importance, that the secondary armament needed to be increased in calibre (to cope with increased ranges and the thicker armour in foreign designs) and that protection needed to be both thicker and more widely distributed. In effect British ships were to be individually superior to their foreign contemporaries and this in turn meant an increase in size. Under the direction of Watts design work on battleships to meet these criteria began in 1902 and resulted in the *Lord Nelson* and *Agamemnon* – the last, largest and most powerfully armed and armoured of Britain's pre-dreadnoughts which retained the then standard speed for British vessels of this type of 18kts.[13]

In January 1902, almost certainly as part of the above investigation and possibly because of Fisher's prompting, the Admiralty requested the Senior Officers' War Course at Greenwich Naval College to investigate whether a lightly armed and protected ship with a 4kt advantage in speed had any tactical advantage over a vessel in which speed was subordinated to gun power and armour. The officer in charge of the course, Captain H J May, concluded in his report, completed on 8 February 1902, that gun power was more important than speed provided both sides were determined to fight. The two ships employed in this investigation (see Table 4), despite being referred to only as 'Type A' and 'Type B' and both being described as battleships, were in fact the very latest US Navy designs for battleship and armoured cruiser respectively.[14] The proposed battle between the two types assumed that fire would be opened at 6000yds and the ships would then close, or attempt to close, to 4000yds and finally 3000yds. It was stated that the lightly-protected ship was more vulnerable to the fire of her adversary, whose better-protected hull and primary gun positions made her immune at all ranges. However, three of the lighter type were considered capable of holding their own against two of the heavier type at long range, where their high rate of fire would help. 'It is evident, therefore, that the "B" ship should so far as possible fight at long range, and that her speed should be used to prevent a heavier antagonist from closing. However close she gets her 6in guns will never become armour piercers. They must, therefore, be looked upon as purely shell guns when pitted against a well-protected modern ship.' It was also stated that the lighter vessel could use her speed to keep her distance in 'fighting a retiring action' but this would only be of use if the heavier ship wanted to chase. The paper concluded 'for fighting a fleet, the "B" ships are much inferior to the "A"s. Their speed may be of the greatest moment strategically, but it is a well nigh negligible quantity tactically.'[15] In July 1902 the DNI, Captain R Custance, commented that this paper

> ... proved that the large armoured cruiser of 22 knots speed, costing upwards of a million sterling is not as efficient in the line of battle as a battleship of 18 knots, and as such a powerful ship should not be detached from the fleet, it is difficult to see how such a ship can be justified.

That enquiry into the strategic conditions may lead to results somewhat similar to those obtained from the investigation of the tactical conditions seems to be not unlikely.

Naval opinion has been and is now under the influence of the traditions of the Napoleonic wars, when we had such a superiority over the forces opposed to us that we were able to blockade them in their ports, and they were forced to evade us whenever they put to sea. We are deeply imbued with the conceit that the enemy must and will still evade us. This idea is a relic of the past, and is no longer fitted to the new conditions. We must look back to the Dutch Wars to find a precedent for the future – to conditions of equality when our supremacy at sea was disputed. No idea of evasion entered into the Dutch mind in the 17th Century, nor will it enter into the German or French mind in the 20th. Neither of these nations will go to war with us alone. We shall have to fight pitched battles to establish our supremacy, and, as Captain May and his officers have shown, these must be decided by fighting power without help from speed.[16]

Printed at the same time as the paper on the tactical value of speed was a series of notes by Captain May on the exercises and problems investigated at Greenwich.[17] Some of the conclusions in this document are particularly relevant and these are briefly summarised below.

Main Armament: The 12in gun was considered more useful than the QF gun at long and short ranges. Given its importance it was concluded that the tactician's task was to keep as many of these weapons bearing on the enemy as possible. To this end the ideal formation was in line-ahead with the enemy on the broadside.

QF Armament: This was of high value at medium ranges for piercing the armour of secondary batteries. However, a gun was required that could pierce 7in to 8in KC armour for which, as the 6in was outclassed and the 7.5in was borderline, the 9.2in QF gun was recommended.

Tactics: Although the ideal tactical manoeuvre was to cross ahead of an enemy fleet (crossing the 'T') this would be extremely difficult to achieve when fighting at long range as any attempt to move ahead of the enemy could be countered by a turn away. This would simply lead to the slower fleet turning inside the circle of the faster fleet at a radius proportional to the difference in speed.

Fisher seems to have been undeterred by these developments, although they no doubt served to modify at least some of his views. He could of course have argued that the armoured cruiser used in the War Course exercise did not meet his requirements for speed or armament. In any case, at this time he was heavily occupied, as Second Sea Lord, in developing new schemes of entry and training for officers and men. Nevertheless, his position on the Board would have kept him in touch with design developments. During this time the designs of the *Lord Nelson* and *Warrior* were being worked out and among the numerous sketch designs for the former were several with a uniform 10in gun armament (12in was also suggested by the DNC's department). It is easy to assume that the idea of the 10in calibre emanated from Fisher, as he no doubt found occasions on which to express his opinions, but it is difficult to tell who was influencing whom, as Watts himself favoured the 10in gun as did his former employer, Noble. Besides, according to Bacon, Fisher kept his plans to himself while at the Admiralty to avoid the possibility of their being watered-down and only partially adopted.[18] It is also doubtful that the Third Sea Lord would have looked kindly upon any direct interference with the departments under his control.

Fisher left the Admiralty in August 1903 to become C-in-C Portsmouth where he once more began detailed work on his plans to modernise the Navy prior to becoming First Sea Lord. On the material side he sought the help of his close advisers, two of whom – Gard (now Chief Constructor of Portsmouth Dockyard) and Bacon (serving as Inspecting Captain of Submarine Boats at Portsmouth) – were readily available.[19] The most notable difference between the armoured ship designs he now proposed and those of his period in the Mediterranean was the adoption of a uniform-calibre armament – sixteen 10in in the battleship and sixteen 9.2in in the armoured cruiser. Both vessels were to be of 15,900 tons, the battleship having a speed of 21kts and the armoured cruiser 25.5kts.

The uniform-calibre main armament resulted from recent development in fire control where it had been found that salvo firing was the best means of controlling guns at long range. Unfortunately guns of differing calibre could not be controlled as a unit owing to the ballistic differences between them and the resulting variations in the sight settings required for different ranges and deflections. At the same time, attempting to control them as separate groups merely caused confusion, as it was almost impossible to distinguish the fall of shot of one group from another. The only answer to this problem was a uniform-calibre main armament that could be controlled as a single group. As a result of this change Fisher reinterpreted his requirement for the 'smallest big gun and the biggest small gun' as meaning that the only guns to be carried other than the uniform main armament were those of the anti-torpedo-boat battery for which, at this time, he favoured the 4in calibre.

Outline designs for the proposed battleship and armoured cruiser, produced by Gard, were available before Fisher became First Sea Lord in October 1904. However, by this time a major shift had occurred in the requirements for the battleship as a result of arguments put forward by his naval advisors (particularly Bacon) regarding the calibre of the main armament. This again developed from the use of spotting for fire control, which required that the fall of shot was registered before the next salvo was fired. Under these circumstances the rate of fire was not controlled by the rapidity with which the guns could be loaded but by the time of flight of the projectiles. This effectively negated one of the primary advantages of the 10in over the 12in gun – its higher rate of fire (in addition, the latest design of heavy gun mounting gave a much improved rate of fire). The 12in gun could also claim:

(a) Greater destructive effect of each hit due to heavier projectile and larger bursting charge.
(b) Improved accuracy and smaller spread of salvo at long range.
(c) Flatter trajectory of projectile and hence greater danger space for target at long range.

Table 5: HMS *Unapproachable*, October 1904

DIMENSIONS:	530ft x 75ft x 26ft 6in
MACHINERY:	40,000ihp = 25.5kts at 110rpm
ENDURANCE:	2425nm at 25kts; 15680nm at 10kts
ARMAMENT:	16 x 9.2in (8 x 2); c12 x 4in
ARMOUR:	6in belt (8in at wing barbettes); 8in barbettes
COAL:	2500 tons
OIL:	600 tons in double bottom
WEIGHTS (tons):	
Equipment	680
Coal (normal)	1100
Armament	1820 (incl gunhouses, torpedoes and stores)
Prop machinery	3400
Armour and backing	3000
Hull	5000 (incl electric motors)
TOTAL:	15,000 tons

Against this the 10in gun could claim lower cost of guns, mountings and ammunition, more economical use of weight for armour and the ability to provide greater numbers of guns on a given displacement.

The choice between a battleship armed with sixteen 10in guns and one armed with eight 12in guns appeared in Fisher's papers in the summer of 1904. In these he expressed the opinion that the arguments in favour of the 12in were 'unanswerable' but, nevertheless, kept the options open for discussion and the decision to adopt the 12in gun was not finalised until after he took up his seat on the Board. In the meantime the armoured cruiser design retained the 9.2in calibre armament and Gard's outline design for this vessel, known as HMS *Unapproachable* (see Table 5: the battleship was HMS *Untakable*), appeared in the papers submitted by Fisher to Selborne in October 1904. However, it seems alternatives *were* discussed as, in these same documents Fisher made the point that for the cruiser the 10in gun was not considered to have sufficient advantage over the 9.2in to justify the additional weight involved and the 12in gun was 'unnecessarily large'. Bacon has recorded that while Fisher's unofficial committee was in full agreement over the adoption of the heavy gun for the battleship, the armoured cruiser's armament was the subject of 'much controversy' and the discussion on the relative merits of the 9.2in and 12in gun continued 'for weeks'. Eventually the 12in gun 'won on the unanswerable plea that ships, of the size and tonnage necessary ... should have an additional use in being able to form a fast light squadron to supplement the battleships in action, and worry the ships in the van or rear of the enemy's line.'[20] The decision to adopt the 12in gun for both the battleship (soon to become HMS *Dreadnought*) and the armoured cruiser was formally taken at a meeting of the Board in December 1904 when the main features to be adopted were finally settled. In part, this may have emanated from a desire by Fisher to retain the similarity of armament of the two types in the hope of maintaining his arguments for replacing battleships altogether. Whatever the reasons, the decision to adopt the 12in gun for the armoured cruiser was critical – it was this, and this alone, that produced the distinct and separate warship type that was eventually to be classified as the battlecruiser. Had the 9.2in calibre been retained the resulting vessels would have been simply a major advance in the evolution of the armoured cruiser in the same way as the *Dreadnought* was a major advance in the evolution of the battleship.

The functions for the big-gun armoured cruisers were essentially the same as those of existing armoured cruisers, the additional speed and gun power being seen as enhancing their effectiveness in these roles. In summary these were:

(a) *To provide a heavy scouting force.* Because of their heavy armament they could push through any existing cruiser screen and report on the composition of an enemy fleet by close observation, following which their speed enabled a rapid retirement. It was assumed that, as their approach and retirement would be end-on, their protection would be sufficient to get reasonably close to an enemy battlefleet, their armour, for most of the time, only being subjected to oblique attack.
(b) *Close support for the battlefleet in action.* They were to be stationed in the van and rear of the battle line where they could defend the battleships against interference by enemy cruisers and worry the enemy battleships with their big guns as opportunity offered. In the latter case they were only to engage battleships already fully occupied in fighting their opposite numbers (it was unlikely in these circumstances that a battleship would shift its fire to the lesser of two dangers). They could also operate as a fast wing and attempt to outmanoeuvre the enemy by enveloping movements across the van or rear of his line – again if opportunity offered and the enemy battleships were otherwise occupied.
(c) *In pursuit of a fleeing enemy.* In a chasing action they were to use their speed and gun power to harass the retiring enemy fleet in the hope of damaging and slowing their ships.
(d) *Trade protection.* To hunt down and destroy enemy surface raiding cruisers and armed merchantmen. Speed was seen as essential for this function, both to give some margin over the likely enemy vessels and in order to reach the area of operations quickly. End-on fire was also of importance in this role as chasing actions would be the norm.

The Committee on Designs

The radical nature of the proposed shipbuilding policy (which also included destroyers and submarines but no intermediate types of cruiser at all) was such as to guarantee controversy. In consequence Fisher and the Board decided to appoint a 'Committee on Designs' ostensibly to investigate and report upon the requirements for future ships. However, its primary purpose was to validate decisions already arrived at and, because it was to consist of eminent and expert men whose opinions could not lightly be ignored, limit the level of criticism that could be aimed directly at the Board in general and Fisher in particular. The resulting Committee did valuable work at a detail level, in particular in sorting out the armament layout and main machinery to be used in the armoured ships, but it did not otherwise have any major influence on events. From the outset the basic requirements were those set by Fisher and he did not provide the Committee with any options to move outside the general parameters set by the Board of Admiralty. The Committee was officially appointed by Admiralty letter, dated 22 December 1904, and included all of Fisher's close advisers and several eminent civilians including the country's leading physicist, Lord Kelvin, and the superintendent of the Admiralty Experiment Works, R E Froude. Fisher himself acted as President of the Committee.[21]

At the first meeting of the Committee, on 3 January 1905, Fisher read the terms of reference, which in simple form stated that the Committee was advisory only and did not relieve the DNC of his responsibility for warship design but was so constituted that the advice it offered to the Board would carry great weight. The instructions given to the Committee outlined the designs to be considered for the battleship, armoured cruiser and destroyers (submarines were not included in the Committee's brief). In the case of the armoured cruiser these were simply that it should be of 25.5kts speed, armed with 12in and anti-torpedo-boat guns only, armoured on the same scale as *Minotaur* and

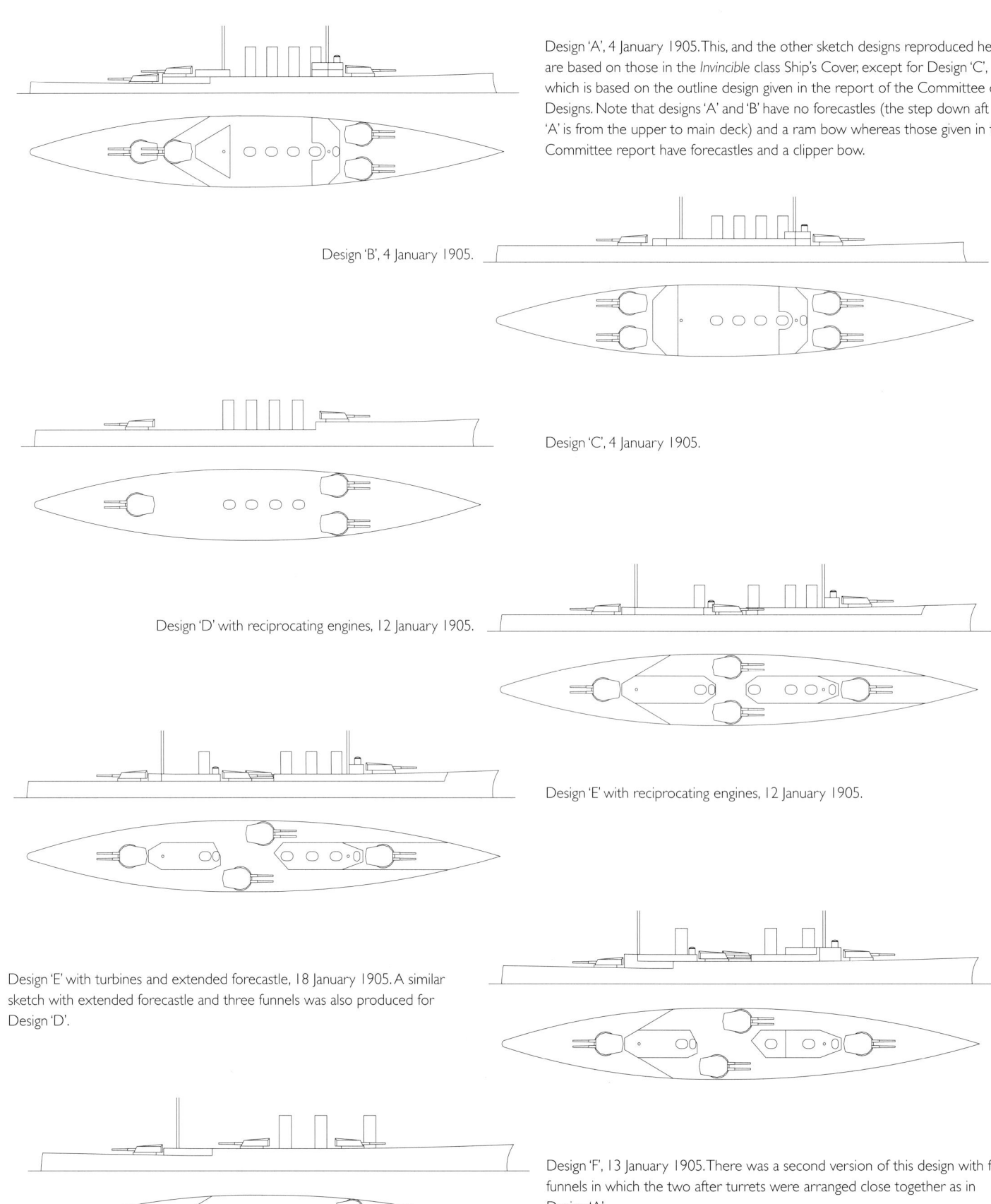

Design 'A', 4 January 1905. This, and the other sketch designs reproduced here, are based on those in the *Invincible* class Ship's Cover, except for Design 'C', which is based on the outline design given in the report of the Committee on Designs. Note that designs 'A' and 'B' have no forecastles (the step down aft in 'A' is from the upper to main deck) and a ram bow whereas those given in the Committee report have forecastles and a clipper bow.

Design 'B', 4 January 1905.

Design 'C', 4 January 1905.

Design 'D' with reciprocating engines, 12 January 1905.

Design 'E' with reciprocating engines, 12 January 1905.

Design 'E' with turbines and extended forecastle, 18 January 1905. A similar sketch with extended forecastle and three funnels was also produced for Design 'D'.

Design 'F', 13 January 1905. There was a second version of this design with four funnels in which the two after turrets were arranged close together as in Design 'A'.

of dimensions suitable for existing docking facilities. However, the Committee also adopted a preliminary statement which was essentially a reiteration of the arguments put forward in the 'Types of Fighting Vessels' section of *Naval Necessities*.[22] There was some additional material concerning recent events in the Russo-Japanese War (February 1904 –September 1905) which were taken to confirm the value of the armoured cruiser, the heavy gun, uniform armament, speed and long-range gunfire.[23]

The Committee first considered the battleship designs and then moved on to the first, and at this time, only, armoured cruiser design. This was design 'A' which was prepared by Constructor C H Croxford on instructions from the DNC, via ADNC W H Whiting. The DNC provided a rough plan showing the layout required for the main armament that, on 28 December, was given as eight 12in/50cal (not 45cal as finally adopted) guns. The machinery was specified as turbines of 42,000hp for a speed of 25.5kts and protection as on the same scale as *Minotaur*. However, when Croxford received his instructions on the following day, the turbines had been replaced by reciprocating engines. It is worth noting that despite a claim by Bacon that 'By the 21st October the sketch designs of the *Dreadnought* and *Invincible* were practically complete, and ... subsequently underwent very little alteration,'[24] none of the sketch designs for the armoured cruiser emanated from Gard and the designs finally adopted, for both the battleship and the armoured cruiser, were produced entirely by the DNC's department after the above date.[25]

The primary requirement for the armoured cruiser layout was to secure good end-on fire and Design 'A' was arranged to allow for four guns firing ahead and astern and six on the broadside. The arrangement was rejected on the grounds that the superfiring turret aft would, cause serious blast interference to the lower turret when firing on after bearings and that the after group of turrets represented a large target which one hit might put completely out of action. At a second meeting, in the afternoon, the DNC was requested to prepare two new sketch designs ('B' and 'C'), and to produce diagrams of blast curves for 12in and smaller guns. These he duly produced at the third meeting on 4

Table 6: **Particulars of armoured cruisers with reciprocating engines considered by Committee on Designs, January 1905**

	Design 'A'	*Design 'B'*	*Designs 'D' & 'E'*
DATE:	4/1/05	4/1/05	12/1/05
LENGTH pp (ft):	540	540	550
BEAM (ft–in):	77	77–6	79
DRAUGHT (ft–in):	26–6	26–6	26–6
DISPLACEMENT (tons):	17,000	17,200	17,750
WEIGHTS (tons):			
General equipment	640	640	640
Armament	2500	2500	2500
Machinery	3500	3500	3600
Coal	1000	1000	1000
Armour	3160	3260	3460
Hull	6100	6200	6450
BM	100	100	100
TOTAL:	17,000	17,200	17,750

Particulars common to all designs: Machinery 41,000hp ('D' & 'E' 42,500) = 25.5kts; Armament 8 x 12in (80rpg), 13 ('D' & 'E' 14) x 4in (200rpg), 2 x Maxims, 5 submerged torpedo tubes; Armour 6in & 4in (3in backing) side, 6in & 3in bulkheads, 8in barbettes, 8in gun shields, 10in ('D' & 'E' 10in & 6in) CT, 6in & 2in com tube, 1.5in & 2in lower deck.

The above design details are taken from the legends of the designs in the Ship's Cover of the *Invincible* class (ADM138/248). The details given with sketch designs 'D' and 'E' in the Design Committee's Progress Report (*Fisher Papers*, Vol 1, pp285–90) do not match these in several respects and in all the designs the speed of 25kts is incorrect. It is possible that these figures were doctored and/or badly recorded some time after the designs were first presented. Unfortunately there is no legend for Design 'C' in the Covers and the only figures available are those from the Committee's report which give the displacement as 15,600 tons and dimensions as 520 x 76 x 26ft. It can be fairly safely assumed that the speed was 25.5kts and that the common particulars given above also applied to this design (except that the main armament was six 12in).

January. The blast diagram revealed that blast problems would also occur between 12in mountings arranged abreast, as in the two new designs, and these were rejected also. The weak broadside fire was also objected to, and it was pointed out that the considerable weight of two mountings and their protection mounted so far forward (and aft in 'B') was likely to have a serious effect on the ships' seagoing qualities due to the excessive pitching that would probably result. It was decided that some wider distribution of the 12in turrets was required which would secure both end-on and broadside fire but reduce blast effects to an acceptable level. The proposal finally adopted was to place one turret forward, one aft and one on each beam giving a broadside of six guns and the ability to fire four guns on forward and after bearings (six on a very limited arc directly fore and aft). This decision resulted in the production of designs 'D' and 'E' which Croxford prepared for the next meeting on 12 January. Design 'E' differed from 'D' only in that the beam turrets were displaced *en echelon* to allow cross-deck firing over a limited arc of fire which, because of the blast effects, was only to be employed if the opposite turret was out of action. The Committee decided they preferred 'E' but asked for the forecastle to be lengthened as far as the after turret, to improve seaworthiness and to give the wing turrets a higher command. Although it was decided to work out this design in greater detail the Committee discussed one further alternative layout. This was design 'F', a variation on 'A' in which the two forward turrets were moved aft to wing positions abreast the forward funnels and the third turret was moved forward to a position between the engine and boiler rooms (basically the same layout as that adopted for the battleship but with the fore turret omitted). Croxford provided sketch layouts for this on the day of the meeting but at the fifth meeting on the following day, at which only the Admiralty members of the

Committee were present, it was decided not to proceed with this design, 'E' becoming the accepted layout for the new ships.

On 7 January the DNC mentioned that a four-shaft turbine arrangement might be adopted and Croxford was requested to produce alternative versions of 'D' and 'E' with this machinery.[26] The sketch designs for these were virtually identical to those of the reciprocating versions except, because they required less boiler power, they had three funnels instead of four. A preliminary discussion on the turbine took place during the 'Admiralty only' meeting on 13 January. Both the DNC and E-in-C urged their adoption on the basis of their simplicity, reliability and because of the great saving in weight that would result. However, several of the naval officers were concerned about the possible loss of manoeuvrability and astern power that was likely to be caused by the use of small, high-speed propellers. On 17 January evidence was taken from Sir Charles Parsons (British inventor of the turbine) and on the following day, when the comparative legends of design 'E' with turbines and reciprocating engines were available, the Committee decided to recommend the adoption of design 'E' with turbines, provided further investigation did not reveal any reason to reverse this decision. This debate, which continued for several weeks, included taking further evidence from Parsons and a detailed examination of the qualities of existing turbine-driven ships. Eventually it was concluded that the advantages far outweighed any disadvantage that might result (see also Machinery chapter).

One further major advance remained to be included in the design – defence against mines and torpedoes. This question had been brought to the fore as a result of recent events in the Russo-Japanese War where losses from mines were heavy. The principle concern was the vulnerability of magazines and in designs 'D' and 'E' provision was made to keep these as near the middle-line, and as far away from the ship's sides as possible. Consideration was also given to providing some form of armoured screen to the magazines and shell rooms. This eventually led to the incorporation of 2.5in-thick internal protective bulkheads abreast these compartments. This innovation was discussed by the Admiralty members of the Committee on 21 February. On the following day comparative legends for design 'E', with and without these bulkheads (version 'A' and 'B' respectively) were placed before the full Committee. To accommodate the additional 250 tons required for these bulkheads without increasing the overall displacement the 'B' version had been modified as follows:

Table 7: Particulars of armoured cruisers with turbine machinery considered by Committee on Designs, January 1905

	Design 'E'	Design 'D' & 'E'	
DATE:	18/1/05	21/1/05	
LENGTH (ft):	530	540* (525**)	
BEAM (ft):	79	79	
DRAUGHT (ft):	26	26	
SPEED (kts):	25.5	25.5	

Armament and armour as reciprocating engine designs (Table 6)

WEIGHTS (tons):			
General equipment	620	620*	600**
Armament	2530	2500	2500
Machinery	2350	3140	2350
Coal	1000	1000	1000
Armour	3350	3370	3300
Hull	6050	6120	5850
BM	100	100	100
TOTAL:	16,000	16,850	15,700

* Assumes 12.5 per cent saving and ** assumes 30 per cent saving on machinery weight. The comparative Design 'E', with reciprocating engines, of 18 January was the same as that of 12 January except for a reduction in the power of the machinery (42,000hp) and in some slight adjustments of weight (displacement 17,600 tons – later modified by Whiting to 17,850 tons).

Table 8: Evolution of Design 'E', February 1905

DATE:	10/2/05*	10/2/05**	22/2/05***	22/2/05****
LENGTH (ft):	540	530	540	540
BEAM (ft):	79	79	79	79
DRAUGHT	26	26	26	26
DISPLACEMENT (tons):	16,750	16,000	16,750	16,750
SPEED (kts):	25.5	25.5	25	25
WEIGHTS (tons):				
General equipment	720	720	720	720
Armament	2470	2470	2450	2420
Machinery	2950	2350	3090	3090
Coal	1000	1000	1000	1000
Armour	3460	3410	3390	3420
Hull	6050	5950	6000	6000
BM	100	100	100	100
TOTAL:	16,750	16,000	16,750	16,750

* Assumes 15 per cent saving on machinery weight by use of turbines.
** Assumes 33 per cent saving on machinery weight by use of turbines.
*** Version 'A' – without magazine protection.
**** Version 'B' – with magazine protection.
Other particulars were as in the previous legends of 'E' except for the changes to protection in Version 'B', as detailed in the text, and the ATB armament which was 17 x 12pdr (300rpg) in the designs of 10 February and 20 x 12pdr (300rpg) in those of 22 February.

Invincible, with *Inflexible* and *Indomitable* astern, at the Spithead Review of July 1909. (Author's collection)

(a) Height of belt armour above the load water line reduced from 7ft 3in to 6ft 9in (the original height was restored in the final legend of June 1905).
(b) 50ft of forward 4in side armour reduced in thickness to 3in.
(c) Sides of 12in gun shields reduced from 8in to 7in.
(d) Barbette armour reduced from 8in to 7in.
(e) Height of axis of forward 12in guns reduced from 34ft to 32ft above load water line.

The Committee approved these changes, except that item (b) was replaced by an alternative suggestion to reduce the heights of the guns' axis of the wing turrets from 29ft 6in to 28ft 6in (subsequently further reduced to 28ft). It was with these legends that the speed dropped from 25.5kts to 25kts. No explanation was offered but it seems likely that the extra 0.5kt could not be guaranteed on the proposed displacement and an increase in the latter for so small a gain in speed was not considered worthwhile.

The 22 February gathering was effectively the Committee's final meeting although various subcommittees (with all naval members) were formed to discuss various details of the designs. Despite this, the report they approved on this day was described as the First Progress Report. To the best of the author's knowledge no further full report was ever produced and one cannot help but feel that at this point in the proceedings the Admiralty had decided that the Committee had served its purpose and it was time to return to the *status quo*.

Design and Construction 1905-14

ADMIRALTY WEEKLY ORDER No.351, 24 November 1911. All cruisers of the *Invincible* and later type are, for the future, to be described and classified as battlecruisers in order to distinguish them from armoured cruisers of the older type. (ADM182/2)

While the Committee on Designs was sitting it effectively took over the role of the Controller and the Board of Admiralty with regard to decisions on the designs being developed. Apart from this difference in consulting with higher authority, the DNC's department functioned normally in providing outline designs and suggestions, and then working out the chosen design in increasing detail. Following upon the Committee's First Progress Report, the Admiralty's design organisation returned to normal and the outline design resulting from the recommendation of Design 'E' by the

Indomitable as completed. (Author's collection)

Table 9: *Invincible* class Legend of Particulars, 22 June 1905

DIMENSIONS:	567ft (oa), 530ft (pp) x 78ft 6in x 25ft (fore), 27ft (aft)
DISPLACEMENT:	17,250 tons load, 19,720 tons deep (excl oil)
MACHINERY:	41,000shp = 25kts
COAL:	1000 tons at load draught, 3000 tons max
OIL FUEL:	700 tons
COMPLEMENT:	708
ARMAMENT:	8 x 12in (80rpg); 18 x 12pdr (300rpg); 5 x 18in torpedo tubes (submerged)
ARMOUR:	Belt 6in amidships, 4in forward (extending 7ft 3in above and 4ft below LWL); bulkheads 7in and 6in; barbettes 7in; turrets 7in; CTs 10in and 6in; communication tubes 4in and 3in
PROTECTIVE PLATING:	Main deck 0.75in forward, 1in & 2in under 'A', 'P' and 'Q' barbettes and on crowns of lower CTs; lower deck 1.5in forward, 1.5in (flat) and 2in (slope) amidships, 2.5in aft; 2in splinter protection to base of barbettes; 2.5in torpedo protection bulkheads abreast magazines
WEIGHTS (tons):	
General equipment	660
Armament	2440
Machinery	3300
Engineer's stores	90
Coal	1000
Armour	3460
Hull	6200
BM	100
TOTAL:	17,250

Committee, was approved by the Board on 16 March 1905. This did not differ substantially from that recommended by the Committee except that the number of 12pdr guns was reduced from twenty to eighteen and there were some minor adjustment of the weights which, by 26 April, had increased the estimated displacement to 17,200 tons. The majority of this increase resulted from additions to the machinery and hull.[1] On 22 June 1905 the sheer, midship section, armour and rig drawings and legend of particulars were presented to and approved by the Board (see Table 9). Detailed calculations had resulted in a 10ft reduction in length, a 6in reduction in beam and a 50-ton increase in displacement, the latter again resulting from an increase in machinery weight, although in this case, entirely due to an additional 70 tons for oil fuel fittings. The detailed calculations for the new design were completed in August. (Detailed tables, for weights, dimensions, stability and construction can be found at the end of this chapter.)

The 1905–6 Programme provided for the construction of the *Dreadnought* and three of the new armoured cruisers. In June 1905 the latter had the provisional names *Invincible,*

Inflexible at Spithead in July 1909. (Author's collection)

Immortalite and *Raleigh* but by the time they were laid down the last two names had been changed to *Indomitable* and *Inflexible*. Why there was only one battleship is not entirely clear but it seems likely that this was the result of her being chosen for rapid construction to prove the type and, in particular, to confirm that the turbine machinery and all-big-gun armament would be successful. In addition the available gun mounting and turbine machinery construction capacity made the accelerated construction of more than one vessel impossible and to the majority of the Board, if not Fisher, the battleship was the more important of the two types. *Dreadnought* was completed in January 1907 and, for a prototype, proved highly successful. She was followed by two further classes of similar design that increased the number of dreadnoughts in service to seven by mid-1910. The first of the *Invincible* class[2] ships was not laid down until February 1906, four months after *Dreadnought,* and the class did not complete until 1908. No further armoured cruisers of this type were to be laid down until 1909 although, as we shall see, this was not from any lack of interest on Fisher's part.

While under construction a number of changes were made to the *Invincible* design, the most important being a decision to fit

Table 10: Approved modifications to *Invincible* class during construction

Sixteen 4in guns in place of 12pdr guns	65 tons
14in torpedoes and stores, and dropping gear for 50ft boats	5 tons
Fittings for keeping cable lockers clean	5 tons
Fittings for separate saluting magazine	2 tons
Substitution of cordite cases for air-tight lockers	40 tons
Armament office and domestics' mess	3 tons
Mastheads raised to 180ft above LWL	5 tons
Air-blast for 12in guns	5 tons
Magazine cooling machinery	30 tons
Increase in complement from 708 to 755	10 tons
Electric ring-main system	30 tons
Additional coal hoists	10 tons
Additions to bridge accommodation	5 tons
TOTAL:	215 tons

Invincible with electrically-powered 12in mountings (see Armament chapter) which involved an additional weight of 130 tons, and the substitution of sixteen 4in guns for the original ATB armament of 12pdr guns. The alterations approved up to the time of completion are given in Table 10. These totalled 215 tons, an excess of 115 tons over the Board Margin, while *Invincible* also had the additional 130 tons excess due to her electrically-powered gun mountings. However, none of the three ships greatly

exceeded their designed displacement on completion and *Invincible,* allowing for her extra armament weight, actually came out slightly light. All three ships exceeded 26kts on their measured mile trials and, *as an interpretation of the design requirements,* they were very successful ships (with the sole exception of *Invincible*'s experimental 12in gun mountings!). For a few years they were also the most powerful cruisers in existence and to a great extent fulfilled Fisher's promise of being capable of sinking any ship fast enough to catch them and fast enough to escape from any ship that could sink them (given, of course, clear visibility, they would not have survived long in a close encounter with a *King Edward VII* or a *Lord Nelson*). However, with the completion of the first German battlecruiser in 1911 all this began to change.

The *Invincible* class were provided with various unofficial classifications to mark their difference from the older armoured cruiser type. These included cruiser-battleship, dreadnought cruiser and battlecruiser (the last used by Fisher himself at least as early as 1908) but it was not until late in 1911, with the issue of the Fleet Order quoted at the head of this chapter, that battlecruiser became their official designation.

Years of economy 1905 to 1908

Although Fisher bowed to the opinion of his fellow officers that the *fully armoured* battleship remained the prime unit of a fleet, he did so with obvious reluctance. Early in 1904 Fisher recorded that 'All are agreed that battleships must *for the present* be continued', the emphasis on the 'for the present' being his; and again, in the papers presented to Selborne in October 1904, 'At the present moment *naval experience is not sufficiently ripe to abolish totally the building of battleships* so long as other countries do not do so.' Fisher claimed on several occasions during his first term as First Sea Lord that while President of the Committee on Designs he wanted to build only the *Invincibles* and not the *Dreadnought* but was 'in a minority of one' (he also, in at least one letter, claimed that this view was supported by Lord Kelvin!). Late in 1905, shortly after *Dreadnought* was laid down and before any of the *Invincible* class had been started, he appears to have tried a different approach by proposing a 'fusing' of the two types. It is known that the DNC's department prepared outline designs for such

Table 11 Design 'X4', 2 December 1905

DIMENSIONS:	580ft (pp), 623ft (oa) x 83ft (max) x 27ft 6in (mean)
MACHINERY:	45,000shp = 25kts
ARMAMENT:	10 x 12in/45; 8 x 4in; 18 x 12pdr; 3 x 18in torpedo tubes
ARMOUR:	Belt (amidships), barbettes, gunhouses and CT 11in
WEIGHTS (tons):	
General equipment	750
Armament	3210
Machinery	3550
Coal	1000
Armour	6540
Hull	7350
Board Margin	100
LOAD DISPLACEMENT:	22,500 tons

ships in about November 1905 as the details of one, designated 'X4' and dated 2 December 1905 (see Table 11), are preserved in the Covers for the *Bellerophon* class battleships. Unfortunately the remainder (there were presumably at least an 'X1' to 'X3')[3] do not appear to have survived. The 'X4' design was essentially a 25kt version of *Dreadnought,* with the same armament and armour but with displacement increased from 17,900 tons to 22,500 tons to accommodate an expansion of the machinery power from 23,000shp to 45,000shp. This remarkable design, in anticipating the advent of the fast battleship by several years, would effectively have rendered the *Invincible* obsolete. Fisher seems to have missed the significance, judging by his continued advocacy of the big-gun armoured cruiser, presumably because he did not value heavy armour. Besides, with a little thought it is not difficult to see that any merging of the two types would result in a new type of battleship rather than an advanced form of armoured cruiser. In fact the whole idea tends to descend rapidly into a debate on semantics.

In December or January the fusion proposal was considered by an Admiralty Committee which concluded that such a great increase in size and cost could not be justified and that the 1906–7 Programme should only provide for the construction of more ships of the dreadnought type and that for the present the three *Invincibles* fulfilled Britain's need for armoured cruisers.[4] This conclusion is understandable when it is considered that Britain was already constructing the most advanced armoured

ships in existence. To move their development forward another stage at this early date must have seemed totally unnecessary. In any case the matter soon became academic as the replacement of the Conservative Government by a Liberal one following the Parliamentary elections of January 1906 quickly resulted in demands for further economy in naval spending. Consequently the Naval Estimates steadily declined over the next three years and there was little scope for any dramatic expansion of the construction programmes, either in numbers or in the power of individual ships. In the case of the armoured ships, the planned programme of four vessels per year was actually reduced to three in 1906–7 and 1907–8 and then two in 1908–9. In effect, Fisher became the victim of his own success. The *Dreadnought* so paralysed foreign warship construction that there was for some time no rival against which to maintain superiority, either in numbers or specification, and the British construction programmes were only required to maintain the existing design standard and build up a reasonable reserve. Fisher, subject to political pressure and attacks on his administration, soon began to justify Admiralty shipbuilding policy on the basis of how much further ahead Britain was in the construction of dreadnoughts (which number he tended to boost by the inclusion of the three *Invincibles*) than Germany, which by this time was regarded as Britain's only serious naval rival. In the case of the battlecruisers a more extended breathing space was obtained than with the battleships as details of the armament and speed of the *Invincible* class were initially kept secret. This led the Germans to the logical but incorrect conclusion that they would be standard armoured cruisers except for a uniform-calibre main armament. Therefore their initial answer was *Blücher,* a 15,590-ton armoured cruiser of 24.25kts armed with twelve 8.2in guns, laid down in February 1907. Germany's first true battlecruiser, the *Von Der Tann,* was not laid down until March 1908, the same year in which the three *Invincibles* were completed.

Despite the apparent lack of any major innovation in the development of the British 12in-gun dreadnoughts, more radical ideas *were* discussed in mid-1906 with regard to the armament to be employed in the 1907–8 Programme ships. These included twin and triple 12in gun mountings (for both 45cal

DESIGN AND CONSTRUCTION 1905-14

Invincible entering Malta harbour in October 1913. By this date she was the only ship of her class which still had funnels of equal height – the fore funnels of *Inflexible* and *Indomitable* had been increased in height in 1911 and 1910 respectively in an attempt to reduce smoke interference to the bridge. The fore funnel of *Invincible* was eventually modified during her refit at Gibraltar in Jan–Feb 1915. (R Ellis)

and 50cal guns) and 13.5in twin mountings. However, by December 1906 it had been decided to employ the same layout as that of the previous year's battleship design and the only important change was in the adoption of the 12in/50cal gun. The 1907–8 programme provided for three of these vessels (the *St Vincent* class) and although no battlecruiser was included in the Programme plans were made, and approved, for such a ship.

The first of these appeared on 20 November 1906 when, it is assumed, they were submitted to the Controller, Rear Admiral Jackson, by the DNC. Designated designs 'A', 'B' and 'C' (see Table 12), they were modified *Invincible*s with the wing turrets moved further apart, longitudinally, to increase their arc of training in cross-deck firing and to allow the use of both turrets simultaneously. In addition, in designs 'B' and 'C' only, the thickness of the belt armour for a length of 200ft on each side had been increased to 9in.[5] Design 'C' also had a 4in after belt, an innovation not present in the other two designs or *Invincible*. On the following day modified versions of 'A' and 'B' were produced ('C' having presumably been rejected) in which 12in/50cal guns were substituted for the 12in/45cal guns and the length, and in the case of 'B' the thickness of the armour belt, had been increased. On 22 November a third design, 'D', was produced, similar to 'B' but with further increases in the armour protection. All these designs were slightly slower than *Invincible* as they were larger but employed the same machinery (except 'D' where the increase in size necessitated a 43,000shp installation to keep the speed up to 24kts).

These designs were discussed at a Sea Lords' meeting on 22 November when the DNC was requested to produce a modified version of design 'D' with some adjustments to the distribution of armour and the 25kt speed of *Invincible* restored. This resulted in design 'E', of 5 December 1906, in which the main and upper belts were reduced in thickness by 1in and increased in length, protection was added aft and the torpedo protection bulkheads extended to cover the machinery spaces as well as the magazines (as had already been adopted in the *Bellerophon* class battleships of the 1906–7 Programme). This design was approved at a Board meeting on 11 December and on 19 December the DNC was authorised to begin the detailed design.[6] Although no battlecruiser was included in the 1907–8 Programme work on design 'E' continued for some time – presumably on the basis that it might be revived in the following year.[7]

In June 1907 political pressure for economy, reinforced by the apparently

Table 12: Battlecruiser designs for 1907–8 Programme

DESIGN:	'A'	'B'	'C'	'A'	'B'	'D'	'E'
DATE:	20/11/06	20/11/06	20/11/06	21/11/06	21/11/06	22/11/06	5/12/06
LENGTH (ft):	550	550	550	560	560	565	565
BEAM (ft):	79	79.5	80	81	81	81	83
DRAUGHT (ft):	26.25	26.5	26.75	26.75	27	27	27
SPEED (kts):	24.5	24.5	24.25	24*	24*	24	25
BELT (amidships):**	6in	9in/6in	9in/6in	9in/6in/4in	10in/6in/4in	10in/8in	9in
WEIGHTS (tons):							
General equipment	680	700	700	720	720	720	720
Armament	2600	2600	2600	2780	2780	2780	2780
Machinery	3420	3420	3420	3450	3450	3500	4100
Coal	1000	1000	1000	1000	1000	1000	1000
Armour	3600	3860	4180	4500	4650	5150	5200
Hull	6700	6820	6900	7150	7200	7450	7500
BM	100	100	100	100	100	100	100
TOTAL:	18,100	18,500	18,900	19,700	19,900	20,700	21,400

* On 22 November speed of 'A' was changed to 24.5kts and that of 'B' to 24.25kts.
** Armour and protective plating in 'A' of 20 November was as *Invincible*; in the other designs it was as *Invincible* except for the side armour. All designs carried an armament of 8 x 12in guns (45cal in those of 20 November and 50cal in rest), 16 x 4in guns and 5 x 18in torpedo tubes (later reduced to three in design 'E'). All designs had a maximum coal stowage of 3000 tons. By June 1907 the following weights had been added to the estimate for design 'E': armament 180 tons, machinery 90 tons, armour 270 tons, hull 60 tons, increasing the load displacement to 22,000 tons.

Inflexible at Genoa on 5 March 1914. Since completion she has had her fore funnel raised in height, additional searchlight platforms added abreast the fore funnel and a new fore top fitted for her Argo rangefinder. Note that the torpedo net booms have been hoisted up parallel to the deck edge. (Author's collection)

advanced state of Britain's dreadnought construction, prompted the Board to put forward a conservative building programme for the 1908–9 Estimates. This included one dreadnought and two armoured cruisers which, it was proposed, should revert to a 9.2in gun armament.[8] It is difficult to believe that Fisher would agree happily to this latter change, which would have meant abandoning his beloved battlecruisers, but it seems fairly certain that, at this time, his fellow Board members did not share his wholehearted belief in these ships. He was, however, still under pressure to reduce expenditure and a 9.2 in gun ship would have been less costly (he was also somewhat preoccupied at this time by a dispute with Admiral Lord Charles Beresford, C-in-C Channel Fleet). Despite these efforts at economy the Cabinet rejected the Admiralty's Sketch Estimates in November and directed the First Lord, Lord Tweedmouth, to get them reduced. The programme was further modified to include, among other reductions, only one armoured cruiser but the Estimates were still rejected. This generated a major dispute between the Admiralty and the Government in which Fisher, who did not at this time see any major danger in a reduced programme and was concerned about accusations of Admiralty overspending, initially followed the government line. However, his hand was forced by the other Sea Lords, Vice Admiral Sir W May and Rear Admirals H Jackson and A Winsloe, who obtained Fisher's support, by threat of resignation, in a campaign to retain the 'modest' programme already proposed. In a memorandum to Tweedmouth dated 3 December, the four Sea Lords pointed out that, far from a reduction, an increase was required to counter the recently published construction plans of the German Navy and to avoid a major compensatory expansion of the 1909–10 Programme. Moreover, if, as suggested, the battleship was dropped from the Programme the effects would be serious not only to the maintenance of Britain's naval supremacy but on her gun and armour plate manufacturing plant (which relied on continuity of orders). The argument dragged on until February when, although the Cabinet did extract a further reduction in the Estimates, the modified Shipbuilding Programme, complete with its single battlecruiser (the 12in gun had by this time been reinstated), was accepted more or less intact.

The *Indefatigable* class

The new battlecruiser design followed the layout of design 'E' but omitted the improvements in side armour and underwater protection and reverted to the 45cal 12in gun. This was design 'A' (see Table 13) of 30 March 1908 which, judging by the designation, may actually have been a reworking of the 'A' design of 20 November 1906. The design was essentially an enlarged *Invincible* on which the only real improvement was the ability to fire the wing turrets across the deck without restriction and over a wider arc of fire (70°). If anything the design was weaker for, although she could claim a true, if restricted, broadside of eight guns and some small improvements in protection, the main belt abreast 'A' and 'Y' turrets was actually reduced in thickness to 4in. In the documents consulted there is no record of any preliminary discussions on this design or any variations for it, but it seems likely that the innovations of design 'E' were abandoned to reduce the size and save cost (the estimated displacement of design 'E' in

Indefatigable as completed. She was easily distinguished from her two half-sisters by the main top, which was not provided in *Australia* and *New Zealand*. (Author's collection)

June 1907 was 22,000 tons). It is also possible, of course, that Fisher objected to the ship being saddled with the extra armour. The final detailed design (see Table 13), with only minor changes from the March estimate, received Board approval in November 1908. It was decided that the new ship was to be named *Indefatigable* on 9 December 1908 and her construction began at Devonport Dockyard in February 1909.

Indefatigable has been greatly criticised as showing no improvement on the *Invincible* class at a time when the Germans had begun the construction of a larger and better protected battlecruiser of their own – the *Von der Tann* (see Table 18), which was launched shortly after the *Indefatigable* commenced building. However, little information was available on the German ship at this time (the Germans having followed Fisher's lead and become very secretive). In the 1909 and 1910 editions of *Brassey's Naval Annual* the ship was credited with twelve 11in guns but even in the 1911 edition, where the armament is given correctly as eight 11in, the protection was still believed to be on a par with that of *Invincible*. The Admiralty did obtain more accurate information on the German ship somewhat sooner than this but not soon enough to allow any improvement to *Indefatigable*. Although she should not therefore be criticised on the basis of comparisons not available at the time, it should have been realised that the construction of battlecruisers by Germany effectively negated Fisher's principal arguments for such ships – which now faced the prospect of fighting an enemy on terms of, at the very least, equality rather than advantage.

Table 13: Design 'A' (*Indefatigable*) Legend of Particulars, November 1908

DIMENSIONS:	555ft (pp), 590ft (oa) x 80ft (max) x 26ft 6in (mean)
DISPLACEMENT:	18,750 tons (load)
MACHINERY:	43,000shp = 25kts
COAL:	1000 tons (load); 3000 tons (max)
OIL FUEL:	850 tons
COMPLEMENT:	737
ARMAMENT:	8 x 12in (80rpg); 16 x 4in (100rpg); 5 x Maxim MG; 2 x 18in submerged torpedo tubes
ARMOUR:	Belt 6in amidships, 4in at ends, 2.5in fore and aft (extending 7ft 6in above and 3ft 6in below LWL); bulkheads 3in and 4in forward, 4.5in and 4in aft; barbettes 7in; gunshields 10in and 7in; CT 10in (fore), 6in (aft); communication tubes 4in (fore), 3in (aft); signal tower 3in
PROTECTIVE PLATING:	Funnel uptakes 1.5in and 1in; torpedo bulkheads abreast magazines 2.5in; splinter protection to 12in gun hoists 2in; main deck 1in; Lower deck 1.5in (flat), 2in (slope) amidships, 2in fore and aft
WEIGHTS (tons):	
General equipment:	680
Armament:	2580*
Machinery:	3655
Coal:	1000
Armour:	3735
Hull:	7000
Board margin:	100
TOTAL:	18,750 tons

* Armament weight excludes shrapnel shells for 12in guns which was under consideration.

The original March 1908 legend differed from the above as follows: length (oa) 585ft, beam 80ft 6in, side armour extended to 7ft above and 4ft below LWL; weights (tons) – general equipment 665, armament 2540, machinery 3650, armour 3800, hull 6995.

The above excuse cannot, however, be offered in the case of *Indefatigable*'s two sister ships, *Australia* and *New Zealand*. These vessels were paid for by the Colonies after which they were named, in the case of the former to form part of the Royal Australian Navy and serve as its flagship, and in the case of the latter as an outright gift to the Royal Navy. These two ships were not laid down until June 1910 by which time British

Germany's first battlecruiser, *Von Der Tann*, seen here at the Spithead Coronation Review in 1911. (Courtesy R A Burt)

Far Left: *New Zealand* viewed from astern in 1913. (Author's collection)

Left: Looking aft from the port side of the bridge of *Australia* in 1917 with *New Zealand* astern. The rangefinder hood of 'P' turret is visible at centre bottom. (Imperial War Museum: Q18718)

designs had moved on (see below) and the nature of German construction plans had become much clearer. A number of reasons might be advanced for the construction of these two ships, none of which can be supported by any direct evidence, but it seems likely that Fisher's influence was at work in giving preference to the battlecruiser type. For Australia the choice was more excusable in that the use of Second Class battleships and large cruisers as flagships on distant stations was standard practice. This was certainly not the case with *New Zealand* and one can only conclude that in this case it was purely financial limits that controlled the choice of design. There was of course, also the fact that Fisher's ability as a publicist had boosted the reputation of these ships in the public mind well beyond their true value.

The *Australia* and *New Zealand* were not exact copies of the *Indefatigable,* differing primarily in the arrangement of their armour forward and aft (see Armour chapter) There were also some minor alterations to the internal arrangements and the bridge structure, and the specified machinery power was increased from 43,000shp to 44,000shp although there was no corresponding increase in the required speed. These changes necessitated a slight alteration of the weights (see Table 14), which resulted in a 50-ton increase in the legend displacement (actually only 10 tons as the *Indefatigable* had by this time lost 40 tons from her Board Margin).

The *Lion class*

On 8 September 1908 Fisher wrote the following, often quoted, passage in a letter to Lord Esher: 'I've got Sir Philip Watts into a new *Indomitable* that will make your mouth water when you see it! (and the Germans gnash their teeth).' It is unlikely, as is often

Left: *Australia* steams towards the battlecruiser anchorage after passing under the Forth Bridge, late in 1917. In the background, left to right, are *Renown, Repulse, Lion* and *Tiger.* (Imperial War Museum: Q18725)

Table 14: Modified weights for Australia and New Zealand, 1909

	Indefatigable	*Australia*
GENERAL EQUIPMENT:	690	690
ARMAMENT:	2610	2615
MACHINERY:	3655	3655
COAL:	1000	1000
ARMOUR:	3735	3670
HULL:	7000	7070
BOARD MARGIN:	60	100
LOAD DISPLACEMENT:	18,750 tons	18,800 tons

assumed, that this refers to the *Indefatigable* as it was written several months after the outline design for that ship had been approved and only a short time before her design calculations were complete. A few days later, on 17 September, he wrote the following to the DNC:

My Dear Watts,
  Kindly send me a few lines to say whether any bright flashes of your genius have further illuminated our very fast big-gun battle cruiser *Indomitable.* We want to see her live! Let us call her 'Sanspareil'! But if we have to accept fewer guns, then let us call her the 'Incompatible'. For it will not be compatible with our brilliant progress if we do no more than just separate the midship guns, which practically is all that a fewer-gun ship will give us in the shape of improvement.
  If we go to work the same way as we did with *Dreadnought,* we shall succeed, because [it is] so obviously silly to refuse an increase of 25 per cent of power in the 'Sansparcil', with only an increase of 4 per cent in cost and 5 per cent in displacement and to go into all the same docks (save one out of three at Malta) as the 'Incompatible' …[9]

Although to some extent this letter is incomprehensible without the background information that prompted it, it contains some clues as to what was under discussion at the time. It was at this time of year that early planning commenced for the following year's Naval Estimates, the proposed building programme, based on preliminary designs, normally being ready for Parliament in the spring. There was already concern about the extent of the German shipbuilding programme and suspicions that their ships would exceed those of the British in size, which meant they would have some advantage – as yet unclear, although they would at least be of closely-equivalent speed to British ships. Fisher must have realised that to maintain the advantages he claimed for the battlecruiser it would be necessary to increase speed still further. Judging by the 'very fast' statement, he had asked the DNC to look into designing such a ship and been told that this meant either a substantial increase in size or a reduction of armament weight. Fisher, in his usual fashion, seems to have been trying to minimise this problem, which was, in any case, soon to evaporate.

Shortly after the argument over the 1908–9 Estimates was settled, Tweedmouth was replaced by Reginald McKenna, a much more capable First Lord who did a great deal to advance the cause of the Navy in the Cabinet and in Parliament. At a meeting with the Sea Lords on 4 May 1908 he agreed that the 1909–10 Programme should include at least four armoured ships to compensate for the reduction in the previous year, and if necessary this might be increased to six. By the end of the year the Admiralty, having received intelligence of the expansion of Germany's shipbuilding and gun manufacturing capabilities, were convinced that Germany was accelerating her proposed construction programme and was about to mount a major challenge to Britain's naval supremacy. Consequently, on 8 December 1908, McKenna recommended the construction of six dreadnoughts to the Cabinet, which precipitated another major conflict between the Cabinet and the Admiralty over the forthcoming estimates. Whatever the Cabinet's doubts concerning the reality of the Admiralty's contention, the argument soon spread to include the Opposition and the Press, and the Government quickly found itself under fire from all directions regarding its guardianship of the country's security. In February 1909, in the hope of quietening the furore, it was decided to put forward a Programme for four ships, as originally intended, but to provide for the possible German expansion by allowing for the construction of a further four 'contingent' vessels if this proved necessary. In announcing this decision in Parliament on 16 March, McKenna said that 'No matter what the cost the safety of the country must be assured' and went on to say that two of the

ships would be laid down in July, two more in November and the remaining four later if required. This statement did not satisfy the Admiralty or the agitators as it was suspected that the last four ships might never be built or, if they were, those of the following year would be cut back. The Government eventually yielded to the continued pressure and in July announced that the four 'contingent' ships would definitely be laid down before the end of the 1909–10 Programme Year and would not prejudice the 1910–11 Construction Programme. Despite the impression given that the extra ships would be late additions, the British were in fact doing what they were accusing the Germans of doing – accelerating the Construction Programme. Battleships were normally laid down toward the end of the programme year (Dec–April) but the first two ships of the 1909–10 Programme (the battleships *Colossus* and *Hercules*) were laid down in July and the next two ships (the battleship *Orion* and the battlecruiser *Lion*) in November. The four contingent ships followed in April 1910 – towards the end of the normal time for construction to begin.

The new programme did not simply allow for an increase in numbers. The Admiralty were also greatly concerned about being outclassed on a qualitative level and gained approval for a substantial increase in the size and power of future battleships and battlecruisers. This was to be achieved by an increase in both gun power and, in the battlecruisers only, speed. The former took the form of the 13.5in gun, firing a 1250lbs projectile (compared with 850lbs for the 12in), approval for the design and manufacture of which had been given by Fisher on 21 October 1908 (one wonders if he picked Trafalgar Day deliberately!). This decision was too late for the first two ships of the Programme and Fisher was concerned that it might also be too late for the 'contingent' ships. On 5 March 1909 he wrote to McKenna: 'What so disquiets me now is that 4 of the German dreadnoughts are of 22,000 tons and that cruiser 'H' will surpass the *Indomitable*. What an uproar there will be if we are over classed. I ought to have pressed my convictions of a year ago to the bitter end for the more powerful 13½-inch gun armament. It is now too late, I fear, for the 4 ships to be laid down on April 1, 1910 [to be so armed]'.[10] It was not in fact too late for these, or the two earlier vessels laid down in November – the

Lion as first completed with her foremast abaft the fore funnel. Note the low height of the second and third funnels, the unprotected 4in gun on the forward shelter deck, water measuring tank (for water consumption trials) abreast the mainmast and the location of the conning tower under the bridge. (Author's collection)

last six vessels, all armed with the 13.5in gun, became the four *Orion* class battleships and the two *Lion* class battlecruisers. That Fisher was still more interested in the battlecruiser type can be seen in another letter to McKenna written at the end of March 1909: 'We have to work hard in the next two years to build 8 'Nonpareils' to meet cruisers 'E', 'F', 'G' and 'H'. Cruiser 'F', the *Blücher*, has 8 11-inch guns and a speed of 25 knots – you want 28 knots to catch her!'[11] He was of course incorrect with regard to *Blücher* but was certainly justified in his concern about the other German ships, which substantially outclassed their British opposite numbers. His demand for eight ships was not fulfilled, a pattern of one battlecruiser to each class of battleship being maintained for the next two Programme years, but he did get 28kts for the battlecruiser.

Before passing on to the *Lion* class design, an occurrence during the discussions on the design of the *Orion* class is worthy of recording as illustrating Fisher's continued obsession with speed and his concern over the quality of German ships. On 12 May 1909 the Board of Admiralty, consisting of McKenna, Fisher, Jellicoe, Winsloe and the Civil Lord G Lambert MP (Bridgeman, the Second Sea Lord, was absent), met to discuss the proposed designs for the 13.5in-gun ships. The discussion on the battlecruiser was postponed for later consideration and effort was concentrated on the battleship designs, which were for alternative 21kt and 23kt ships, the higher speed in the second design being obtained by an increase in size. The Board decided on the slower of the two, much to Fisher's disgust and he had his protest recorded in the Board Minutes in the following terms.

> In my judgement the alternative design for a battleship of 23 knots is preferable for tactical reasons to the 21 knot design adopted by the Board, in view of the evidence that the new German battleships are to have 30,000 Horse Power with a probable speed of 23 knots. It is not desirable we should be outclassed in any type of ship.
> The increased cost of £150,000, or £200,000, would be worth spending for the sake of equalling the alleged German speed.[12]

Discussion on the battlecruiser design was again postponed at Board Meetings on 17 and 26 May but on 27 May it was decided to adopt an eight-gun design with all turrets on the centre-line, two forward (with 'B' mounting superfiring over 'A'), one amidships and one aft. This decision simply followed the pattern set with the *Orion* class, the arrangement being identical except for the omission of the superfiring turret aft. Unfortunately the details of the designs which led up to this decision do not appear to have survived. The first design mentioned in the Ship's Covers is Design 'CV' (again one presumes there was a 'CI' to 'CIV' and possibly an 'A' and 'B') which was submitted by the DNC to the Controller, Jellicoe, on 7 June 1909 with the statement that it had been carefully revised and differed only slightly from that presented previously. Among the other comments that accompanied the rough drawings and legend (see Table 15) was that the DNC considered that 'For the purposes of comparison and in consequence of the increased armoured protection the new vessel may be regarded as a battleship as well as a cruiser.'[13] He also stated that if the ship's length was increased by three frame spaces (12ft) an additional twin 13.5in mounting could be added aft to superfire over 'X' mounting (which in such a case would have been redesignated as 'Y' mounting). This was expected to add little to the cost of the ship but would add about £175,000 to the armament cost, which, the DNC pointed out, was only a 7 per cent increase in overall cost for a 25 per cent gain in broadside fire. This idea was not taken up by the Board but it can be safely assumed that Fisher, at least, would have found this a very attractive proposal. The completed design for 'CV' was approved by the Board on 18 August 1909.

Table 15: Design 'CV' (*Lion* class) Legend of Particulars, 7 June 1909

DIMENSIONS:	700ft (oa), 660ft (pp) x 88ft 6in x 28ft (mean)
DISPLACEMENT:	26,350 tons
MACHINERY:	70,000shp = 28kts
COAL:	1000 tons at load draught, 3800 tons max
OIL FUEL:	1000 tons
COMPLEMENT:	920
ARMAMENT:	8 x 13.5in (80rpg); 16 x 4in 150rpg); 5 x Maxim MG; 2 x 21in torpedo tubes (submerged)
ARMOUR:	Belt 9in (main), 6in (upper) amidships, 6in and 5in forward, 5in aft (extending 16ft above and 3ft 6in below LWL); bulkheads 5in forward, 9in and 5in aft; barbettes 9in and 8in; gunshields 10in and 7in; CT 10in; communication tube 4in
PROTECTIVE PLATING:	Upper deck 1in over citadel; lower deck 1in–1.25in amidships, 2.5in at ends; 1.5in and 1in funnel uptakes; 2.5in, 1.5in and 1in torpedo protection bulkheads abreast magazines
WEIGHTS (tons):	
General equipment	760
Armament	3260
Machinery	5840
Coal	1000
Armour	5930
Hull	9460
BM	100
TOTAL:	26,350 tons

The final approved legend of 18 August 1909 was as above except for the following:
Max coal stowage 3700 tons, oil fuel 1100 tons.
Complement 960.
Armour: after bulkheads 8in and 5in, barbettes 9in and 8in, gunshields 9in, communication tube 4in and 3in, Weights (tons) – general equipment 800, machinery 5340, armour 6140, hull 9710.
By early 1910 the armour had been further modified, the complement increased to 984 and the design weights adjusted as follows (tons) – general equipment 805, armament 3270, armour, 6400, hull 9660. The Board margin had been entirely absorbed and the design load displacement had increased to 26,475 tons.

The improvement over the earlier British battlecruisers was dramatic: apart from the major increase in firepower, the design provided for a 3kt increase in speed and a substantial increase in protection. The latter included a 9in belt and barbettes, while a 6in upper belt extended the side armour to the upper deck. However, the side armour abreast the forward and after 13.5in mountings was little better than that of *Indefatigable* and overall the design did not compare well with its German equivalents. This and other weaknesses in the protection meant that, despite the DNC's comment, they fell well short of the 'fast battleship' ideal. The cost of the high speed was marked – compared with the *Orion*, which had much heavier armour and carried ten 13.5in guns, the *Lion* was 7kts faster and 4000 tons heavier. From this time on British battlecruisers were consistently larger than their contemporary battleships.

Lion after her 1912 reconstruction with the fore funnel and bridge moved aft, the second and third funnels increased in height and the foremast altered from tripod to pole, now fitted forward of the fore funnel. Note that the 4in guns on the forward shelter deck are provided with a blast screen but are yet to be enclosed in a casemate. (Author's collection)

Lion, like *Indefatigable,* was built by Devonport Dockyard, these two being the only battlecruisers built in a Royal Dockyard. Her sister ship, *Princess Royal* was put out to tender on 7 August 1909 and that from Vickers (dated 5 November) was accepted by telegram on 18 December.

In December 1909 the arrangement of armour was reconsidered, and resulted in a reworking of the protection at the forward and after end of the citadel (see Armour chapter). These changes involved a total additional weight of 210 tons. As 5.5 tons had already been appropriated from the Board Margin (3.5 tons for an increase in complement of 29, and 2 tons for an additional 30ft cutter), this left a surplus of 115.5 tons. On 24 January 1910 Jellicoe proposed that this be carried as additional weight and the fuel stowage be reduced to compensate. No reduction in fuel seems to have occurred and the completed ships were actually just light of their designed displacement.

All the ships of the 1909–10 Programme were designed with their fore funnels placed forward of the foremast. This layout, which had not been employed since the *Dreadnought,* was adopted because these ships, following decisions relating to fire control (see Armament chapter), had no main mast and it had therefore been decided to use the foremast as the main (heavy boat) derrick post – an arrangement that could only be employed if the mast was abaft the funnel. Unfortunately, under certain conditions of wind direction and ship's heading, the smoke and heat from the funnel could seriously interfere with the foretop and bridge to a much greater extent than was the case with the more normal arrangement. The heat was a particular problem as it could so raise the temperature of the mast that access to the foretop (which was via ladders inside the tripod struts) was totally cut-off.

These problems first revealed themselves in 1911 during the trials of *Hercules* and *Colossus* and, to a lesser extent, in *Orion* (her fore funnel served only six boilers whereas those of the two earlier ships served twelve). Although not ideal, it was decided that the existing arrangement in these ships could be accepted. The *Lion,* however, proved a very different case as a result of the considerably greater heat and smoke generated by her boilers. Following her steam trials in January 1912 the Controller, Rear Admiral Charles Briggs, reported that he had seen the ship's Captain, A A M Duff, and

> it appears to be quite certain that the arrangements for control from the top and spotting from the spotting tower would be of little or no value for war. Presumably no ship would go into action without having fires in all boilers and in these conditions the fumes from the fore funnel would suffocate the operators in the top, who would also have a good chance of being burnt. It is not to be expected that the delicate instruments would be of any value there.
>
> The bridge is placed almost on top of the spotting tower and consequently obscures the view with a slight roll.

Princess Royal as completed; her forward shelter deck 4in guns are enclosed in casemates. (Author's collection)

Rangefinders are placed in two turrets and guns could be controlled from them but I consider that neither of the turrets are suitable for the primary control. It therefore appears necessary to alter this state of things at once at the expense of delaying the completion of the ship and extra cost.

Proposals include to steer from the conning tower always and to fit a control tower abaft the conning tower, thus simulating the arrangement to those lately approved for the *King George V* class. The cost will probably not be less than £25,000 and time three months. As the ship is now in hand until middle of March for opening up machinery prior to acceptance, if this work is commenced at once the ship could be completed in early May. These remarks apply also to *Princess Royal*.[14]

In addition to these problems the upper bridge was 'uninhabitable' due to the heat and fumes, the manoeuvring compass was difficult to use and unreliable due to the proximity of the funnel and the signal flags and halyards were in danger of being burnt. In short her value as a fighting ship was seriously impaired. After some discussion it was concluded that the only solution was a complete rearrangement of the forward superstructure with the positions of mast and funnel reversed. The estimated cost was £25,000 per ship (the *Princess Royal* which was still fitting out had also to be altered) and it was hoped that the work would be completed in three months. In fact it cost over £30,000 per ship and the work took a few weeks longer. The main alterations were as follows:

(a) New fore funnel, 14ft in external diameter, fitted further aft.
(b) Heights of second and third funnel raised to same height as fore funnel (81ft above LWL).
(c) Existing mainmast fitted in place of foremast, forward of new funnel.
(d) Positions of heavy and light boats reversed, former being repositioned abaft mainmast and latter between first and second funnels.
(e) Foremast, without struts, refitted as mainmast complete with boat derrick.
(f) Stump masts and derricks fitted abreast second funnel to serve light boats.
(g) New bridge structure constructed between CT and fore funnel. All structure within 20ft of compass built from naval brass.
(h) Conning tower enlarged and spotting tower removed.

Queen Mary

The battlecruiser of the 1910–11 Programme, although generally listed separately, was virtually a third unit of the *Lion* class with some minor improvements and changes. With her displacement increased to 27,000 tons it was necessary to increase the beam by 6in to restore the load draught to 28ft and, to maintain the speed of 28kts, the machinery power from 70,000shp to 75,000shp. In addition the forward 4in gun battery was provided with 3in armour protection and there were some minor changes to the distribution of the belt armour.

In December 1911, following the problems with *Colossus*, *Hercules* and *Orion*, it was decided to reverse the positions of her

Table 16: Legend of Particulars of *Queen Mary*, 1910

DIMENSIONS:	700ft (oa), 660ft (pp) x 89ft x 28ft (mean)
DISPLACEMENT:	27,000 tons
MACHINERY:	75,000shp = 28kts
COAL:	1000 tons at load draught, 3700 tons max
OIL FUEL:	1100 tons
COMPLEMENT:	999
ARMAMENT:	8 x 13.5in (80rpg); 16 x 4in (150rpg); 5 x Maxim MG; 2 x 21in torpedo tubes (submerged)
ARMOUR:	Belt 9in (main), 6in (upper) amidships, 6in, 5in and 4in forward, 5in and 4in aft (extending 16ft above and 3ft 6in below LWL); bulkheads 4in forward and aft; barbettes 9in and 8in; gunshields 9in; CT 10in forward, 2in aft; communication tube 4in and 3in forward; forward 4in battery 3in
PROTECTIVE PLATING:	Shelter deck 1in over 4in gun battery; forecastle deck 1.25in and 1in; upper deck 1in over citadel; lower deck – 1.25in amidships, 2.5in at ends; 1.5in and 1in funnel uptakes; 2.5in, 1.5in and 1in torpedo protection bulkheads abreast magazines
WEIGHTS (tons):	
General equipment	805
Armament	3300
Machinery	5460
Coal	1000
Armour	6575
Hull	9760
BM	100
TOTAL:	27,000 tons

fore funnel and foremast. The changes were along generally similar lines to those later adopted in *Lion* and *Princess Royal* except that the trunking for the fore funnel and the

Queen Mary in 1914. She could be distinguished from the *Lion* and *Princess Royal* by her wider second funnel, the absence of 4in guns on the forward shelter deck and the provision of a stern walk and the after torpedo/control tower. (Author's collection)

design of the bridge structure were slightly different and there were some minor changes to the distribution of the belt armour.

In February 1911, following a decision to adopt heavier projectiles for her 13.5in guns (see Armament chapter), 52 tons was appropriated from the Board Margin for the extra load and in May 1911 a further 20 tons to provide for an after control tower with 6in armour walls. The remainder of the Board Margin was absorbed in April 1912 when a third hydraulic pump was fitted for the main armament. As completed the ship was 230 tons light of her designed load displacement.

Tiger

The debate on the design of the 1911–12 Programme battlecruiser continued somewhat longer than in the case of earlier ships. As usual there appears to be no record of the early development of the design but in July 1911 Watts submitted three outline designs, 'A', 'A1' and 'C' (see Table 17) to the Controller for circulation to the Sea Lords; there is no mention of a design 'B' in the Ship's Covers and one must assume that this was rejected earlier. In the two 'A' designs the 13.5in mountings were disposed two forward and two aft, with 'B' and 'X' superfiring over 'A' and 'Y' turrets. In design 'C' the third turret was placed further forward, between the engine rooms and boiler rooms, which position, the DNC explained was found convenient because of the altered positions of bulkheads resulting from the introduction of an after torpedo room. This placed the turret abaft the masts and funnels and, unlike that in *Queen Mary*, gave it a clear arc of fire across the stern. The 'A' designs also had a 6in secondary gun battery, following upon a decision already arrived at for the battleships of the 1911–12 Programme (the *Iron Duke* class), with 5in armour protection which effectively increased the height of the side armour amidships by one deck. To accommodate the additional top weight the beam in the 'A' designs was increased to 91ft

Table 17 Battlecruiser designs for 1911–12 Programme

Design:	'A'	'A1'	'A2'	'C'	'A2'	'A2*'	'A2**'
Date:	July 1911	July 1911	July 1911	July 1911	12 Dec 1911	15 Dec 1911	15 Dec 1911
Length (ft):	660	660	660	660	660	660	660
Beam (ft):	91	91	91	89	90.5	90.5	90.5
Draught (ft):	28.5	28.25	28.25	28.25	28.25	28.33	28.5
Displacement (tons):	28,450	28,100	28,100	27,250	28,200	28,300	28,500
SHP:	80,000	79,000	79,000	76,000	82,000	100,000	108,000
Speed (kts):	28	28	28	28	28	29.5	30

ARMAMENT (all designs): 8 x 13.5in (80rpg)
Designs 'A' and 'C' 16 x 4in (150rpg), rest 16 x 6in (150rpg – increased to 200rpg in design 'A2' by November 1911)
Two 12pdr (design 'A' only)
Five Maxim MG
Four submerged 21in torpedo tubes.

ARMOUR (all designs): Main belt 9in (amidships), 5in and 4in (fore and aft); upper belt 6in (amidships), 5in and 4in (fore), 5in (aft); lower belt 3in (not in design 'C'); Side armour extending from 24ft 3in (24ft 6in in design 'C') above to 6ft (3ft 9in in design 'C') below LWL; bulkheads 4in (additional 2in bulkhead added forward in 'A2' design of December 1911); barbettes 9in and 8in; CT 10in (fore), 6in (aft); gun-shields 9in; communication tubes 4in and 3in (forw), 4in (aft); secondary gun battery 5in (4in in design 'C'; increased to 6in in 'A2' design of December 1911).

PROTECTIVE PLATING: Shelter deck 1in over 6in gun battery in design 'A2' only, 1in over 12pdr guns in design 'A' only; forecastle deck 1.5in (1in and 1.5in in design 'A' and in design 'A2' of December 1911); upper deck 1in over citadel except under secondary gun battery; main deck 1in outside citadel; lower deck 1in amidships, 3in (2.5in in design 'C') forward; torpedo bulkheads 2.5in, 1.5in and 1in; funnel uptakes 1.5in and 1in.

Weights (tons):							
General equipment	820	820	820	820	840	840	840
Armament	3860	3650	3650	3450	3650	3650	3650
Machinery	5780	5720	5720	5500	5550	5650	5900
Fuel	1000	1000	1000	1000	1000	1000	900
Armour	7030	6980	6980	6730	7360	7360	7360
Hull	9860	9830	9830	9650	9650	9650	9770
BM	100	100	100	100	100	100	100
Total:	28,450	28,100	28,100	27,250	28,200	28,300	28,500

and to maintain the required speed the specified engine power was also increased.

In discussing these designs the Sea Lords rapidly concluded that they preferred the 'A1' design generally but criticised the limited arcs of fire of the 6in guns on forward and after bearings and asked the DNC to look into improving this. In addition it was decided that in general layout design 'C' was preferable because 'two turrets so close together practically form one target, when sufficiently separated as in 'C' it means the enemy has three separate targets to fire at which complicates his fire control, this is important up to 10,000 yards.'[15] This resulted in the production of design 'A2', a variation on 'A1' with the armament layout of 'C', the embrasures of the forward 6in guns being altered to allow them to fire 3° across the bow and the battery armour increased to 6in thickness. This (together with the three previous designs), was submitted to the Sea Lords on 14 August and received Board approval four days later. The DNC was asked to proceed with the design as rapidly as possible and this, apart from the usual minor changes, would probably have been an end to the matter but for a major political change in the Board of Admiralty as a result of demands for the formation of a Naval War Staff.

In October 1911 the Home Secretary, Winston Churchill, exchanged posts with Reginald McKenna and shortly afterwards the Board was reconstituted in line with the new First Lord's wishes. Of the original Sea Lords only the Controller, Rear Admiral Briggs, was to remain. Admiral Sir A K Wilson (the First Sea Lord since Fisher's departure) was replaced by Admiral Sir Francis Bridgeman, Vice Admiral Sir G Le C Egerton (the Second Sea Lord) was replaced by Vice Admiral Prince Louis of Battenberg and Captain C E Madden (the Fourth Sea Lord) by Captain W Pakenham. One of Churchill's first moves was to seek the advice of Fisher who, during three days of discussion at Reigate Priory, was 'most of all … stimulating in all matters related to the design of ships'.[16] Churchill was soon infected with Fisher's great obsessions for speed, gun power and all oil-fired boilers, and carried these back to the Admiralty where the new Board took up its duties on 5 December 1911.

Churchill was much more inclined to become involved in the details of warship design than was normal for a First Lord and on 20 November 1911 requested that the tender for the armoured cruiser be delayed while he made a few inquiries into the design. This inquiry appears to have resulted in a proposal to increase the speed of the new ship. On 12 December 1911 the final design of 'A2' was approved by the Board 'subject to certain modifications to secure additional horse power.' On the same day Churchill asked if the boilers of all the armoured ships of the 1911–12 Programme could be adapted to use oil fuel only.

On 15 December Watts submitted to the Controller modified legends designated 'A2*' and 'A2**'. In 'A2*' the machinery power was increased to 100,000shp for a speed of 29.5kts at the cost of an additional 100 tons displacement and an increased sinkage of 1in. In 'A2**' the power was further increased to 108,000shp for a speed of 30kts, which added 300 tons to the displacement and 3in to the draught, and her fuel was modified to half coal/half oil. It was also necessary in 'A2**' to increase the width of the boilers and boiler rooms. Watts added that the machinery could be modified to oil-fuel only but that 'to carry the same amount of fuel oil would require some to be carried above the protective deck which is undesirable and the loss of protection by giving up coal above this deck would be considerable.'[17]

Rear Admiral Briggs appears to have passed on the details of 'A2**' only, with the comment that all oil-fuel arrangements could be adopted at little added cost provided the decision was not delayed. However, he was more inclined to favour the increased oil stowage in combination with coal, as recommended by the DNC, as the additional oil would assist in attaining the speed and valuable experience would be gained in the design and construction of the oil stowage arrangements. On 20 December, the day after design 'A2**' received approval, the DNC suggested that the inner bottom compartments could be employed for additional oil-fuel stowage and if all these were fitted with the necessary pipes, valves etc, the maximum fuel stowage could be increased to 7350 tons (3750 tons oil/3600 tons coal) in an emergency. This proposal was approved by Briggs on the following day. Detailed design resulted in a reduction of these figures to 6800 tons (3480 tons oil/3320 tons coal) in the completed ship; however, under normal circumstances the maximum stowage was not expected to exceed 2450 tons oil and 2450 tons coal, and during the First World War the normal maximum actually carried was 800 tons oil and 3240 tons coal.

On 2 March 1912 a tender from J Brown (dated 23 January) was provisionally accepted for the new ship which was to become HMS *Tiger*. A final letter of acceptance was sent on 3 April 1912 and the contract was signed on the following day.

The main alterations made to the ship between the approval of the design and completion were:

(a) On 10 February 1912 it was approved to fit anti-rolling tanks and these were

Tiger in 1916–17. Note the searchlight mounted on the roof of 'Q' turret. (Imperial War Museum: SP1674)

The German battlecruiser *Moltke* interned at Scapa Flow, 1919. (Author's collection)

Table 18: German battlecruiser designs 1907–13

Ships	Laid down	Completed	Load displacement (tonnes)	Armament	Belt armour (in)	Barbettes armour (in)	shp	Speed (kts)
Blücher	1907	1911	15,600	12 x 8.2in 8 x 5.9in 4 x 17.7in TT	7	7	34,000(ihp)	24.25
Von Der Tann	1908	1911	19,000	8 x 11in 10 x 5.9in 4 x 17.7in TT	10	9	43,600	24.75 (27)
Moltke	1908	1912	22,600	10 x 11in	11	9	52,000	25
Goeben	1909	1912	22,600	12 x 5.9in 4 x 19.7in TT				(28)
Seydlitz	1911	1913	24,600	10 x 11in 12 x 5.9in 4 x 19.7in TT	12	9	63,000	25.5 (28)
Derfflinger	1912	1914	26,200	8 x 12in	12	10	63,000	26.5
Lützow	1912	1916	26,200	12 x 5.9in 4 x 19.7in TT				(28)
Hindenburg	1913	1917	26,500	8 x 12in 14 x 5.9in 4 x 23.6in TT	12	10	72,000	27 (28.5)

Notes: The armoured cruiser *Blücher* is included for comparison. 8.2in gun = 21cm; 11in gun = 28cm; 12in gun = 30.5cm; 5.9in gun = 15cm; 17.7in TT (torpedo tube) = 45cm; 19.7in TT = 50cm; 23.6in TT = 60cm. The gunshield armour was generally equal to the barbette armour. The main belt armour extended over the full length of the machinery and magazine spaces. The figures in parentheses under speed are the maximum service speeds at full power with clean hull, clean boilers and reasonable sea conditions (the horsepower given is the nominal design figure which was always greatly exceeded on trial).

incorporated in the design. In June 1912 it was decided that these should not be fitted and the bilge keels were increased in depth from 18in to 2ft 6in instead.

(b) On 27 February 1912 the funnel heights were raised 5ft to 81ft above the LWL, in line with alterations already incorporated in the *Queen Mary* and the *Lion* class.

(c) On 27 July 1912 it was approved to fit additional oil-fuel sprayers to the boilers. The additional weight of 27.5 tons was appropriated from the Board Margin.

(d) In 1913 it was approved to fit the ship with two 3in AA guns.

(e) The number of 3pdr saluting guns was reduced from six to four.

Princess Royal in 1917, with *Lion* in the background, astern. (Imperial War Museum: Q18132)

(f) In 1913 it was approved to omit the torpedo net defence, saving 95 tons.

On completion the ship was 70 tons light of her designed load displacement.

The *Tiger* was the last, and easily the best, of the pre-war British battlecruisers. Her deeper side armour (courtesy of the 6in gun battery), heavier secondary armament, higher speed and improved arcs of fire made her a major step forward in the design evolution of the British battlecruiser. She was nevertheless, like the *Queen Mary*, a derivative of the *Lion* design and still retained some of the weaknesses of that ship – in particular a reduction in the side armour abreast the forward and after barbettes.

The 1912–13 Programme included the five *Queen Elizabeth* class battleships, which marked a major advance in the evolution of the type in that they revived the idea of a true 'fast battleship' of the type envisaged during 1905–6. They were designed for the same speed as the *Invincible* class – 25kts – but were 10,000 tons larger and armed with 15in guns. They also had heavier protection than any of the earlier British dreadnoughts and represented a true 'fast wing' squadron that was more than capable of standing in the line against opposing battleships. They were by no means perfect but were, for their time, a major advance in armoured ship technology that should have brought the development of the battlecruiser to an end. This they did for a while but shortly after the outbreak of the First World War Fisher returned to the Admiralty with his faith in the original battlecruiser concept undimmed.

Table 19: Battlecruiser construction 1906–14

Name	Builder	Machinery	Laid down	Launched	Commissioned
Invincible	Armstrong Whitworth	Humphrys, Tennant	2 Apr 1906	13 Apr 1907	20 Mar 1909
Inflexible	J Brown	J Brown	5 Feb 1906	26 Jun 1907	20 Oct 1908
Indomitable	Fairfield	Fairfield	1 Mar 1906	16 Mar 1907	20 Jun 1908
Indefatigable	Devonport Dky	J Brown	23 Feb 1909	28 Oct 1909	24 Feb 1911
Lion	Devonport Dky	Vickers	29 Nov 1909	6 Aug 1910	4 Jun 1912
Princess Royal	Vickers	Vickers	2 May 1910	29 Apr 1911	14 Nov 1912
New Zealand	Fairfield	Fairfield	20 Jun 1910	1 Jul 1911	19 Nov 1912
Australia	J Brown	J Brown	23 Jun 1910	25 Oct 1911	21 Jun 1913
Queen Mary	Palmers	J Brown	6 Mar 1911	20 Mar 1912	4 Sep 1913
Tiger	J Brown	J Brown	6 Jun 1912	15 Dec 1913	3 Oct 1914

Table 20: Summary of design calculations for battlecruisers 1905–12

Class:	Invincible	Indefatigable	Lion	Queen Mary	Tiger
Date*:	10 Aug 1905	cDec 1908	25 Sep 1909	cAug 1910	cJan 1912
Coef of fineness:	0.558	0.558	0.564	0.575	0.554
Load condition (tons):					
General equipment	660	680	800	805	845
Armament	2440	2580	3260	3295	3660
Machinery	3300	3555	5190	5310	5630
Engineer's stores	90	100	150	150	125
Coal	1000	1000	1000	1000	450 coal/450 oil
Armour and protective plating	3460	3735	6140	6575	7400
Hull	6200	7000	9710	9765	9580
Water in anti-rolling tanks (Tiger only)					250
Board margin	100	100	100	100	100
Load displacement:	17,250	18,750	26,350	27,000	28,490
Deep condition (tons):					
General equipment	740	872	1038	994	980
Armament	2480*	2628*	3346*	3390*	3660
Machinery	3300	3591	5190	5310	5630
Engineer's stores**	90	100	150	150	125
Coal	3000	3100	3700	3700	2450
Armour and protective plating	3460	3735	6140	6575	7400
Hull	6200	7000	9710	9765	9580
Reserve feed water	350	427	590	590	620
Overflow feed water	n/a	27 (half full)	140 (full)		80
Oil fuel	700	850	1130	1130	2450
Water in anti-rolling tanks (Tiger only)					395
Board margin	100	100	100	100	100
Deep displacement:	20,420	22,430	31,234	31,844	33,470
Light condition – items to be removed from legend condition (tons):					
Coal	1000	1000	1000	1000	450
Oil	n/a	n/a	n/a	n/a	450
Fresh water	70	70	84	84	90
Provisions	40	40	48	49	50
Officers' stores and slops	45	45	45	45	50
Half WOs' stores	33	37	45	47	47
Half Engineer's stores	45	50	75	75	63
Water in anti-rolling tanks (Tiger only)					250
Total:	1233	1242	1297	1300	1450
Light displacement:	16,020	17,508	25,053	25,700	27,040

Table 20: *(Continued)*

Class: Date*: Coef of Fineness:	*Invincible* 10 Aug 1905 0.558	*Indefatigable* cDec 1908 0.558	*Lion* 25 Sep 1909 0.564	*Queen Mary* cAug 1910 0.575	*Tiger* cJan 1912 0.554
Summary of general equipment at load draught:					
Fresh water	70	70	84	84	90
Provisions	40	40	48	49	50
Officers' stores and slops	45	45	45	45	50
Crew and effects	90	94	124	125	140
Masts, yards, etc	124	126.6	110	110	90
Anchors	24	22.7			
Cables	84	95	160***	160***	160***
SW Hawsers	7	6			
Boats	55	51.7	71	71	75
WOs' Stores	65	75	90	93	95
Net Defence	50	54	68	68	95
Canvas furniture	6	n/a	n/a	n/a	n/a
Total:	660	680	800	805****	845
Additions to equipment for deep condition:					
Admiral's Boats	10	14	n/a	n/a	n/a
Admiral's Stores	10	10	10	10	10
Canteen Stores	20	20	20	20	20
Provisions	–	32	42	43	145
Freshwater	40	116	166	116	59
Total for deep:	740	872	1038	994	979

Notes: Date is time at which calculations were completed and approved; the above figures do not take account of subsequent changes.
* Added armament weight in deep condition was for practice ammunition, water in hydraulic tanks and (in 13.5in gun ships only) shrapnel projectiles. All these items were included in the load displacement in *Tiger*.
** Engineer's stores included general stores, lubricating oil, firewood and coal sacks.
*** Total of cables, anchors and SW hawsers.
**** Taken in legend as 800 tons.
Armour weights included protective plating for decks, torpedo bulkheads and funnel uptakes. From *Lion* onward it also included the plating behind the side and bulkhead armour. It did not include gunshields, which were part of armament weight. *Tiger* was also calculated for extreme deep condition with an additional 890 tons coal and 1350 tons oil giving an extra deep displacement of 35,710 tons.

Table 21: Dimensions

	Length (oa)	Length (pp)	Beam (extreme)***	Beam (moulded)	Depth (moulded)
Invincible class (designed)	567ft	530ft	78ft 7.75in	78ft 5in	40ft 6in* 48ft 2in**
Invincible (actual)		530ft 0.75in	78ft 8.5in	78ft 5.75in	40ft 8.81in* 47ft 11.88in**
Inflexible (actual)	567ft 1.25in	530ft 1in	78ft 10.13in	78ft 6.63in	40ft 5.94in*
Indomitable (actual)	567ft 5.75in	530ft 1.75in	78ft 7.75in	78ft 4.25in	48ft 2.75in**
Indefatigable class (designed)	590ft	555ft	80ft	79ft 10.5in	48ft 9in**
Indefatigable (actual)		555ft 0.25in	79ft 10.25in	79ft 8.75in	48ft 10.5in**
New Zealand (actual)	590ft 3.5in	555ft 1in			
Australia (actual)		555ft 0.13in	79ft 11.75in	79ft 10.25in	41ft 3.5in* 48ft 7.38in**
Lion class (designed)	700ft	660ft	88ft 6in	88ft 4.5in	53ft 1in**
Lion (actual)		660ft 0.5in	88ft 6.75in	88ft 5.25in	53ft 2in**
Princess Royal (actual)		660ft 0.81in	88ft 6.44in	88ft 4.69in	53ft 0.25in**
Queen Mary (designed)	700ft	660ft	89ft	88ft 4.5in	53ft**
Queen Mary (actual)	700ft 0.63in 703ft 6in (over sternwalk)	660ft 0.13in	89ft 0.5in	88ft 5.25in	53ft 0.81in**
Tiger (designed)	704ft	660ft	90ft 6in		

* Depth from underside of flat keel to edge of upper deck at side (to top of corticene deck covering).
**Depth from underside of flat keel to edge of forecastle deck at side (to top of deck planking).
***Excludes barbette armour on side in 12in gun ships.
NB: The 'actual' dimensions given are those recorded at the time of launch but would be subject to variation both from inaccuracies in measurement and from temperature changes. Some anomalies can occur in relation to the extreme beam figures depending on whether the dimension is to the extreme outside of shell plating or the mean line of shell plating.

Freeboards as designed to LWL

	Forward	Amidships	Aft
Invincible class	30ft	22ft	17ft 2in
Indefatigable class	30ft	22ft	17ft
Lion class	30ft	25ft	19ft
Queen Mary	30ft	25ft	19ft
Tiger	30ft	24ft 6in	19ft

Heights to centres of gun axis as designed from LWL

Turret	'A'	'B'	'P'	'Q'	'X'
Invincible class	32ft	–	28ft	28ft	21ft
Indefatigable class	32ft	–	28ft	28ft	21ft
Lion class	33ft	42.5ft	–	31ft	23ft
Queen Mary	33ft	42.5ft	–	31ft	23ft
Tiger	33ft	42.5ft	–	31ft 9in	23ft

Dimensions of bilge keels

Ship	Length	Breadth (max/min)	Area per side	Period for double roll
Indomitable	240ft	3ft 6in/15in	530sq ft	14 sec
Indefatigable	266ft	3ft 8in/9in	710sq ft	14.5 sec
Lion	298ft	3ft 8in/9in	850sq ft	13.5 sec
Queen Mary	328ft	3ft 8in/9in	960sq ft	–
Tiger	297ft	3ft 8in/2ft 6in	1275sq ft	–

Table 22: Displacements and stability

Condition	Displacement (tons)	Draught (ft–in) Fore	Aft	Mean	TPI	GM (ft)	Angle of Max Stability (deg)	Angle at which Stability vanishes (deg)
Invincible class design:								
Load	17,250	25–0	27–0	26–0	69.5	4.0		
Deep	20,420			30–0	71	5.0		
Light	16,020			24–6		3.5		
Deep (less oil)	19,720			28–10		4.1		
Invincible (given in Ship's Book):								
Load	17,482		26–0	69.84				
Deep	20,866		30–0	71.2				
Invincible as inclined 21 February 1909:								
Load	17,330	24–7	27–0	25–9.5	69.8	3.5	42	76
Deep	20,700(e)			29–10	71.2	4.7	43	73
Light	16,100(e)			24–3		3.15	43	85
Deep (less oil)	19,940			29–0		3.75	42	78
Indomitable as completed:								
Load	17,408	25–6	26–7	26–0.5	69.8			
Deep	20,722			29–9.5(e)				
Deep (less oil)	20,125			29–3(e)				
Indomitable Results of inclining (date unknown but later than time of completion):								
Load	17,800			26–5.25	69.8	3.63		
Deep	20,900			30–0	71.5	4.71		
Light	16,500			25–0	69.4	3.24		
Deep (less oil)	20,400			29–6.25	71.25	4.18		
Inflexible as completed:								
Load	17,290	25–1	26–8	25–10.5	69.8	3.8		
Deep	20,700(e)			29–9(e)				
Deep (less oil)	19,975			29–2		4.22		
Indefatigable as designed:								
Load	18,750	26–0	27–0	26–6	75.1	3.56		
Deep	22,430			30–7	76.4	5.0		
Light	17,508			25–1		3.12		
Deep (less oil)	21,580			29–8.5		4.05		
Indefatigable as inclined 11 March 1911:								
Load	18,500(e)	25–4.5	27–0.5	26–2.5	69.8	3.45	43	74
Deep	22,130	29–4	30–6.5	29–11.25	71.2	4.78		
Light	17,100	22–11	25–8	24–3.5		2.95	43	83
Deep (less oil)	21,260	28–9	29–3	29–0		3.9	47	76
Australia as completed:								
Load	18,500	24–9	27–0	25–10.5				
Deep (less oil)	21,240							
Lion class as designed:								
Load	26,350	27–0	29–0	28–0	98	4.85	43	76
Deep	31,234			32–3	99.3	5.83	42	84
Light	25,053			26–11		4.66		
Deep (less oil)	30,104			31–4		4.98	42	
Lion as inclined 1 June 1912:								
Load	26,270	26–5	28–10	27–7.5	98	5.0	43	76
Deep	30,820	30–8	32–5	31–6.5		6.0	42	85
Light	24,970		26–9					
Deep (less oil) 29,580		30–3	30–10	30–6.5		5.0	42	78

Condition	Displacement (tons)	Draught (ft–in) Fore	Aft	Mean	TPI	GM (ft)	Angle of Max Stability (deg)	Angle at which Stability vanishes (deg)
Princess Royal as inclined on completion:								
Load	26,100	25–8	29–3	27–5.5		4.95		
Deep	30,620	30–4	32–4	31–4		5.95		
Light	24,820			26–9				
Deep (less oil)	29,490	29–11	30–11.5	30–5		5.05		
Queen Mary as designed:								
Load	27,000			28–0		4.73	43	75
Deep	31,844	31–11	31–2.5	32–1		5.7	42	82.5
Light	25,700			26–10.5		4.64	43	74
Deep (less oil)	30,714	30–6	31–9	31–1.5		4.9	42	77
Queen Mary as completed:								
Load	26,770	26–11	28–4	27–7.5	99	4.99	42	76
Deep	31,650	31–0	32–4	31–8		5.92	42	84
Light	25,383					4.9	42	74
Deep (less oil)	30,480			30–9		5.08	42	78
Tiger as designed:								
Load	28,500			28–6	100.7	5.3 (4.9*)	43	74
Deep	33,470			32–7	101	6.2 (5.5*)	43	80
Light	27,040	26–0	28–4	27–2		5.0	43	71
Extreme deep	35,710	35–2.5	33–9.5	34–6	102	7.0 (6.3*)	44	86
Tiger as completed:								
Load	28,430			28–5	101	5.2	43	74
Deep	33,260			32–5		6.1	43	80
Light	27,000(e)			27–3		5.0	43	71
Extreme deep	35,560			34–3		6.7	44	86

* GM with allowance for free surface water in anti-rolling tanks

(e) = estimated

Battlecruiser Revival

> In all probability the Board [of Admiralty], who knew much more about requirements than about technicalities, would have asked for more qualities than could by any means be embodied in any one design of the approximate displacement laid down by them.
>
> It would, in fact, be correct to say that every single ship is in the end a compromise.
>
> Sir Eustace T D'Eyncourt, DNC 1912–19

At the end of October 1914 Admiral Fisher returned to the Admiralty to replace Admiral Prince Louis of Battenberg as First Sea Lord. He immediately set to work on organising a large war construction programme in which his talents as an administrator came to the fore. By circumventing the standard bureaucratic procedures of the Admiralty and dealing directly with the design department, shipbuilding firms, material suppliers etc, he was able to get things moving very quickly. It was a system to a large extent based on mutual support and trust – the contracts and other red tape followed when convenient. Within the next few months he had set in train the construction of a large fleet of new vessels including destroyers, submarines, patrol craft, and a large group of vessels of various types intended to support amphibious operations. He also wanted to build new battlecruisers to strengthen the Grand Fleet against the latest German ships of this type, the armament and speed of which tended to be exaggerated in intelligence reports.

Fisher had returned with his concept of the original battlecruiser type unchanged. As far as he was concerned the key, as always, was speed and the tactical and strategic advantages that would be gained from it. If the enemy had fast ships, then the Royal Navy must have ships that were faster still and if this meant increases in size and reductions in armour it was of little importance compared with, in Fisher's view, the great advantages that could be gained. The arguments were not new to Churchill. In April 1912 Fisher had written to him concerning the design of the armoured ships of the 1913–14 Programme: 'There must be sacrifice of armour ... There must be further VERY GREAT INCREASE IN SPEED ... your speed must vastly exceed [that of] your possible enemy!'[1] At the time Fisher was advocating that *all* armoured ships should have speeds in excess of 30kts but his plea went unheeded – the 1913–14 ships were the *Royal Sovereign* class battleships, heavily-armoured vessels with the standard battlefleet speed of 21kts.

As First Sea Lord, Fisher was in a much better position to advance his ideas, particularly as under war conditions resources rather than cost was the controlling factor. He soon set the DNC to work on a design for a 32kt battlecruiser, armed with 15in guns, which he christened 'Rhadamanthus', and began a campaign which lasted into the new year, to get three such ships built.

Initially he suggested to Churchill that two battleships, *Renown* and *Repulse* – ordered before the war from Fairfields and Palmers respectively but suspended on 26 August 1914 on the grounds that they would not be completed in time to take part in the war – should be converted to battlecruisers. The

Renown proceeds down the Clyde after completion at Fairfield's. She and her sister were originally provided with funnels of equal height, it being assumed that the increased distance between the fore funnel and bridge would be sufficient to avoid smoke interference. This proved not to be the case and the fore funnels of both ships were raised very soon after completion. (Author's collection)

Table 23: Rough outline particulars for battlecruiser 'Rhadamanthus', December 1914

	19 December 1914	*21 December 1914*
LENGTH (pp):	630ft	750ft
BEAM:	74–75ft	90ft
DRAUGHT:	26–27ft	25ft
DISPLACEMENT:	18,750 tons	25,750 tons
SHP:	105,000	?
SPEED:	32kts	32kts
ARMAMENT:	4 x 15in	6 x 15in
	20 x 4in	20 x 4in
		2 x 21in torpedo tubes
ARMOUR: Belt	6in, 4in, 3in	6in, ?
Barbettes	8in	
WEIGHTS:		Not given
General equipment	700	
Armament	2200	
Machinery	4800 (5100*)	
Oil fuel	800	
Armour	3000 (3200*)	
Hull	7400	
TOTAL:	18,900	
Say	19,000 tons	

* Corrected figures, added later

term 'convert' was used somewhat loosely, as to modify the design of the battleship in such a way was impractical and the ships did not, in any case, exist except on paper and in the material gathered at the shipyards and ordered for their construction. Churchill argued that such large ships would absorb too many resources and interfere with other construction programmes and reiterated the point that they would in any case not be completed in time. Fisher, however, expected the war to last some time and insisted he could repeat his performance with the battleship *Dreadnought* in 1905–6 and get them built very quickly. He could save time by continuing the contracts for any material for the battleships which might be used for the battlecruisers, particularly the eight 15in twin gun mountings which had been ordered on 1 May 1914 as these items took almost as long to manufacture as the ships in which they were mounted, and this assuming normal and not accelerated construction times.[2]

Fisher's campaign was greatly strengthened by the Falklands victory on 8 December, which he interpreted as a vindication of the battlecruiser concept despite the fact that this proved little with regard to the battlecruisers' role in support of the battlefleet. He also enlisted the help of Jellicoe and Beatty. On 23 December he wrote to the former:

I am now here fighting the battle for more battlecruisers. I wish, when you have leisure, you would write me a casual sort of letter which I can show the Cabinet (*not as if you were responding to my request; not an official memorandum*) that the supposed existing superiority we have in fast battleships that we now have is FALLACIOUS! more especially in quoting *Queen Elizabeth*s as they do. *None of our existing ships have the necessary FUTURE speed!* The new German *Lutzow* battle cruiser, with possibly 14-inch guns, or even 16-inch, will have certainly *over 28-knots speed!* We must have 32-knots speed to give us a margin for being long out of dock, and to give the necessary speed to CATCH a 28-knot ship! ... SPEED IS EVERYTHING ... It would save me an immense amount of trouble if you would kindly send this letter to Beatty, as being the Admiral commanding the Battle Cruiser Squadron, if he could support me with a private letter *written in a casual* way! I have to resort to every stratagem to gain my mind! If I don't get these 3 battle cruisers of 32 knots speed, I shall have to leave the Admiralty on January 25 next.

Churchill finally gave in to the pressure and on 28 December obtained Cabinet approval for the construction of two new battlecruisers – not the three that Fisher had been pressing for. The new ships took the contracts and the names of the two *Royal Sovereign* class ships ordered from Fairfields and Palmers but it was later found that Palmers did not have a slip long enough for the new design and the contract was transferred to John Brown at Clydebank. Fisher interviewed the contractors on the 29 December and obtained agreement to an accelerated construction time of fifteen months from the date of order (30 December 1914). The difference in progress between Fisher and the Admiralty contracts department can be judged by the fact that the modified contracts were not available until 10 March, over six weeks after the ships concerned had been laid down!

Fisher was still not satisfied and was soon campaigning for the construction of a pair of somewhat bizarre vessels described as large light cruisers but in fact representing a kind of light battlecruiser each armed with two twin 15in turrets. The 'light cruiser' description was a subterfuge to obtain Cabinet approval because, while the construction of further battlecruisers and battleships had been vetoed, the construction of light cruisers had not! Work on these two ships, *Courageous* and *Glorious*, began in January 1915. Shortly after a third ship (*Furious*) was added, but in this case with the 15in turrets modified to take a single 18in gun, three of which were ordered from Armstrong in the spring of 1915.

Renown and *Repulse*

D'Eyncourt in his memoirs and in official documents stated that the first indication that a new battlecruiser design was required occurred on 19 December 1914. However, the first mention of the requirement in the Ship's Cover is dated 18 December and indicates that the DNC had received a request from Fisher for the size of a ship to meet the following characteristics:

(a) A long, high, flared bow, like *Renown* (the pre-dreadnought) but higher.

(b) Four 15in guns in two twin mountings, as high above water as in the original *Dreadnought*.
(c) An ATB armament of twenty 4in guns on the upper deck, mounted high up and with shield protection only.
(d) No other guns or torpedoes to be fitted.
(e) Speed 32kts.
(f) Oil fuel only.
(g) Armour on the same scale as *Indefatigable*.

A rough estimate for this vessel was produced on the following day but Fisher then modified his requirements by increasing the number of 15in guns to six and adding two torpedo tubes (see Table 23).[3] A new estimate was produced on 21 December and a model of the proposed design three days later which, after some modification at Fisher's request, was completed on 26 December. After Churchill's agreement to the new ships, design work started on 30 December along normal lines but at an accelerated pace, a preliminary legend being produced on the same day (see Table 24). It is obvious from his references to these ships that D'Eyncourt was very proud of the rapidity with which his department produced the design and oversaw the production of these two ships. Regardless of their value as fighting vessels they were a remarkable demonstration of design expertise under pressure and met the requirements set for them with very little exception.

During the first week of January the material on order and received at the yards of Fairfield and Palmers for the two battleships was examined by the DNC's department to see how much of it could be used in the new ships and the Palmers material was transferred to John Brown. By mid-January the builders had been supplied with enough information to order additional material and build the hulls out as far as the turn of the bilge and on 25 January 1915, Fisher's 74th birthday, both ships were laid down. By the end of the month the contractors had sufficient information to prepare the drawings for the hull structure and order all the steel required for its construction. The DNC's department completed all the drawings, specifications and calculations normally prepared for a new design on 12 April 1915 and these received Board approval ten days later. The design had changed little since the preliminary legend of 30 December. Primarily as a result of modifications to the machinery and armour, displacement had increased by 500 tons and there had been some adjustment of the weights to accommodate this and the production of more detailed calculations. An additional weight of 115 tons had been appropriated from the Board Margin for the addition of torpedo net defence but in August 1915 it was decided not to fit this equipment and the margin was restored to its original 130 tons. The original 4in gun battery, protected at least in part by 3in armour, was replaced by upper deck mountings in open shields and reduced in number from twenty-five to seventeen. Fifteen of the latter were fitted in new triple mountings intended to provide a high volume of fire and ease the problem of distributing the guns of the ATB armament clear of blast from the heavy guns and each other. Alterations after approval of the design were as follows:

(a) In April 1915 it was decided that the ships should not be fitted with wood decks in order to economise on weight and construction time. Lagging was fitted under the weather decks in living spaces to compensate for the loss of insulation (totalling 70 tons) and deck strips (totalling 7 tons) were fitted to improve the foothold on the steel deck. Corticene was to be fitted on the forecastle deck in the area of the Admiral's accommodation.
(b) In May 1915 it was decided to fit additional stiffening to the forward section of the hull following experience in the battleship *Queen Elizabeth*, which had

Table 24: *Renown* class Legends of Particulars

	Renown	Repulse
DATE:	30 December 1914	22 April 1915
LENGTH:	750ft pp	750ft pp, 794ft oa
BEAM:	90ft	90ft
DRAUGHT:	25ft fore, 26ft aft	25ft fore, 26ft aft
DISPLACEMENT:	26,000 tons	26,500 tons
SHP:	112,000	110,000
SPEED:	32kts	32kts
OIL FUEL:	1000 tons; 3500–4000 tons max	1000 tons, 4000 tons max
ARMAMENT:	6 x 15in (80rpg)	6 x 15in (80rpg)
	25 x 4in (150rpg)	17 x 4in (150rpg)
	4 x 3pdr saluting (150rpg)	2 x 3in HA
	5 x Maxim MG (5000rpg)	5 x Maxim MG
	2 x 21in TT (14 x 21in torp)	2 x 21in TT (5 x 21in torp)
ARMOUR:		
Side	6in amidships, 4in at ends	6in amidships, 4in fore, 4in and 3in aft
Bulkheads	4in fore	4in, 4in and 3in fore, 4in and 3in aft
Barbettes	7in	7in
Gunshields	8in	9in and 7in.
CT	10in	10in
Communication tube	4in and 3in	3in
After CT	–	3in
4in battery (for'd)	3in	3in
Funnel uptakes, etc	1.5in sides, 1in ends	1.5in sides, 1in ends
Main deck	1in flat; 2in slope	1in flat; 2in slope
Lower deck	–	2.5in fore
WEIGHTS:		
General equipment	750	800
Armament	3400	3335
Machinery	5325	5660
Eng Stores	125	120
Oil Fuel	1000	1000
Armour	4470	4770
Hull	10,800	10,800
BM	130	15
TOTAL:	26,000	26,500

shown some weaknesses in this area.
(c) In January 1915 Fisher had instructed that arrangements be made for the ships to carry twenty-five mines each. This presented some constructional difficulties and on 21 July (after Fisher had resigned his post) the DNC requested that this instruction be reconsidered. On the following day the omission of the mine gear was approved.
(d) In November 1915 it was discovered that the revolving weight of the 15in mounting had been underestimated by 20 tons. The additional 60 tons was appropriated from the Board Margin.

In February 1916 the estimated alterations of the weights for *Repulse* were as follows:

Additions:
Hull and protective plating (including
   50 tons excess of estimated weight
   for hull castings)   339 tons
Excess weight of 15in mountings
                                                   60 tons
Additional weight for 4in
   mountings   34 tons
Turbine pump and fittings in each
   boiler room   20 tons
Total: 453 tons

(There was also an additional 7 tons in the armament weight for the 4in gun director towers and their platforms but this seems to have been absorbed in the original weight estimates)

Deductions:
Net defence   115 tons
Mines and fittings   20 tons
4in BL ammunition in place of QF
   ammunition (see Armament
   chapter)   16 tons
Total: 151 tons

(There was also a saving in the hull weight of 37 tons incidental to the net defence and 9 tons due to the omission of a bow fire-control compartment both of which were allowed for in the hull weight given above)

These changes, with the Board Margin omitted, produced a total estimated load displacement of 26,787 tons, 287 tons in excess of the design. The actual figure from the inclining of *Repulse* was 26,854 tons while that for *Renown* was somewhat larger at 27,420 tons.

The ships actually completed a few months late, in the autumn of 1916, partly no doubt because Fisher was no longer in a position to push them forward. However, this was still a remarkably rapid construction period for ships of such size, particularly under war conditions. *Repulse* ran her trials in August 1916 and achieved 31.7kts in moderately heavy weather on a displacement of 29,900 tons. *Renown*, in September 1916 made 32.6kts on a displacement much closer to the designed load – 27,900 tons. They proved good seaboats but had some minor structural problems forward that were cured by fitting additional stiffening and pillars under the forecastle deck.

That *Renown* and *Repulse* completed so close to their intended displacements and achieved the high speed for which they were designed is a very creditable achievement. Unfortunately they joined the Grand Fleet

Renown in the spring of 1917 with raised fore funnel. Note the searchlight platform on the second funnel, the design of which served to distinguish her from *Repulse* until both ships were refitted with searchlight towers in 1918. The triple 4in gun mountings of the secondary armament provided, in theory, maximum firepower in a minimal space but in practice they were not a great success as it was difficult to organise the rapid loading of such closely-spaced guns. (Author's collection)

Repulse in 1918 with aircraft flying-off platforms on 'A' and 'Y' turrets and dark grey camouflage on the funnels and superstructure. (Imperial War Museum: SP720)

Renown in 1918. (Author's collection)

after Jutland and were justifiably pilloried for their lack of protection. They were subsequently considerably modified to improve their defensive qualities, details of which are given in the chapter on Armour.

Courageous, Glorious and *Furious*

The origin of these ships, and often that of *Renown* and *Repulse*, is normally put down to Fisher's Baltic Project. However, there seems little doubt that *Renown* and *Repulse* were built primarily to strengthen the Grand Fleet's battlecruiser force while the evidence in the case of the three large light cruisers is far from clear. It seems likely that while Fisher did, initially, see them primarily for this role, he never had an absolutely fixed plan in mind. His statements as to their purpose varied from time to time and it seems much more rational that he envisaged a number of roles for the ships which affected the requirements of the design.

Courageous as completed. (Imperial War Museum: SP1673)

The Baltic Project was an old idea which Fisher first outlined several years before the war. Essentially it consisted of landing a Russian army on the Baltic coast of Pomerania, 90 miles from Berlin whence the direct threat to the German capital and the need for the enemy to redistribute his troops would not only relieve pressure on the Russian front but would ultimately lead to his panic and collapse. During 1914–15 it was one of several schemes discussed at the Admiralty for using the Navy to break the deadlock between the armies fighting in Europe. Others included outflanking the German army in the west by landing troops on the Belgian coast, an assault on the Dardanelles (Churchill's pet scheme which eventually won the day) and the taking of either the islands of Heligoland or Borkum in the southern North Sea. The last would have served to provide an advance base from which to harass and observe the movements of the German Fleet – a kind of substitute close blockade. Borkum was also considered as a possible jumping-off point for the invasion of Schleswig-Holstein and the capture of the Kiel Canal. This was directly linked to the Baltic Project in that before the Grand Fleet could be transferred to the Baltic, it was necessary to either defeat the German Fleet or prevent its entry into the North Sea. Fisher was rather prone to fanciful ideas of sowing the southern North Sea with a gigantic minefield, despite the fact that Britain did not have the vast number of mines required and that those that were available were of dubious efficiency. As usual he did not consider human ingenuity, which would have found a means of clearing a path through any such static barrier unless it was very closely defended – and in force. Moreover, Heligoland, and to a lesser extent Borkum, were on the doorstep of the German Fleet, making the organisation of their containment a much simpler matter than their support by the British, whose lines of supply would be long and vulnerable. To be fair, Fisher had long been of the opinion that the mine and the submarine, and more recently aircraft, would revolutionise naval warfare and that these weapons rather than the battleship would control the outcome of any conflict. The occupation of one of the German islands was partially intended to provide a submarine base that would have increased their time on patrol and their relative number by reducing the distance to the operational area. However, the wartime record of both British and German submarines in intelligence-gathering and the infliction of damage while operating off enemy bases fell well below Fisher's expectations. In general the Baltic Project appears to have been taken much more seriously after the event, when Fisher used this proposal, and the plans he made for it – including the light battlecruisers – as a defence of his position with regard to the Dardanelles Campaign, which had proved a very costly failure.

What then was the purpose of the large light cruisers? In January 1915 Fisher told both Churchill and Jellicoe that their primary function was as support vessels for the Baltic Project. However, on the 6 March 1915 Fisher wrote to D'Eyncourt:

I've told the First Lord that the more I consider the qualities of your design of the Big Light Battle Cruisers, the more I am impressed by its exceeding excellence and simplicity – all *the three vital requisites of gunpower, speed and draught of water* so well balanced!

Beardmore and Vickers [neither of whom was to build one of these ships] are absolutely sure they can produce two ships in 11 months, which alone is a testimony to the goodness of the design as regards simplicity.

However, I fear we are not going to get even two out of the four owing to the parliamentary bugbear of delaying 4 last ships of *Royal Sovereign* type!

It's a great pity as it will be very greatly regretted!

The present light small cruisers get their speed knocked down at once to 15

Glorious raising steam in 1917. (Imperial War Museum: Q18040)

knots in heavy weather so will be no use to accompany and scout for the Battle Cruisers and may fall prey to the enemy's Battle Cruisers if caught by them scouting in heavy weather.[5]

Fisher had also told D'Eyncourt that he proposed that they be 'used against any of the enemy cruisers that might get out into the open seas and attack merchant ships '.[6] Finally, in describing the 18in-gunned *Furious*, and presumably in answer to the criticism that two guns were inadequate for any sensible system of fire control, Fisher wrote that: 'Her guns with their enormous shells were built to make it impossible for the Germans to prevent the Russian Millions from landing on the Pomeranian Coast! … The "Furious" (and all her breed) was not built for salvoes! They were built for Berlin, and that's why they drew so little water and were built so fragile, so as to weigh as little as possible, and so go faster.'[7] In the same passage he describes the probable effects of the 20in gun (intended for yet another Fisher battlecruiser project – which did not go beyond the 'idea' stage) whose shells would fall 'out of sight' but with 'exact accuracy' producing a crater 'like that of Vesuvius or Mount Etna and consequently you can then easily imagine the German Army fleeing for its life from Pomerania to Berlin.' Fisher had a very exaggerated idea of the value of heavy naval artillery against shore targets and does not seem to have realised that anything that fell 'out of sight' could not at this time be 'exact' in its impact. Moreover, the proposition that a few 20in or 18in shells would either produce the effect described or scatter the German Army is ludicrous. It is also worth noting that if shore bombardment was the ship's primary function one would have expected them to be supplied with mostly HE shell, whereas the intended and actual outfit supplied was a mixture of APC and CPC for use against ships.

In Fisher's comments can be found most of the functions expected of the battlecruiser, including trade protection and scouting for the battlefleet, together with shore support. The major exception is their use as a 'fast wing', which is hardly surprising. The specified shallow draught, also provided in *Renown* and *Repulse* and later in the *Hood* class, is also far from a straightforward 'Baltic' requirement. Shallow draught was necessary for close inshore operations and could have been used to enable them to use waters denied to enemy heavy ships of deep draught, but it was also seen as valuable for other reasons.

Earlier ships, particularly the *Iron Duke* and *Queen Elizabeth* class battleships, were seen as having an excess of draught and insufficient freeboard under actual service conditions in which deep load was more common than the designed load displacement. The desire to improve seakeeping, reserve of buoyancy and safety against underwater attack from mines and torpedoes therefore led to a reconsideration of hull proportions. In addition there was concern about the size of the underwater target and the fact that damage low in the hull was more dangerous at deep draughts owing to the greater pressure of water on bulkheads, etc. The target size argument is, however, something of an oddity because, while the reduced depth would improve the remote chance of a deep running torpedo going under the hull, the increased length of ship was a positive advantage to an attacking submarine. It is of course difficult to tell which requirement came first, the need to operate in shallow water or the improvement in hull proportions, but the latter was certainly the primary purpose of the shallow draught designs of late 1915 which led up to the construction of *Hood*.

The legend for *Courageous* and *Glorious* was submitted for approval on 28 January 1915. The ships were essentially reduced editions of the *Renown* with 'B' turret omitted and the hull armour reduced to the scale of a light cruiser. They did, however, gain something on the earlier design as they adopted small-tube boilers and geared turbines, which saved weight and improved the efficiency of their machinery installation.

Early in March 1915 Fisher instructed D'Eyncourt to thicken up the 0.75in torpedo protection bulkheads in *Renown, Repulse* and the large light cruisers. D'Eyncourt pointed out that this would add considerable weight, increase the draught and reduce the speed, but Fisher, who had been concerned about the dangers of underwater attack since the losses to mines in the Russo-Japanese War, merely said that this would have to be accepted. In the case of *Renown* and *Repulse* the lower section of the bulkhead was to be increased to 2in and the upper section to 1.5in. The ships were so far advanced that the

The single 18in gun turret of the light battlecruiser *Furious*. (© National Maritime Museum, London: E13/276)

Table 25: Large light cruisers, Legends of Particulars

	Courageous class (28 January 1915)	*Furious*
LENGTH:	735ft pp	735ft pp
BEAM:	80ft (later increased to 81ft)	88ft
DRAUGHT:	21ft 9in mean	21ft 6in mean
DISPLACEMENT:	17,400 tons (later increased to 17,800 tons)	19,200 tons
SHP:	90,000	90,000
SPEED:	32kts	31.5kts
FUEL OIL:	750 tons, 3250 tons max	750 tons
ARMAMENT:	4 x 15in (80rpg)	2 x 18in
	16 x 4in (120rpg)	8 x 5.5in
	3 x 3in HA (150rpg)	3 x 3in HA
	5 x Maxims (5000rpg)	5 x Maxims (5000rpg)
	2 x 21in sub TT (10 x 21in torp)	2 x 21in sub TT (10 x 21in torp)
ARMOUR:		
Side	3in amidships, 2in forward	3in amidships, 2in forward
Bulkheads	2in fore, 2.5in aft	3in and 2in fore, 3in aft
Barbettes	7in and 6in	7in and 6in
Gunshields	13in, 11in and 7in	9in and 5in
CT	10in	10in
Communication tube	4in and 3in	3in
Torpedo CT	3in	3in
Torpedo bulkheads	0.75in	0.75in
Funnel uptakes	0.75in	0.75in
Forecastle deck	1in	1in
Main deck	0.75in flat, 1in slope	1.75in and 0.75in flat, 1in slope
Lower deck	1in fore, 1.5in and 3in aft	1in fore, 1.5in and 3in aft
WEIGHTS (tons):		
General equipment	650	775
Armament	2250	2420
Machinery	2350	3030
Oil Fuel	750	750
Armour	2800	3780
Hull	8500	8345
BM	100	100
TOTAL:	17,400	19,200

change would have delayed their completion by at least two months. This was considered unacceptable and the modification was cancelled. However, the *Courageous* and *Glorious* had not yet been laid down and their bulkheads were increased in thickness to a uniform 1.5in, which added 500 tons to the displacement, increased the draught by 6in and reduced the estimated speed by 0.25kts. This change was approved by Fisher on 14 March, the *Courageous* being laid down two weeks later and the *Glorious* on the 20th of the following month. The ships do not appear to have received any other major alterations while under construction apart from the provision of additional deck plating after the Battle of Jutland and this, combined with a number of minor additions, added a further 400 tons to their displacement. There must, however, have been other major alterations in the early design stages as the completed ships were over 1700 tons heavier than the original legend estimate (no later legend seems to have survived). It seems more than likely that one of these changes was the installation of the triple 4in mounting (the original legend provided for sixteen 4in which is not divisible by three).

Both ships took approximately eighteen months to build, the *Courageous* running her trials in October 1916 and the *Glorious* in

Furious as first completed with a single 18in turret aft and the fore turret replaced by a flight deck and hangar. (Imperial War Museum: SP1669)

After the removal of her after 18in mounting and the fitting of a second flight deck between the funnel and stern during the winter of 1917–18, *Furious* became a fully-fledged aircraft carrier. She was later modified to include a full-length flight deck as were her half-sisters *Courageous* and *Glorious* and thus, despite their unpromising start, the large light cruisers became true representatives of the capital ship of the future. (Imperial War Museum: Q23192)

December 1916. During the trials of *Courageous* the ship sustained structural damage while working up to full speed against a rough head sea. The forecastle, from the forward barbette to the breakwater and the side plating in this area between the forecastle and upper decks were buckled; there were also leaks in some of the oil tanks, in the reserve feed water tank and elsewhere. Subsequent enquiries were inconclusive as to whether this was due to structural weakness or the ship being driven too hard but in any case it was decided to fit an additional 130 tons of stiffening in the ship – a modification also extended to *Glorious* although in this case the work was not carried out until 1918.

Table 26: Legends of Fast Battleship Designs 1915–16

Design:	'A'	'B'	'C1'	'C2'	'D' (Mod 'A')
Date:	29/11/15	1/1/16	18/1/16	18/1/16	1/2/16
Length (pp):	760ft	750ft	660ft	610ft	710ft
Beam:	104ft	90ft	104ft	100ft	104ft
Mean draught:	23ft 6in	25ft 9in	23ft 6in	24ft 9in	23ft 6in
Displacement:	31,000 tons	29,500 tons	27,600 tons	26,250 tons	29,850 tons
Shp:	75,000	60,000	40,000	40,000	65,000
Speed:	26.5–27kts	25kts	22kts	22kts	25.5kts
Armament (all):	8 x 15in				
	12 x 5in ('C1' and 'C2' 10 x 5in, 'D' 12 x 5.5in)				
	2 x 3in HA (1 x 3in HA in 'C1', 'C2' and 'D')				
	4 x 21in TT (2 x 21in in 'C1', 'C2' and 'D')				
Armour (all):					
Main Belt	10in				
Barbettes	10in max (9in max in 'C1', 'C2' and 'D')				
Gunshields	11in–9in				
Weights (tons):					
General equipment	750	750	700	700	700
Armament	4750	4750	4650	4650	4700
Machinery	3550	3250	2450	2450	3350
Oil Fuel	1000	1000	1000	1000	1000
Armour	9150	8600	7860	7770	8500
Hull	11,650	11,000	10,800	9500	11,400
BM	150	150	140	130	150
Total:	31,000	29,500	27,600	26,250	29,850

Also on 1 Jan 1916 a design as 'B' above with shp increased to 75,000 for speed of 27kts increasing displacement to 30,350 tons and mean draught to 26ft 3in.

Hood

At the end of 1915 the Admiralty gained Treasury approval for the construction of an experimental battleship the design of which was to be based on war experience. What was wanted was a ship with the same armament and speed as the *Queen Elizabeth* but of improved seaworthiness and with an underwater protection system based on more recent ideas and the latest experiments. A primary requirement was for a high uninterrupted freeboard, it having been found that the embrasures cut in the sides of earlier ships to accommodate the secondary armament casemates not only 'spoiled the ships as seaboats, making the [6in] guns very nearly useless and the ships almost dangerously wet in heavy weather' but also reduced the apparent reserve of buoyancy as the casemates were not watertight.

This situation was made worse by the fact that ships seldom operated in their designed load condition. They went to sea deep, with a full fuel load and were generally running at deep draughts and low freeboard in the operational area, lighter loading conditions only being likely when returning to base after an extended period at sea.

The high freeboard was to be combined with shallow draught, to reduce the underwater target and the difficulties of dealing with underwater damage, the length and beam being increased accordingly. Between November 1915 and the end of January 1916 the DNC produced several designs for battleships (see Table 26) of varying proportions, the great length of the earlier designs being reduced in the later ones due to concerns about difficulties with docking facilities, particularly the fact that there was no floating dock that could accommodate them. The DNC generally preferred those designs with greater beam, experiments having shown that the underwater protection could be greatly improved with increased depth, and was also urging the adoption of small-tube boilers in order to save space and weight.

These designs were submitted to Jellicoe for comment in January 1916 and were not received well. He stated that the Grand Fleet was not in need of new battleships but of escort vessels and the fleet's only potential weakness with regard to large ships was in battlecruisers. He was greatly concerned about the battlecruisers under construction in Germany, the three most recent of which

Table 27 Legends of Battlecruiser Designs, February 1916

Design:	'1'	'2'	'3'	'4'	'5'	'6'
Length (pp):	835ft	790ft	810ft	710ft	780ft	830ft
Length (oa):	885ft	840ft	860ft	757ft	830ft	880ft
Beam:	104ft	104ft	104ft	104ft	104ft	104ft
Draught (mean):	26ft	25ft	26ft	25ft	25ft	26ft
Displacement (tons):	39,000	35,500	36,500	32,500	35,500	39,500
Shp:	120,000	120,000	160,000	120,000	120,000	120,000
Speed:	30kts	30.5kts	32kts	30kts	30.5kts	30kts
Armament:	8 x 15in	8 x 15in	8 x 15in	4 x 18in	6 x 18in	8 x 18in
	12 x 5.5in	12 x 5.5in	12 x 5.5in	12 x 5.5in	12 x 5.5in	12 x 5.5in
			2 x 21in TT (in all)			
Armour (all designs):						
Belt			8in (10in in '3')			
Barbettes			9in max			

All designs had small-tube boilers, forced draught and narrow boiler rooms, except '1' which had large-tube boilers and '3' which had wide boiler rooms.

Table 28: Legend of Battlecruiser Designs 'A' and 'B', 27 March 1916

Length:	810ft pp, 860ft oa
Beam:	104ft
Draught:	25ft fore, 26ft aft, 29ft 6in mean deep
Displacement:	36,250 tons ('B' = 36,300 tons)
Shp:	144,000
Speed:	32kts
Oil fuel:	1200 tons; 4000 tons max.
Armament:	8 x 15in (80rpg)
	12 x 5.5in (design 'B' 16 x 5.5in), (150rpg) 2 x 3in HA, 2 or 4 above-water 21in torpedo tubes (Design 'B' 2 x 21in submerged tubes)
Armour:	
Belt	8in, 5in and 3in amidships; 5in and 4in fore; 4in aft
Bulkheads	4in, 4in and 3in fore and aft
Barbettes	9in max
Gunshields	11 and 10in
CT (forward)	10in
Tube and Support	3in–3.5in
Torpedo CT	6in
Torpedo CT tube	4in
Torpedo bulkheads	1.5in and 0.75in
Funnel uptakes	1.5in
Forecastle deck	1.5in and 1in
Upper deck	1in aft
Main deck	1.5in
Lower deck	1in–2in fore, 1in–2.5in aft
Weights (tons):	
	'A'	'B'
General equipment	750	750
Armament	4750	4800
Machinery	5200	5200
Oil Fuel	1200	1200
Armour	10,100	10,100
Hull	14,070	14,070
BM	180	180
Total:	36,250	36,300

Table 29 Legends of Battlecruiser and Fast Battleship Designs, 5 July 1916

	Modified Battlecruiser	*Battleship Design 'A'*
LENGTH:	810ft pp, 860ft oa	810ft pp, 860ft oa
BEAM:	104ft	104ft
DRAUGHT:	25ft 9in fore, 26ft 9in aft, 29ft 6in mean deep	27ft 9in fore, 28ft 9in aft, 31ft 6in mean deep
DISPLACEMENT:	37,500 tons	40,600 tons
SHP:	144,000	144,000
SPEED:	31.75–32kts	31.5kts
OIL FUEL:	1200 tons; 4000 tons max	1200 tons; 4000 tons max
ARMAMENT:	8 x 15in (80rpg)	8 x 15in (80rpg)
	16 x 5.5in (150rpg)	16 x 5.5in (150rpg)
	2 x 4in HA	2 x 4in HA
	2 x 21in submerged tubes	2 x 21in submerged tubes
		2 x 21in above water tubes
ARMOUR:		
Belt	8in, and 3in amidships; 5in, 4in and 3in fore; 4in aft	12in and 6in amidships; 7in and 6in fore; 6in aft
Bulkheads	4in and 3in fore and aft	6in and 4.5in fore and aft
Barbettes	9in max	12 in max
Gunshields	15in and 11in	15in and 12in
CT (forward)	10in	12in
Tube and Support	3in, 6in, 3.5in, 2in	3in and 6in
Torpedo CT	6in	6in
Torpedo CT tube	4in	4in
Torpedo bulkheads	1.5in and 0.75in	1.5in and 0.75in
Funnel uptakes	2.5in	2.5in
Forecastle deck	1.25in and 2in	1.25in and 2in
Upper deck	0.75in and 1in	0.75in and 1in
Main deck	1in, 1.5in and 2in	1in, 1.5in and 2in
Lower deck	1in, 1.5in and 2in fore; 1in, 2.5in aft	1in, 1.5in and 2in fore; 1in, 2.5in aft
WEIGHTS (tons):		
General equipment	750	750
Armament	4950	5000
Machinery	5300	5300
Oil Fuel	1200	1200
Armour	10,600	13,400
Hull	14,520	14,750
BM	180	200
TOTAL:	37,500	40,600

were believed to be capable of 30kts and armed with 15.2in guns. He did not care for the intermediate speeds of some of the designs and said that future ships should be either 21kt battleships or 30kt battlecruisers. He also commented that the *Renown* and *Courageous* types, although of sufficient speed, would not meet the needs of the fleet as they were inadequately protected. These views were supported by Beatty, who did not expect the older 12in gun battlecruisers to be of much use in action due to their lack of speed and was concerned that he might be outnumbered as well as outclassed by a faster, more powerfully armed German battlecruiser force. He was anxious to see the *Renown* and *Repulse* completed to help restore the balance but, like Jellicoe, did not much care for the large light cruisers which he described as 'freak' ships.

The views of the senior officers afloat were not taken lightly and the DNC was immediately switched from battleship to battlecruiser designs. On 1 February 1916 he submitted two legends, designs '1' and '2', which were essentially a continuation of the battleship project with the emphasis shifted to speed at the expense of protection. However, the reduction in the thickness of the latter fell a long way short of compensating for the great increase in weight required for the machinery which was not only itself heavier but, as it occupied a greater length, required proportional increases in both the hull and armour weight. Design '1' with the same requirements of proportion and armament as the battleships was 835ft long and displaced 39,000 tons, 8000 tons more than the largest of the battleship designs. Seeing in this an opportunity to advance the cause of lightweight machinery, the DNC produced design '2', essentially the same as the first design but with small-tube boilers substituted for the large-tube type. This saved 3500 tons in displacement and 1ft in draught and, as the machinery was of the same power, gave a 0.5kt improvement in the estimated speed. In addition, as the boilers were of reduced width, the boiler rooms were proportionally smaller, which allowed an increase in the depth of the torpedo protection system abreast those compartments. This seems to have convinced the Sea Lords as the DNC was asked to work out some more small-tube boiler designs, a further four of which were submitted for discussion on 17 February. One, design '3', was a modification of '2' with the machinery power increased to give a speed of 32kts – the same as that of the *Renown* and *Courageous* types and no doubt intended to ensure a margin of speed over the most recent German designs. The remaining three, designs '4' to '6', were again based on design '2' but with four, six and eight 18in guns respectively. This followed a request from Jellicoe that a larger gun than the 15in should be fitted if such a weapon was available and if it was not it should be given serious consideration. However, he also stated that the minimum number of guns should be eight as any less produced difficulties in accurate fire control and reduced the weight of broadside. This would have made designs '4' and '5' unacceptable and the eight-gun design was probably rejected as being too large. It may also have been anticipated that delays would occur due to supply problems with the 18in guns and their mountings (only Armstrong had plant capable of dealing with guns of this size adequately).

After some discussion the DNC was asked to work out design '3' in greater detail and to provide an alternative version of the same design with the secondary armament increased to sixteen 5.5in guns. These two designs, designated 'A' and 'B' (see Table 28) were submitted to the Board on 27 March

1916 and it was generally agreed that the alternative 'B' design was preferred. The final design was approved by the Board on 7 April and on 19 April orders for three ships were placed with John Brown, Cammell Laird and Fairfields. A fourth ship was ordered from Armstrong Whitworth on 13 June and on 14 July the four ships were allocated the names *Hood, Howe, Rodney* and *Anson* respectively. The first ship of the class, *Hood,* was laid down on 31 May but on the same day events were occurring in the North Sea that were to drastically alter her design.

The Battle of Jutland made it clear that improvements were required in the armouring of British dreadnoughts and in particular that the inadequacies of deck protection were much more serious than had hitherto been supposed. During June the *Hood* design was reconsidered in light of this experience, which included consultation with Jellicoe during a conference at the Admiralty. These deliberations resulted in the production of two modified legends, dated 5 July 1916 (see Table 29). In the first, which was based directly on the instructions given to the DNC, the primary changes were directed toward improving the deck protection and the turret and barbette armour (between decks), some compensation for the added weight being obtained by reducing the upper belt from 5in to 3in thickness. In addition, the funnel protection was increased, the height of the 8in belt raised by 1ft 8in, the 5.5in ammunition hatches and dredger hoists on the main deck enclosed with 1in bulkheads and the number of dynamos increased from four to eight (the latter was already under consideration before Jutland). This produced a 1200-ton increase in displacement and a 9in

Hood under construction at Clydebank. This view is taken from the upper deck aft looking forward with the barbettes of 'X' and 'Y' 15in mountings in the foreground. (Imperial War Museum: Q19450)

BATTLECRUISER REVIVAL | 59

Table 30: Legend of 'Admiral' Class, 20 August 1917

LENGTH:	810ft pp, 860ft oa
BEAM:	104ft
DRAUGHT:	28ft fore, 29ft aft, 31ft 6in mean deep
DISPLACEMENT:	41,200 tons
SHP:	144,000
SPEED:	31kts
OIL FUEL:	1200 tons; 4000 tons max
ARMAMENT:	8 x 15in, 16 x 5.5in, 4 x 4in HA, 2 sub 21in TT and 8 aw 21in TT
HT OF SIDE ARMOUR:	21ft 6in above LWL (extending 3ft 3in below LWL)
ARMOUR:	
Belt	12in, 7in, 5in amidships; 6in and 5in fore; 6in aft (extending 21ft 6in above and 3ft 3in below LWL)
Bulkheads	5in and 4in fore and aft
Barbettes	12in max
Shields	15in front, 12in and 11in sides, 5in roof
CT (for'd)	11in, 10in and 9in
Torp Control tower	9in and 7in
Communication tube	6in and 3in
Torpedo bulkheads	1.5in, 1in and 0.75in
Funnel uptakes	2.5in and 1.5in
Forecastle deck	1.5in and 1.75in
Upper deck	0.75in, 1in and 2in
Main deck	1in, 1.5in, 2in and 3in (5in glacis plates at 'A' and 'Y' barbettes)
Lower deck	1in and 1.5in fore; 1.5in, 1in and 3in aft
WEIGHTS (tons):	
General equipment	800
Armament	5255 (inc 55 tons for heavier gunshields)
Machinery	5300
Oil Fuel	1200
Armour	13,550
Hull	14,950
BM	145 (with 55 tons appropriated)
TOTAL:	41,200 tons

increase in draught. The second, 'Design A', produced at the instigation of the DNC, was for a much more drastic improvement to the protection aimed at converting the ship into a fast battleship. This involved increasing the thickness of the vertical armour generally by 50 per cent, which, together with some minor additions to the deck protection, added a further 3100 tons to the displacement and 2ft to the draught. Although this negated the shallow draught requirement, the ship still drew 2ft less water than the *Queen Elizabeth* class battleships and the loss in speed was negligible. The ultimate result was a ship equal in most respects to the *Queen Elizabeth* but with a 7kt advantage in speed and much improved torpedo protection, at the cost of an additional 13,000 tons in designed load displacement. An additional feature of this design was the provision of four above-water torpedo tubes on each side of the upper deck which in part substituted for the lack of an after submerged torpedo room. The latter had been requested earlier but was found to be impossible to fit owing to the amount of space taken up by the propeller shafts etc, in what was a comparatively restricted area of the hull.

The DNC's proposal resulted in a request for him to consider further variations on this theme employing triple 15in gun mountings. On 20 July another three designs were submitted with the same particulars as design 'A' except for the following:

Design 'B': 43,100 tons; twelve 15in guns (4 x 3); 30.5kts; mean draught 30ft (load), 33ft 3in (deep). The total ammunition stowage for this design remained the same as design 'A' that reduced the number of rounds carried per gun from 120 to 80. This could not be increased without lengthening the shell rooms, which would have meant either a reduction in the machinery spaces, and hence speed, or an increase in size beyond available docking limits. This restriction also applied to designs 'C' and 'D' but with a lesser effect as they had fewer guns.

Design 'C': 41,700 tons; ten 15in guns (2 x 3 + 2 x 2); 30.5-30.75kts; mean draught 29ft (load), 32ft 3in (deep); ammunition stowage 96rpg.

Design 'D': 40,900 tons; nine 15in guns (3 x 3); 30.75kts; mean draught 28ft 6in (load), 31ft 9in (deep); ammunition stowage 106rpg.

These four designs were submitted to the Controller on 26 July with the comment from the DNC that the triple mountings involved a further increase in draught and loss of speed. After some consideration the Board approved design 'A' and the *Hood* was recommenced to this new design on 1 September 1916. However, in the same month the protection was reviewed again following a more detailed analysis of the lessons of Jutland and the design further modified as follows:

(a) Thickness of side armour between upper and forecastle decks reduced from 6in to 5in and between main and upper decks increased from 6in to 7in.
(b) Forecastle deck amidships increased from 1.75in to 2in.
(c) Upper deck forward increased from 1in to 2in and areas of 2in and 1in plating aft extended.
(d) Main deck over magazines increased from 2in to 3in and aft from 1.5in to 2in.
(e) Lower deck aft increased from 1in to 1.5in and 1in.

These changes were intended to ensure that a total minimum thickness of 9in of protection would have to be penetrated by a projectile striking at angles of descent up to 30°. The alterations were approved by the Board on 2 October 1916 but the protection continued to be the subject of debate between the Admiralty and the C-in-C Grand Fleet, first Jellicoe and then Beatty, until the end of the war. The final legend, after some further modification, including an additional 55 tons (appropriated from the Board Margin of 200 tons) for heavier gunshields – 15in front plates and roofs increased from 4.25in to 5in – was submitted on 20 August 1917 and received Board approval ten days later (see Table 30). By this time the displacement had increased by a further 600 tons and the draught by 3in, the estimated speed having fallen by 0.5kts to 31kts. By the end of 1917 the following modifications had been approved for allocation from the Board Margin of 200 tons:

Hood

5.5in gun dredger hoists	80 tons
Lagging to magazine walls and crowns	45 tons
15in front and 5in roof plates to turrets	55 tons
Total:	180 tons
	(surplus 20 tons)

Rest of Class

5.5in gun dredger hoists	80 tons
15in front and 6in roof plates to turrets	115 tons
Alterations to armour bulkheads	152 tons
Total:	347 tons
	(excess 147 tons)

From this point on the designs for *Hood* and her three sister ships began to diverge because *Hood* was too far advanced to incorporate major changes without excessive delay and expense. Her sisters, however, had been suspended on 9 March 1917, it having been decided that the enormous amount of labour and material they absorbed was of more value employed in the construction and repair of merchant ships and escort vessels in the face of the increasing seriousness of the German U-boat assault on British shipping. This was not an easy decision as there was still great concern that the British battlecruiser force was about to be seriously outclassed by German new construction. In fact the Germans had six battlecruisers under construction but only one was to be completed before the end of the war – the *Hindenburg* (eight 12in guns, 27.5kts), which entered service in October 1917. Seven battlecruisers of the *Mackensen* class (eight 13.8in guns, 28kts) were ordered in 1915, of which five were laid down and two were launched but none were ever completed. One of those laid down, and two which were never begun, were redesigned in early 1917 to accommodate an armament of eight 15in guns with a speed of 27.25kts. Although these ships did not have the speed or armament that the British attributed to them, they did have armour on the same scale as that of a battleship and only the *Hood* class ships would have been a match for them. Not knowing how far behind the German programme was (like the British they had more important work), Beatty was continuously pressing to get the construction of *Hood* expedited and that of her sisters restarted. The Admiralty were also concerned but could not obtain the authorisation of the War Cabinet for the resumption of construction on the three sisters, particularly as the Naval Staff was unable to find anything in the shipbuilding programme which could be sacrificed to achieve this end. Some effort was put into *Hood* which might otherwise have never been completed but no further progress was

Hood in 1921. (Author's collection)

Table 31: Battlecruiser construction 1915–20

Name	Builder	Machinery	Laid down	Launched	Completed
Renown	Fairfield	Fairfield	25 Jan 1915	4 Mar 1916	20 Sep 1916
Repulse	J Brown	J Brown	25 Jan 1915	8 Jan 1916	18 Aug 1916
Courageous	Armstrong	Parsons	28 Mar 1915	5 Feb 1916	28 Oct 1916
Glorious	Harland & Wolff	Harland & Wolff	1 May 1915	20 Apr 1916	14 Oct 1916
Furious	Armstrong	Wallsend	8 Jun 1915	18 Aug 1916	26 Jun 1917
Hood	J Brown	J Brown	1 Sep 1916	22 Aug 1918	15 May 1920
Anson	Armstrong	–	9 Nov 1916	Cancelled Oct 1918	
Howe	Cammell Laird	–	16 Oct 1916	Cancelled Oct 1918	
Rodney	Fairfield	–	9 Oct 1916	Cancelled Oct 1918	

made on the construction of *Anson*, *Howe* and *Rodney* and with the end of the war and the realisation that its lessons were not fully represented in these ships the Board decided to cancel them on 27 February 1919.

Modifications made to the design of the suspended ships which were not incorporated in *Hood* included a redesign of the bridge structure and moving the funnels closer together to make the ships' inclination more difficult to estimate. In addition it was approved in August 1918 to exchange the positions of the shell rooms and magazines for which it was necessary to fill out the after body of the ships to fit in the handing room of 'Y' magazine with a consequent slight loss in speed and ammunition stowage.

Modifications to *Hood* up to the time of her completion in 1920 were as follows:

August 1918: Approved to increase thickness of crowns of magazines from 1in to 2in. To compensate for the added weight the 1in and 2in protection to the funnel uptakes above the forecastle deck was omitted.

February 1919: Rig modified to incorporate main topgallant mast and W/T yard 175ft above LWL.

May 1919: Main deck at side increased to 3in thickness abreast magazines. To compensate for added weight of about 100 tons, four of the 5.5in guns and their ammunition supply arrangements were omitted.

July 1919: Approved to increase thickness of main deck over the after magazines to a total of 6in and over the forward magazines to 5in. To compensate for the added weight the above-water torpedo tubes and their protection were to be omitted and the armour walls of the torpedo control tower were reduced from 6in to 1.5in thickness. However, the additional deck protection was never fitted while four of the eight above-water torpedo tubes (less their protection) were retained as a 'peacetime' fitting only – presumably for training purposes.

Hood in 1932–3. (© National Maritime Museum, London: PX235A)

HMS *Hood* was commissioned in May 1920 as a battlecruiser. The DNC's original design description of her as a battleship never seems to have been adopted despite the fact that she was in almost every respect, except her higher speed, an equal to the *Queen Elizabeth* class battleships. Given this and post-war designs, it seems that the Admiralty had begun to regard 'battlecruiser' as a designation for 'fast battleship'. *Hood* was, however, something of a paradox. On completion she was the largest, fastest and in many ways one of the most powerful capital ships in existence. Compared with pre-Jutland designs she was a vast improvement, partly because she was of a size that would have been totally unacceptable in pre-war years – and partly because she incorporated a substantially improved underwater protection system. However, she was still an extension of pre-war ideas and having evolved directly from the *Queen Elizabeth* class, did not fully incorporate the lessons of the war, particularly with regard to protection, which had been improved and patched together piecemeal since the time of Jutland. Major improvements in the design of capital ships were envisaged for post-war ships but the imposition of International Treaty restrictions over the construction of such ships soon brought these plans to an end and enabled *Hood* to remain one of the world's most advanced designs well into the 1930s.

Table 32: Summary of design calculations for *Renown* and *Repulse*, May 1915

LOAD CONDITION (tons):		Provisions	50
General equipment	685 (+ 115 for torpedo net defence)	Officers' stores and slops	50
Armament	3335	Half WOs' stores	44
Machinery	5660	Half Engineers' stores	60
Engineer's stores	120	TOTAL:	1284 (say 1300)
Oil fuel	1000	LIGHT DISPLACEMENT:	25,200
Armour	2440		
Protective plating	2330	SUMMARY OF GENERAL EQUIPMENT AT LOAD DRAUGHT:	
Hull	10,800	Fresh water	80
Board margin	15	Provisions	50
LOAD DISPLACEMENT:	26,500	Officers' stores and slops	50
ORDINARY DEEP CONDITION WITH 4000 TONS OF OIL (TONS):		Crew and effects	120
General equipment	950	Masts, yards, etc	110
Armament	3775	Anchors, cables and	
Machinery	5660	SW Hawsers	130
Engineer's stores	120	Boats	55
Oil Fuel	4000	WOs' Stores	88
Armour	2440	Net Defence	114
Protective plating	2330	TOTAL:	797 (taken in legend as 800)
Hull	10,670	ADDITIONS TO EQUIPMENT FOR DEEP CONDITION:	
Reserve feed water	610	Admiral's boats	15
Overflow feed water	110	Admiral's stores	10
Water in feed tank	40	Canteen stores	18
Board Margin	15	Provisions	35
ORDINARY DEEP DISPLACEMENT:	30,720	Fresh water	70
LIGHT CONDITION – items to be removed from legend condition (tons):		Total	148 (taken in legend as 150)
Oil Fuel	1000	TOTAL FOR DEEP:	950
Fresh water	80		

Renown steaming at high speed in 1919–20. (Author's collection)

Table 33: Dimensions

	Length (oa)	Length (pp)	Beam (extreme)	Beam (moulded)	Depth (moulded)
Renown class (designed)	794ft	750ft	90ft	89ft 8in	41ft 0.5in* 49ft 0.94in**
Renown (actual)	794ft 1.5in	750ft 2in	90ft 1.75in	89ft 9.75in	41ft 1.5in*
Repulse (actual)	794ft 2.5in	750ft 1.13in	89ft 11.5in	89ft 7.5in	49ft 1in**
Courageous class (designed)	786ft 3in	735ft	81ft (over bulges)		
Courageous (actual)		735ft 0.13in	80ft 2in		36ft 1.25in*
Glorious (actual)		735ft 1.5in	81ft 5.25in (over bulges)		
Furious (designed)	786ft 6in	735ft	88ft		
Furious (actual)		735ft 2.25in	88ft 0.63in		35ft 7.19in*
Hood (designed)	860ft	810ft	104ft		
Hood (actual)	860ft 7in	810ft 5in	104ft 2in 105ft 2.5in extreme over rubbing pieces	103ft 11.5in	50ft 6in**

* Depth from underside of flat keel to edge of upper deck at side.
**Depth from underside of flat keel to edge of forecastle deck at side.
NB: The 'actual' dimensions given are those recorded at the time of launch but would be subject to variation both from inaccuracies in measurement and from temperature changes.

Heights to centres of gun axis as designed from LWL

Turret	'A'	'B'	'X'	'Y'
Renown class	35ft	45ft	–	23ft
Courageous class	33ft	–	–	23ft
Furious	35ft	–	–	28ft
Hood	32.25ft	42.25ft	32ft	22ft

Table 34: Displacements and stability

Condition	Displacement (tons)	Draught (ft–in) Fore	aft	Mean	GM (ft)	Angle of Max Stability (deg)	Angle at which Stability vanishes (deg)
Renown as inclined on 2 Sept 1916							
Load	27,420	25–5.5	27–0	26–3	3.5	43	64
Deep	32,220	30–2	30–1	30–1.5	6.2	44	73
Light	26,145	24–1	26–3.5	24–2.25	2.95		
Repulse as inclined Sept 1916							
Load	26,854	25–0	26–7	25–9.5	3.45		
Deep	31,592	29–9	29–7	29–8	6.1		
Light	25,579	23–6	25–10.5	24–8.25	2.8		
Courageous as inclined 8 October 1916							
Load	19,180			22–8.25	4.0	44	85
Deep	22,560			25–10	6.0	40	94
Light	18,180						
Glorious as completed							
Load	19,180						
Deep	22,360						
Furious as inclined on 25 May 1917							
Load	19,513	19–8	24	21–10	3.75	44	81
Deep	22,890			24–11	5.33	44	93
Light	18,480						
Hood as designed (1917)							
Load	41,200			28–4	4.15		69
Deep	45,620			31–4.5	4.9		76
Light	39,630			27–3.5	4.4		
Hood as inclined 21 February 1920							
Load	42,670			29–3	3.25	36	66
Deep	46,680			32–0	4.2	37	73
Light	41,000			28–3	3.2	36	64

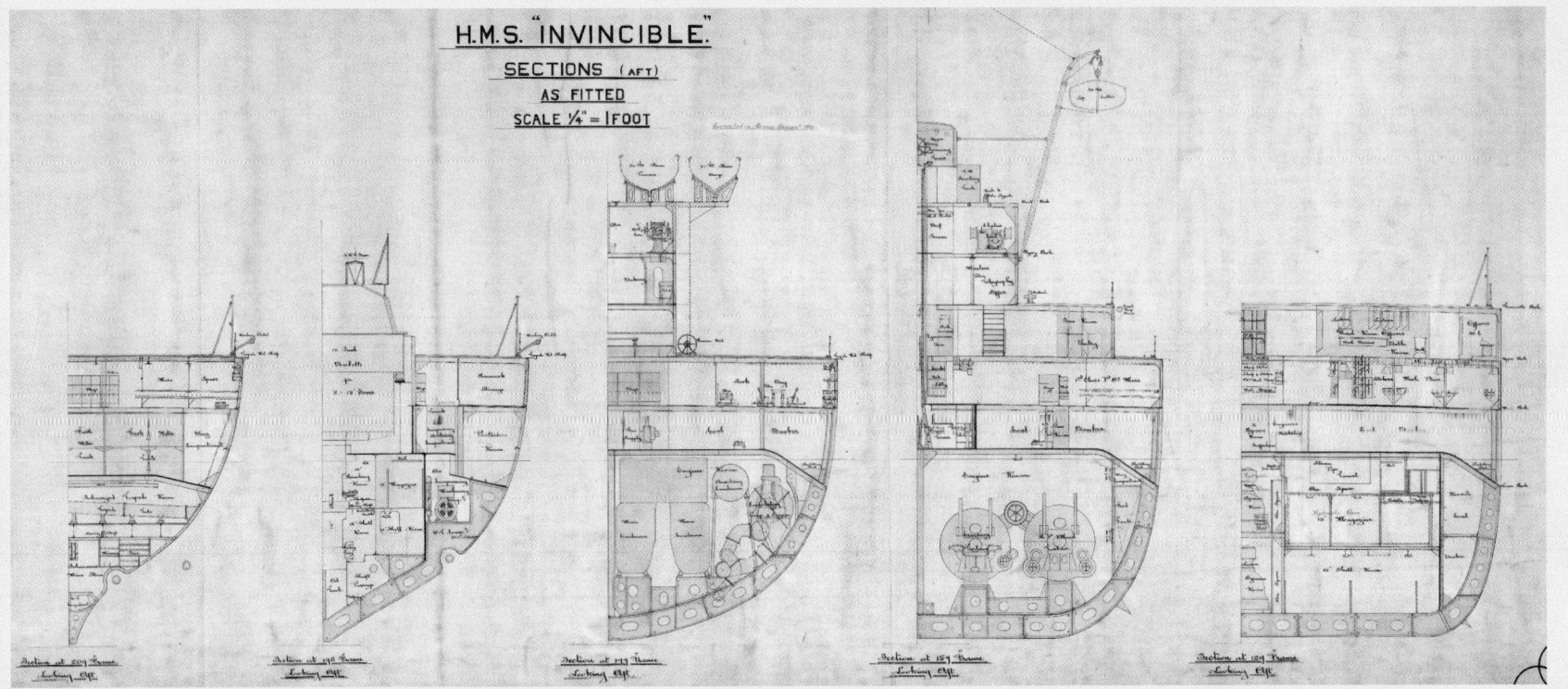

H.M.S. "INVINCIBLE".
SECTIONS (AFT)
AS FITTED
SCALE ¼" = 1 FOOT

H.M.S. "INVINCIBLE".
SECTIONS (FORWARD)
AS FITTED
SCALE ¼" = 1 FOOT

Invincible forward and after sections 'as fitted'. These and the following drawings show the ship as completed but also include modifications (in green) added to the drawing in August 1914 at the end of her major 1914 refit. Unfortunately the alterations are rather faint and incomplete. Several changes made during the refit are not shown and there is some indication of changes that were not made. It seems probable that the outbreak of war and the resultant hurry to return *Invincible* to service resulted in the abandonment of the updating of the 'as fitted' drawings for more important work. (© National Maritime Museum J9364 and J9365)

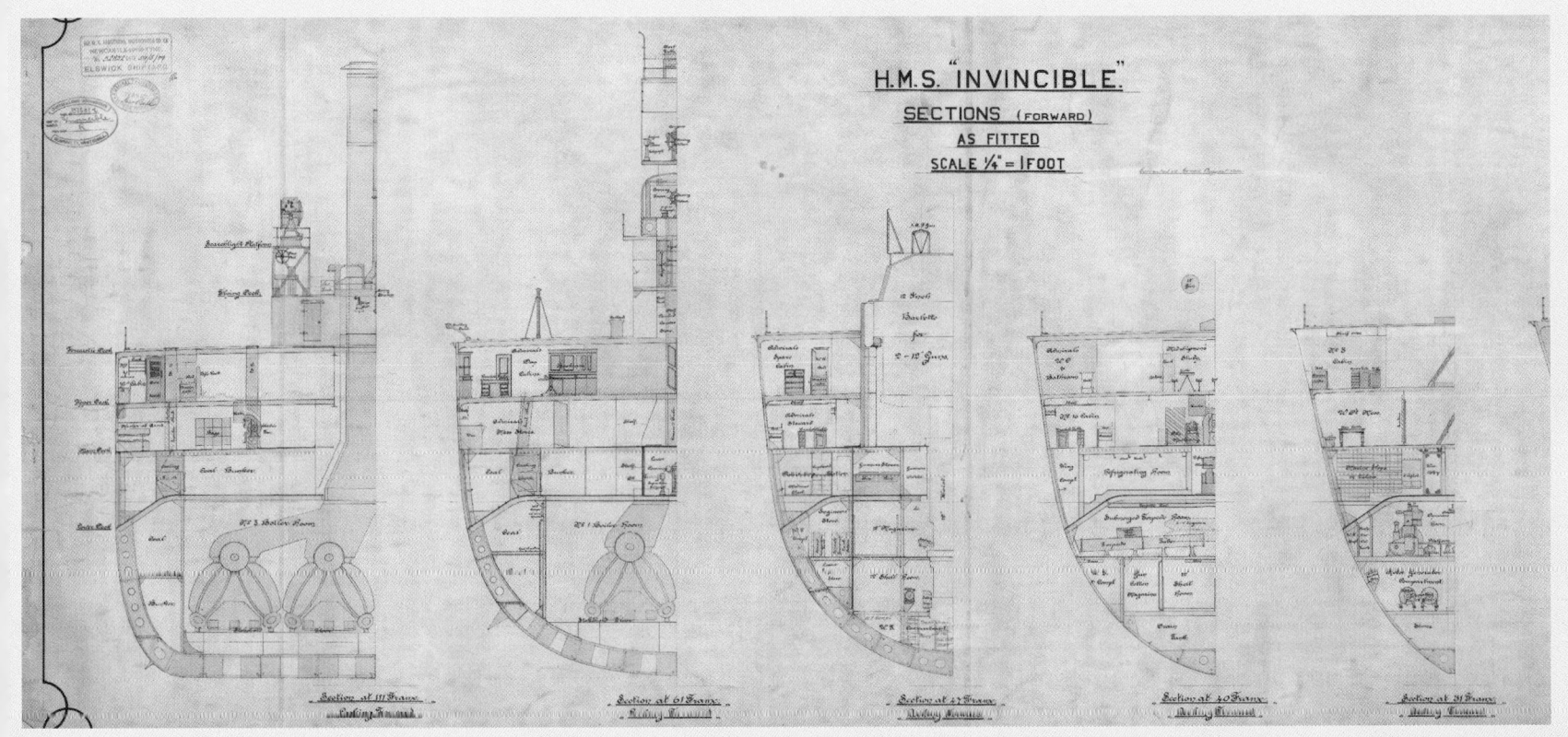

Overeaf top: *Invincible* boat stowage and bridge platforms 'as fitted'. Following standard practice the boats are only shown in outline. The heavy boats are stowed on skid beams above the after superstructure while the lighter types are similarly arranged forward between the funnels. These two positions accommodated the entire outfit of boats apart from the two 32ft life cutters carried on davits abreast the after funnel. She has forward and after armoured conning towers, both serving as conning and torpedo control positions. On the aft side of the forward conning tower is the armoured signal tower intended to provide a protected position for flag signalling during action. The August 1914 modifications on this drawing are limited to an outline of the extension of the navigating platform and the additional 36in searchlights provided abreast the fore funnel, a plan view of the director tower platform fitted below the fore top and (together with the flying deck 'as fitted') an indication of the partial re-arrangement of her secondary armament of 4in guns. (© National Maritime Museum J9363)

Overeaf bottom: *Invincible* flying deck 'as fitted'. The term 'flying deck' is something of a throwback to earlier terminology and was soon to be superseded by 'shelter deck'. Note that the aftermost 4in gun mounting on the starboard side of the after flying deck and the right 4in gun mounting on the roof of 'A' turret are the only ones shown in detail – all other positions are indicated only by a circle for the mounting and the training arcs. The same comment applies to the boat hoists and winches on the forward and after flying decks where only those to starboard are shown in detail. The limited modifications made to the drawing in August 1914 include the addition of a rangefinder hood on the roof of 'A' turret. (© National Maritime Museum J9362)

H.M.S.
PLAN OF SKID
AND BRI
SCA

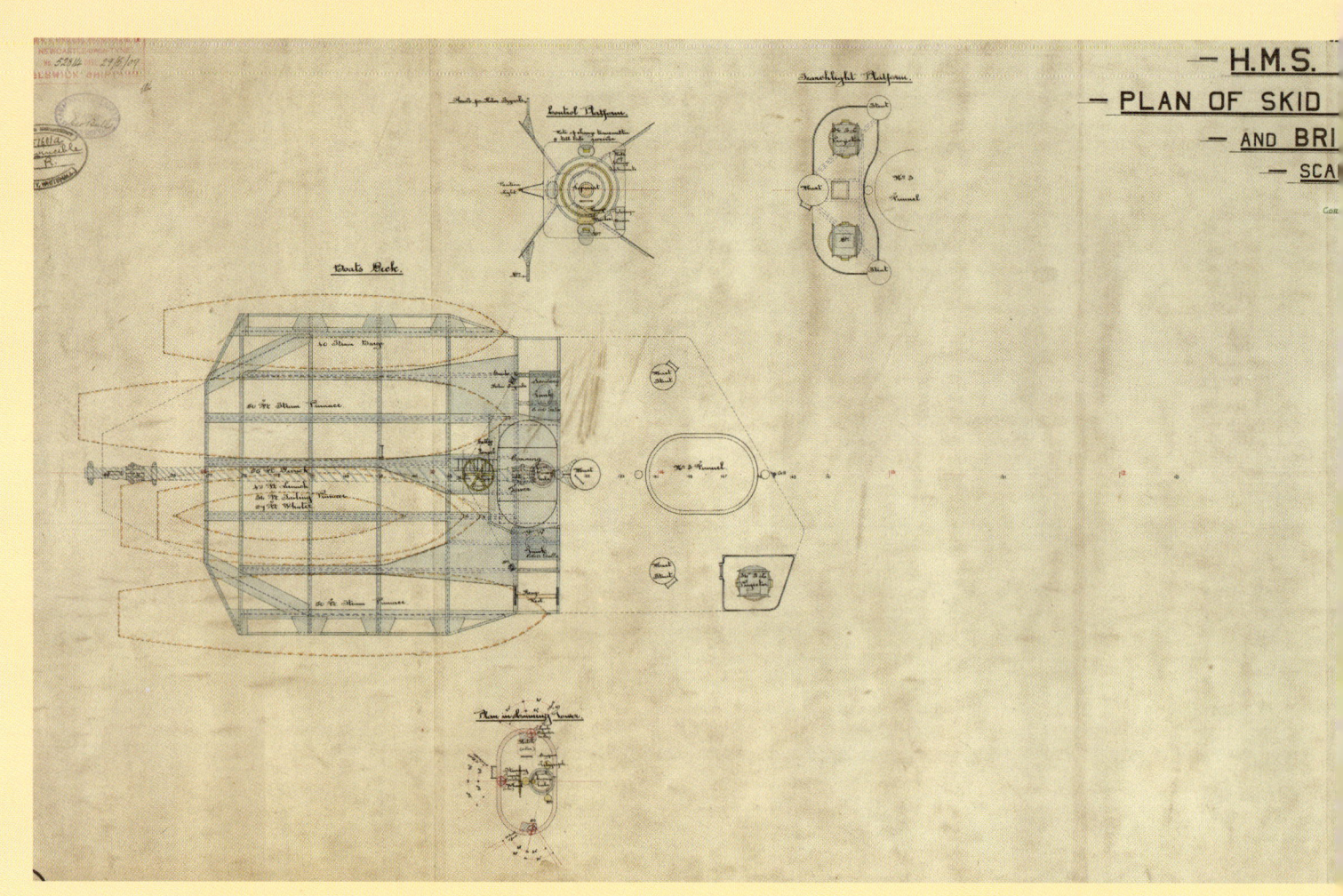

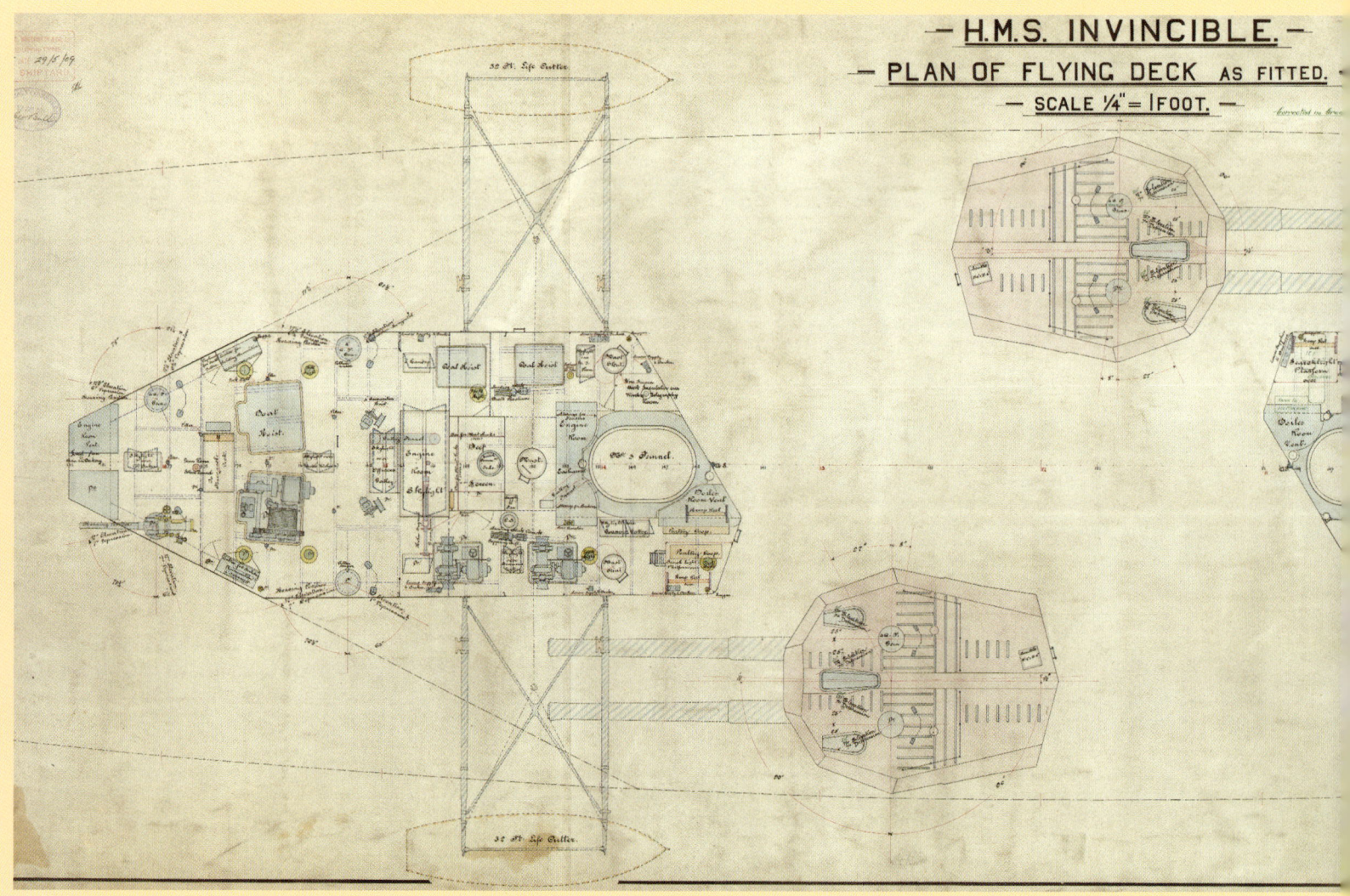

H.M.S. INVINCIBLE.
PLAN OF FLYING DECK AS FITTED.
SCALE ¼" = 1 FOOT.

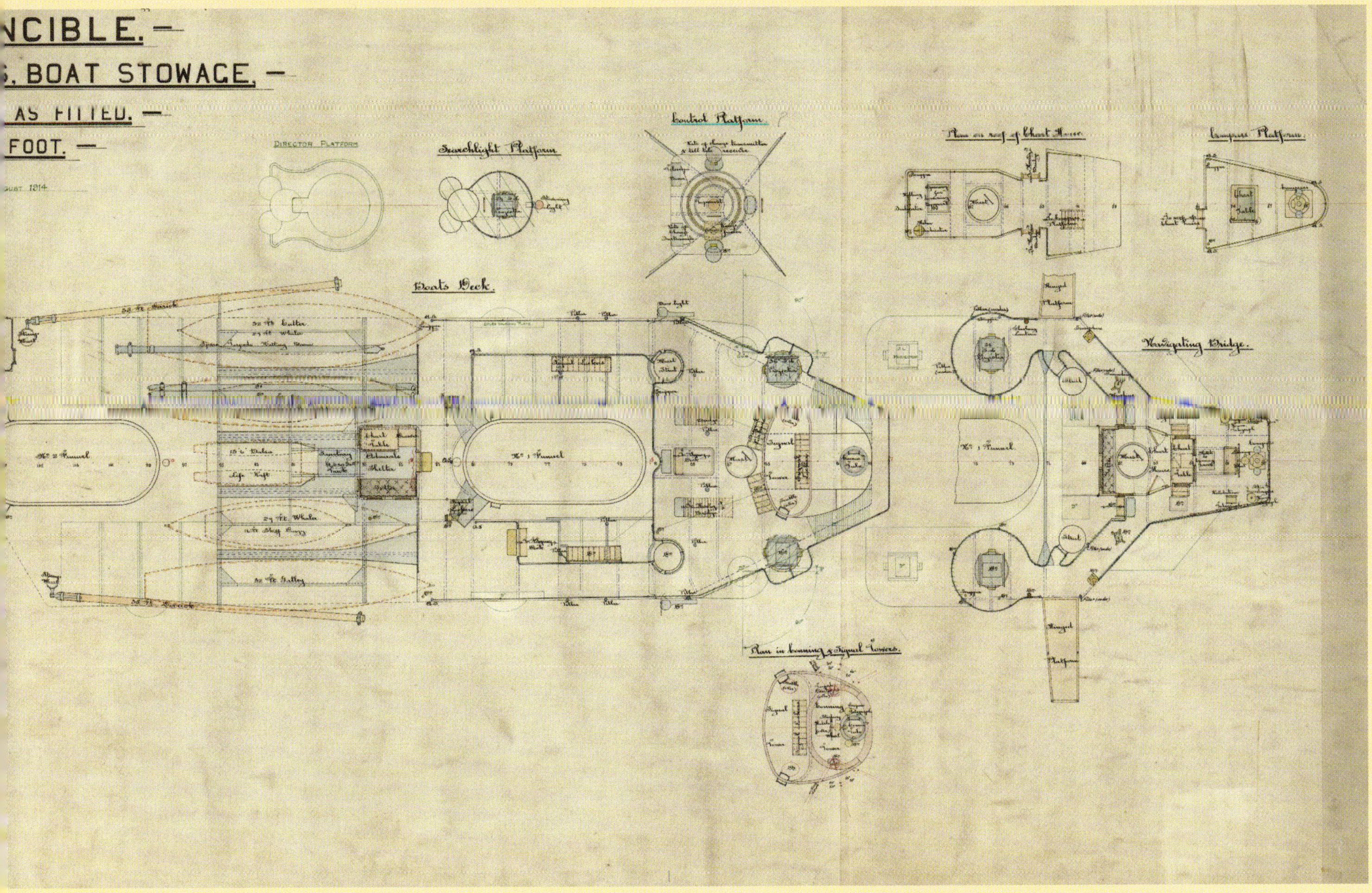
NCIBLE. —
S. BOAT STOWAGE. —
AS FITTED. —
FOOT. —
DIRECTOR PLATFORM
Searchlight Platform
Control Platform
Plan on roof of Chart House
Compass Platform
Boats Deck
Navigating Bridge
Plan in Conning & Signal Towers

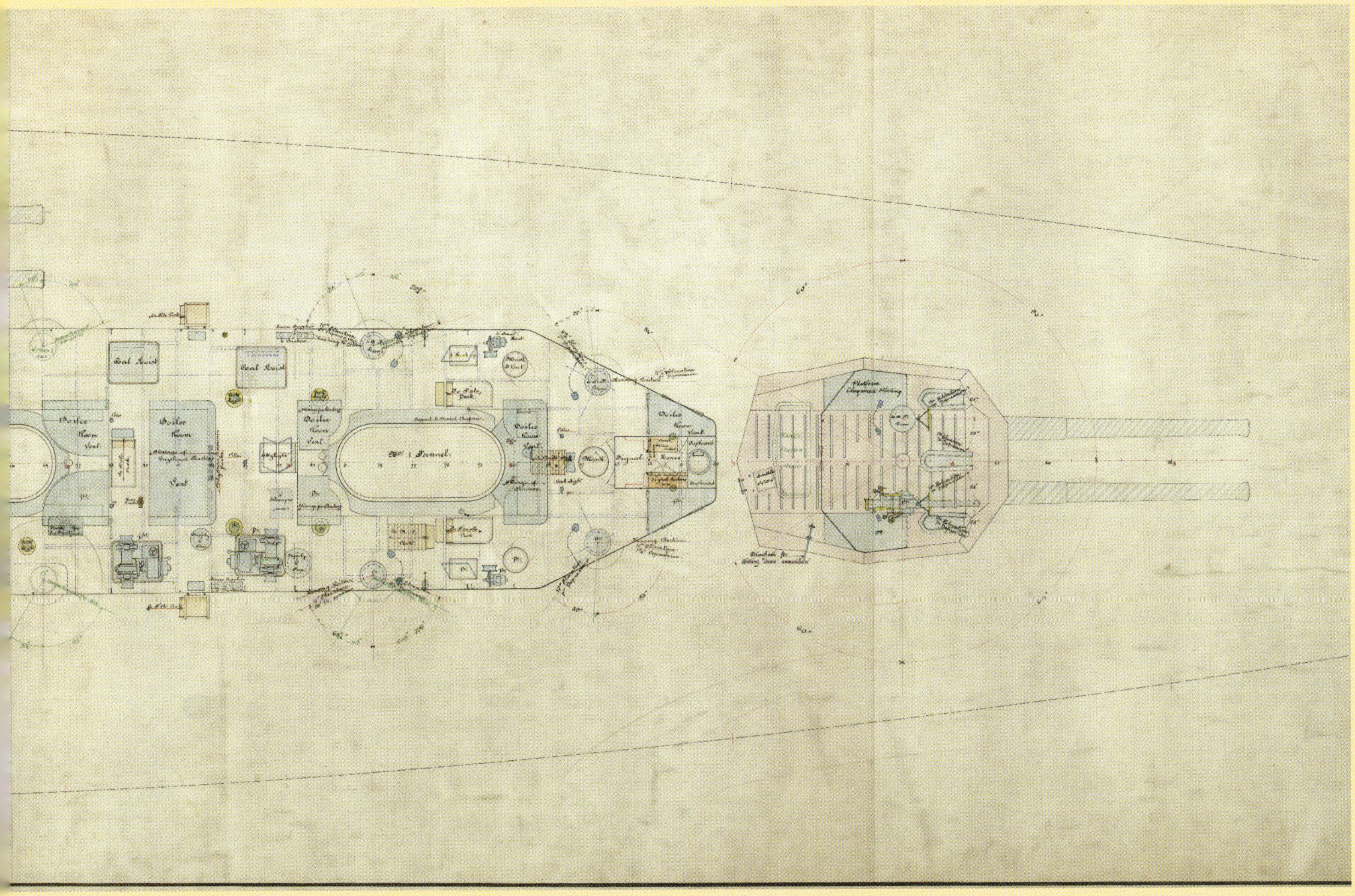
No 1 Funnel

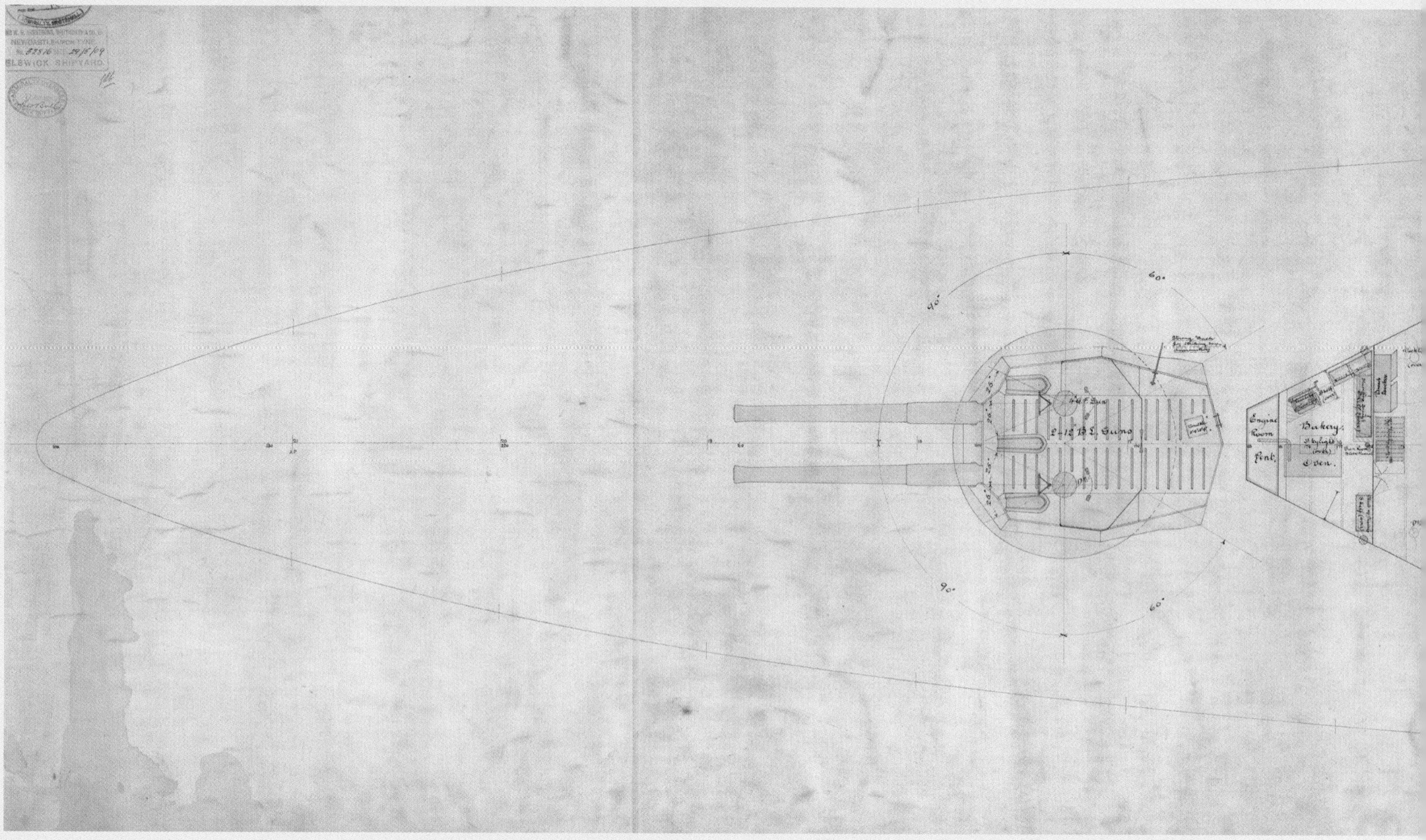
NEWCASTLE-UPON-TYNE
ELSWICK SHIPYARD
Engine Room
Vent
Bakery
Oven

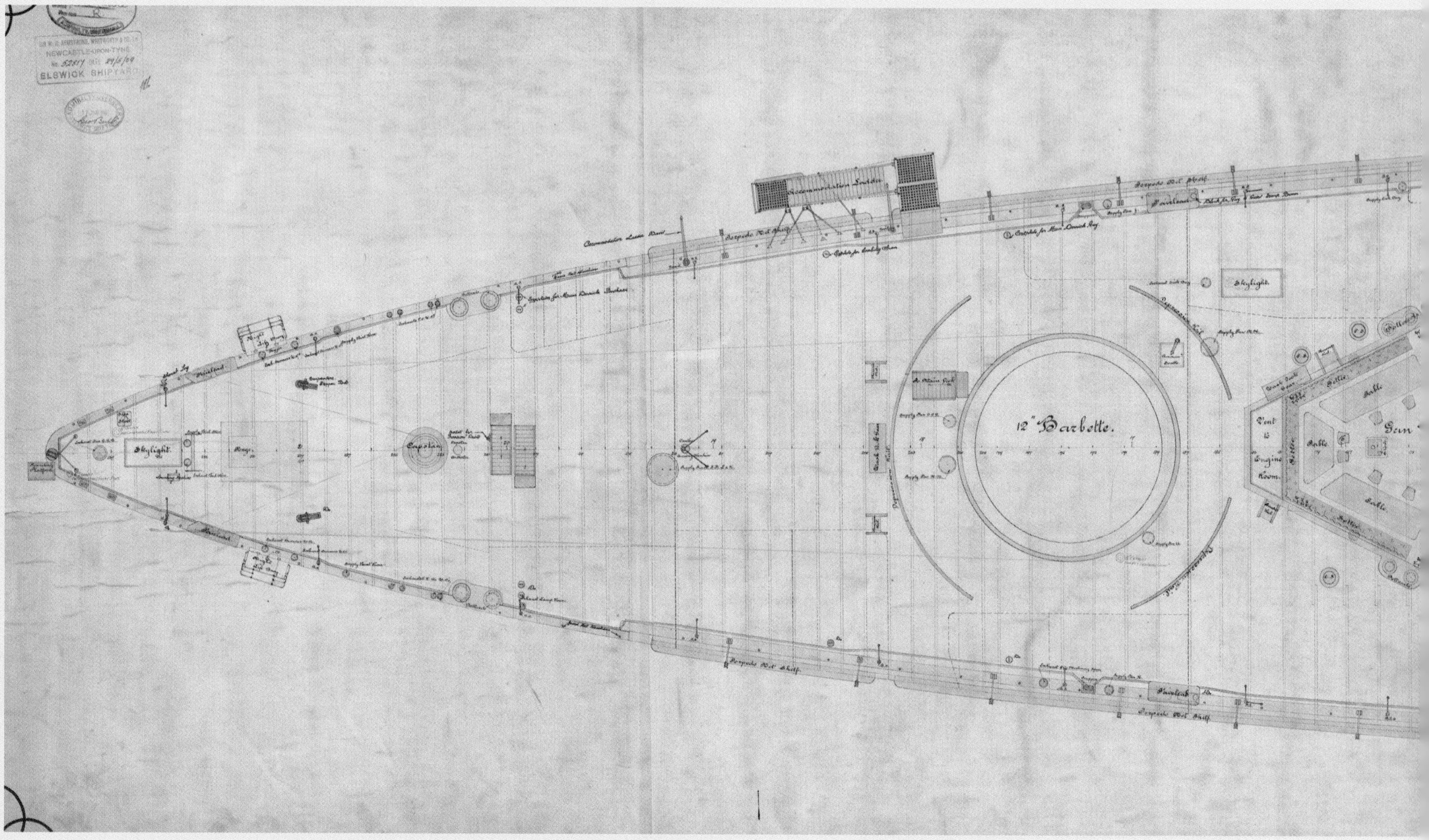
NEWCASTLE-UPON-TYNE
ELSWICK SHIPYARD
Accommodation Ladder
Skylight
Capstan
12" Barbette.
Skylight
Vent
Engine Room

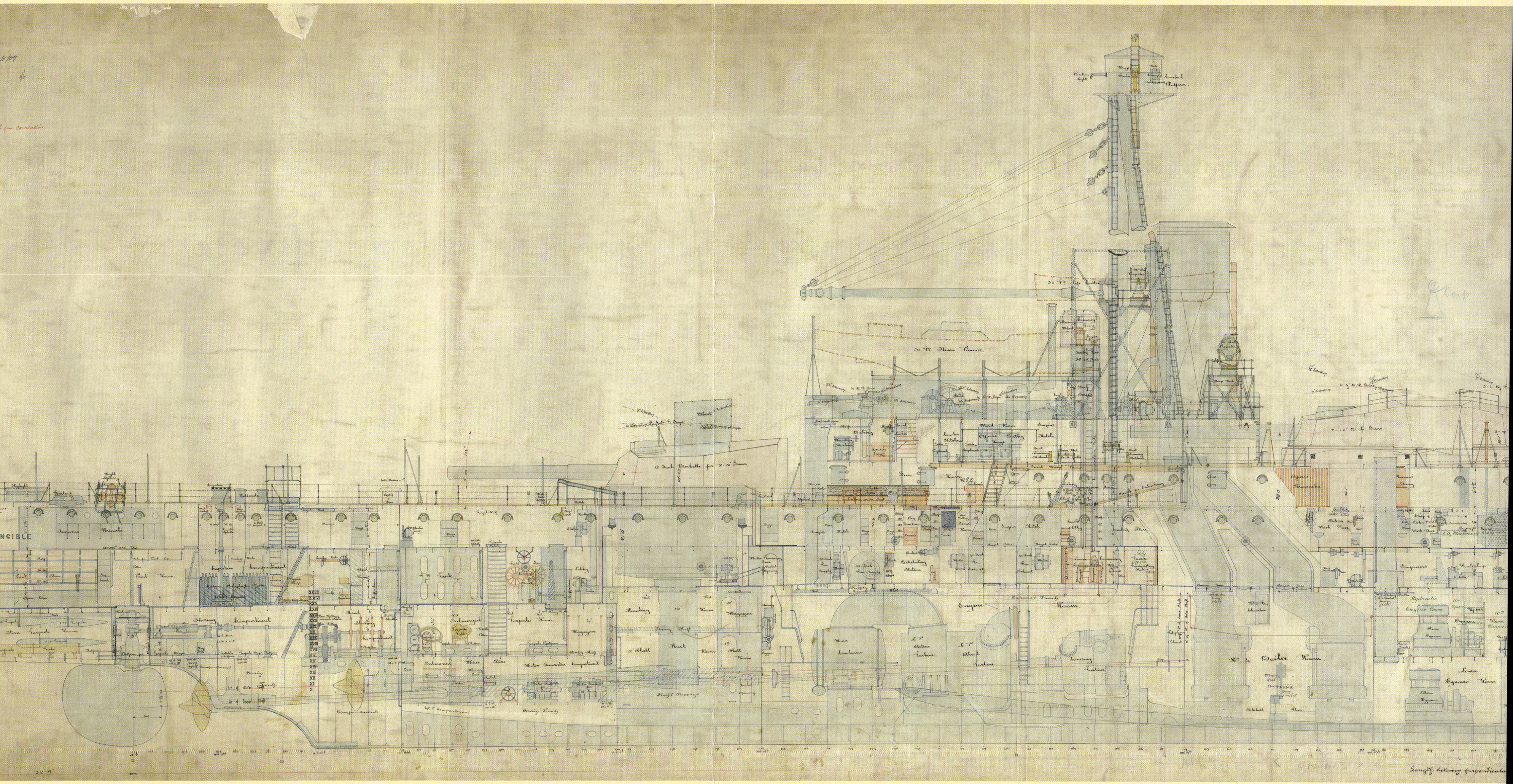

vious page top: *Invincible* forecastle deck 'as fitted'. 1914 refit included the transfer of the 4in untings on 'A' and 'X' turrets to the forward perstructure (abreast the conning tower platform and the flying deck abreast the second funnel). There is an indication of a probable intention to mount four guns on the forecastle deck as there are circles of correct diameter for these mountings within both forward superstructure (one to starboard of the ond funnel and one further forward to port –

ie further from the blast of 'P' turret) and abreast the after end of the after superstructure. It seems likely that if such a change was intended it was abandoned due to the need to complete the refit early following the outbreak of war. It also seems likely that the guns would have been transferred from the roofs of 'P' and 'Q' turrets. (© National Maritime Museum J9361)

Previous page bottom: *Invincible* upper deck 'as fitted'. This drawing illustrates the effect of a decision of

1905 to reverse the normal accommodation arrangements of men forward and officers aft so that the latter would be closer to their command positions. The area under the forecastle from the after screen bulkhead to well forward of 'A' barbette is almost entirely taken up with compartments and cabins for the ship's officers. In particular, the cabins for the senior officers (Admiral, Captain, Chief of Staff) are located immediately below the bridge. (© National Maritime Museum J9360)

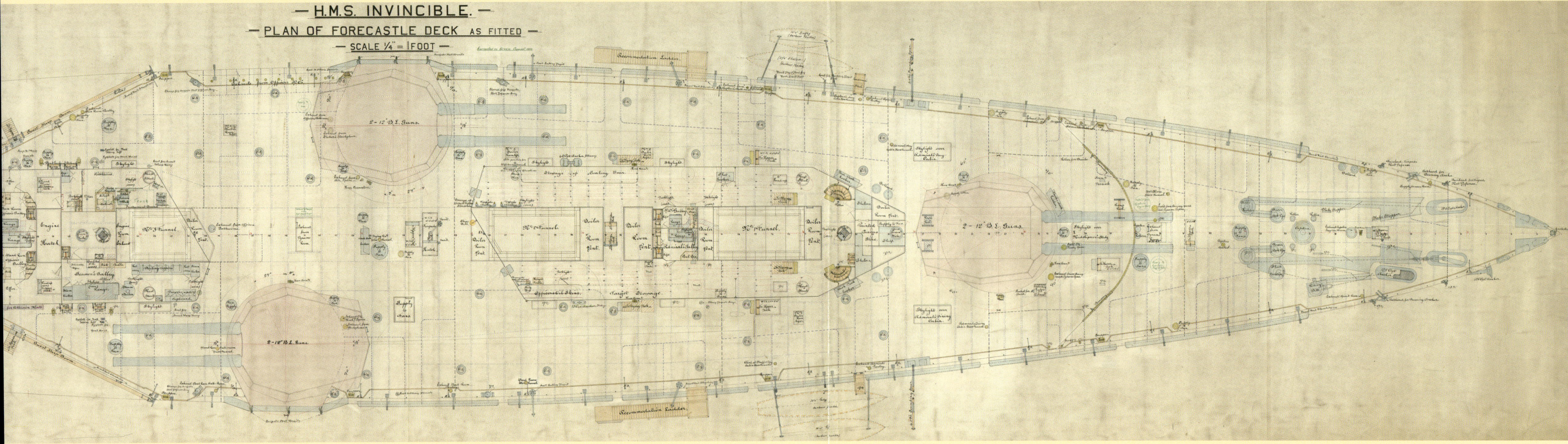

H.M.S. INVINCIBLE.

PLAN OF FORECASTLE DECK AS FITTED
SCALE ¼" = 1 FOOT

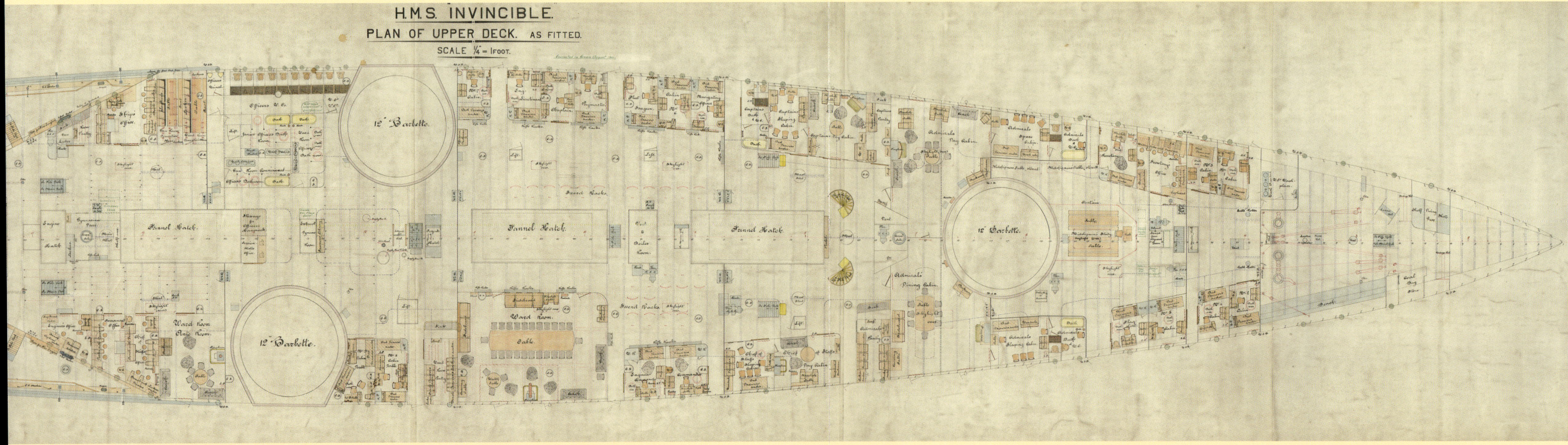

H.M.S. INVINCIBLE.

PLAN OF UPPER DECK AS FITTED.
SCALE ¼" = 1 FOOT.

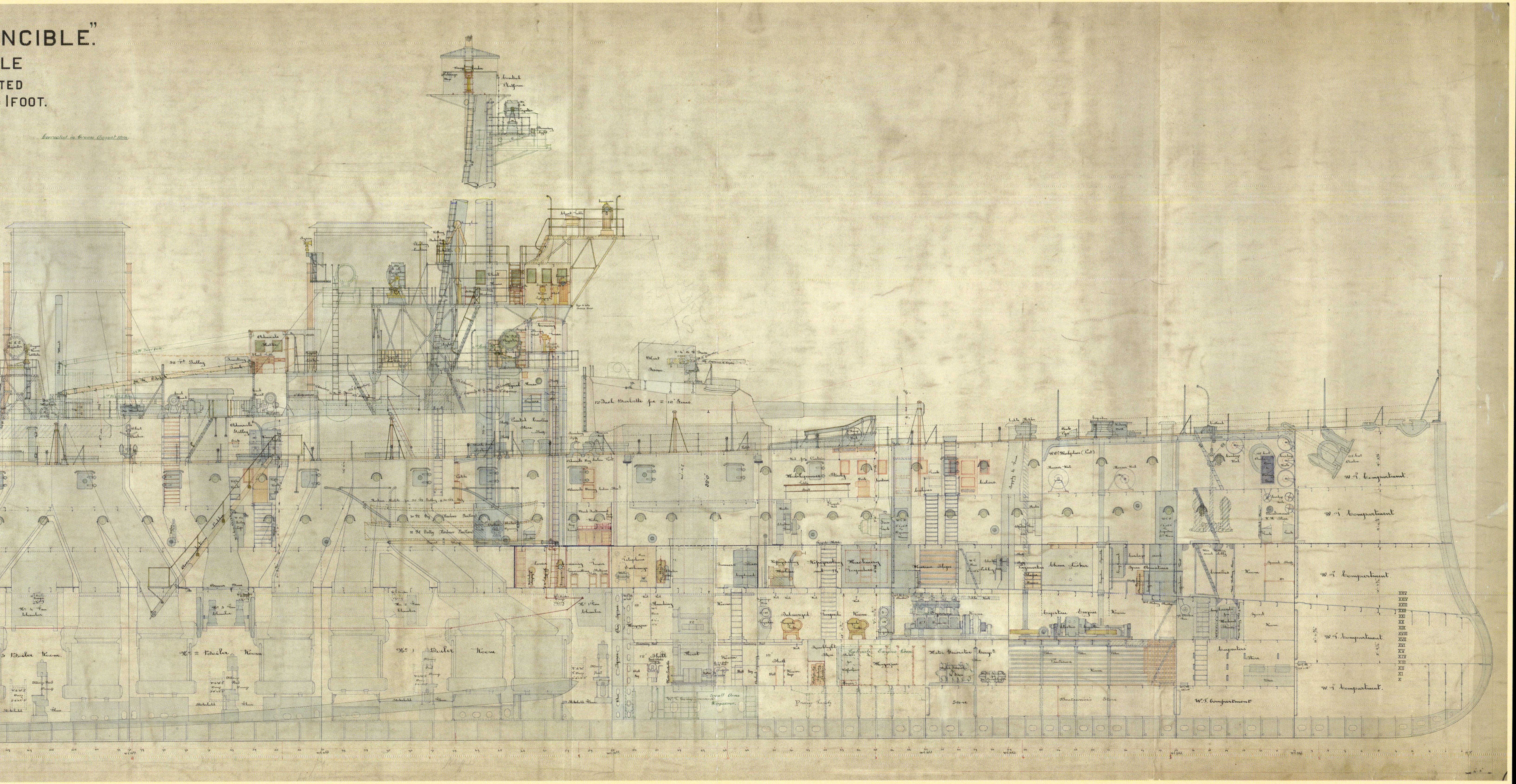

"NCIBLE".
LE
TED
1 FOOT.

profile 'as fitted'. This shows clearly the state of the changes made to the drawing 1914. Included are the director platform foretop, the rangefinder hood on 'A' turret rations to the positions of the 4in gun mountings and the extension of the navigating bridge with its additional 36in searchlight. Not shown are the ship's new foretop (fitted in 1912) and the lowering of the position of the compass platform to extend forward from the roof of the chart house. It was also intended to raise her fore funnel but this was not done until she refitted at Gibraltar in Jan-Feb 1915. (© National Maritime Museum J9358)

Above: *Princess Royal* profile 'as fitted'. This and the other plans of this ship show her as completed. As with all the British battlecruisers, in having no middle deck the ship has one less deck than contemporary battleships. This was in part due to their origin as 'cruisers' and in part a result of the different hull proportions. (© National Maritime Museum J9081).

Below: *Princess Royal* platform deck 'as fitted'. This plan clearly illustrates the cost of increased speed and displacement. She has 42 boilers compared with 31 in *Invincible* and 18 in the contemporary battleships of the *Orion* class. In addition the engine and condenser rooms occupy a length of 112ft compared to 88ft in *Orion*. (© National Maritime Museum J9368).

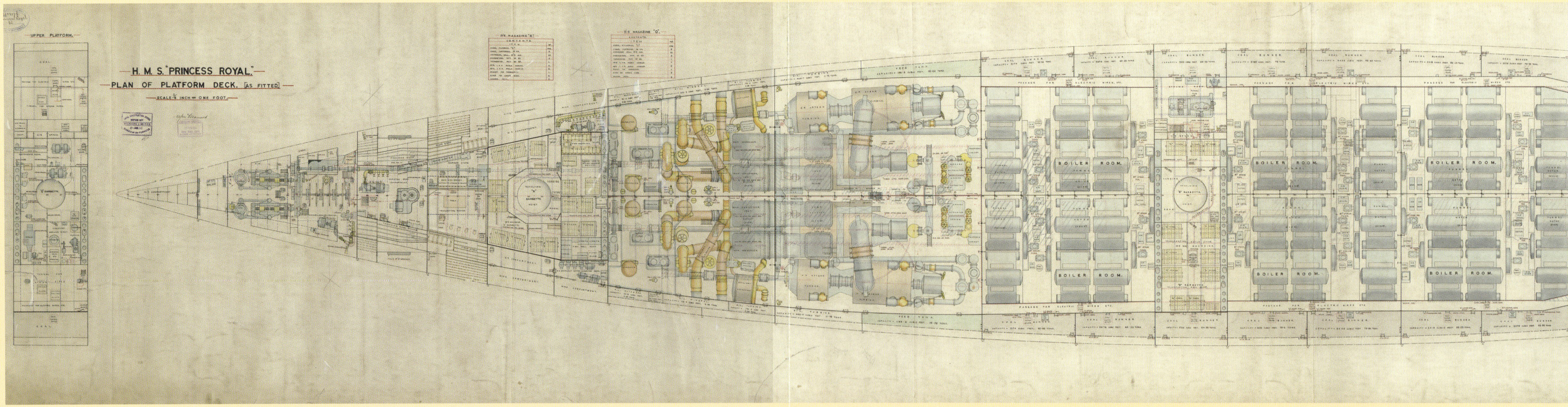

PROFILE.

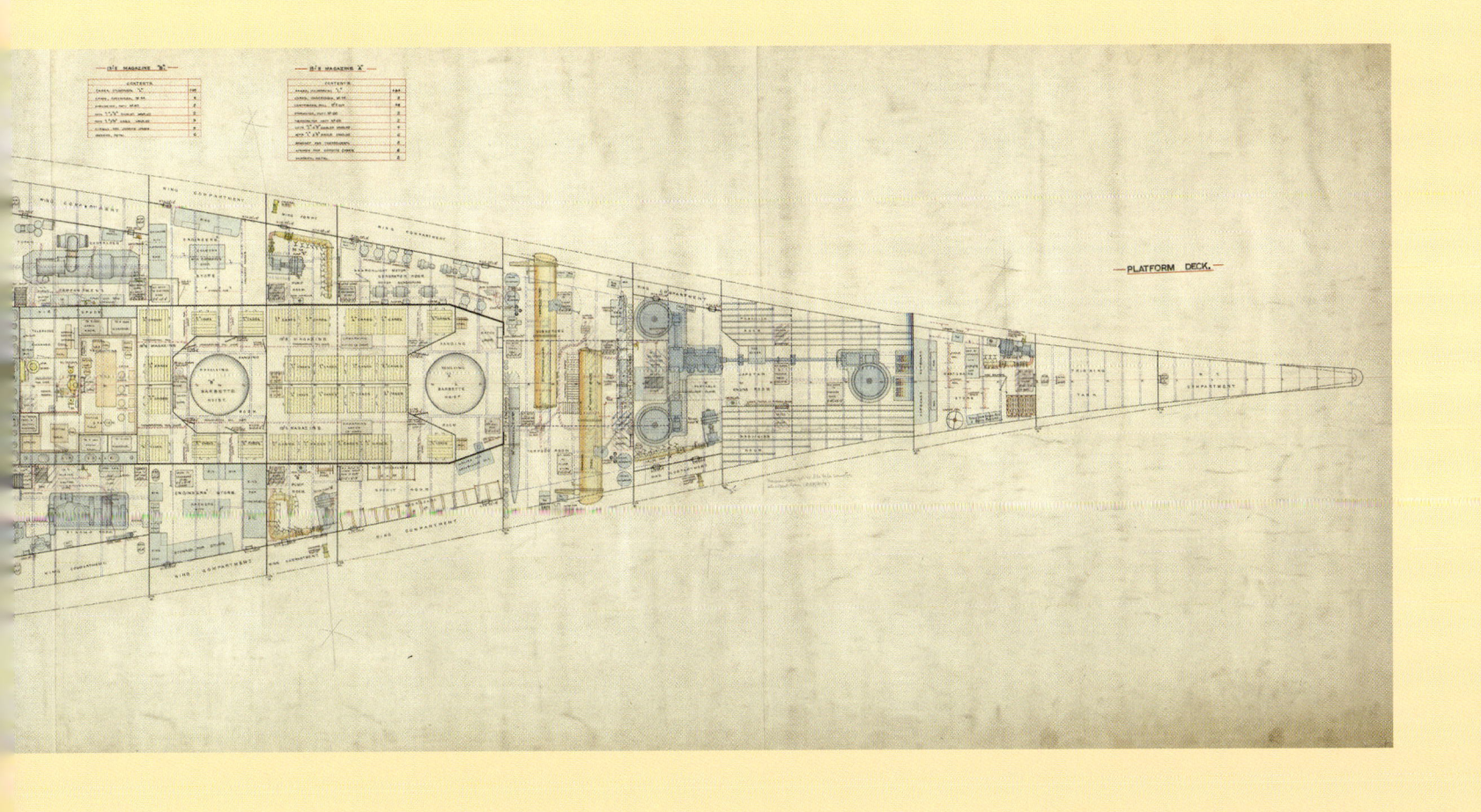

PLATFORM DECK.

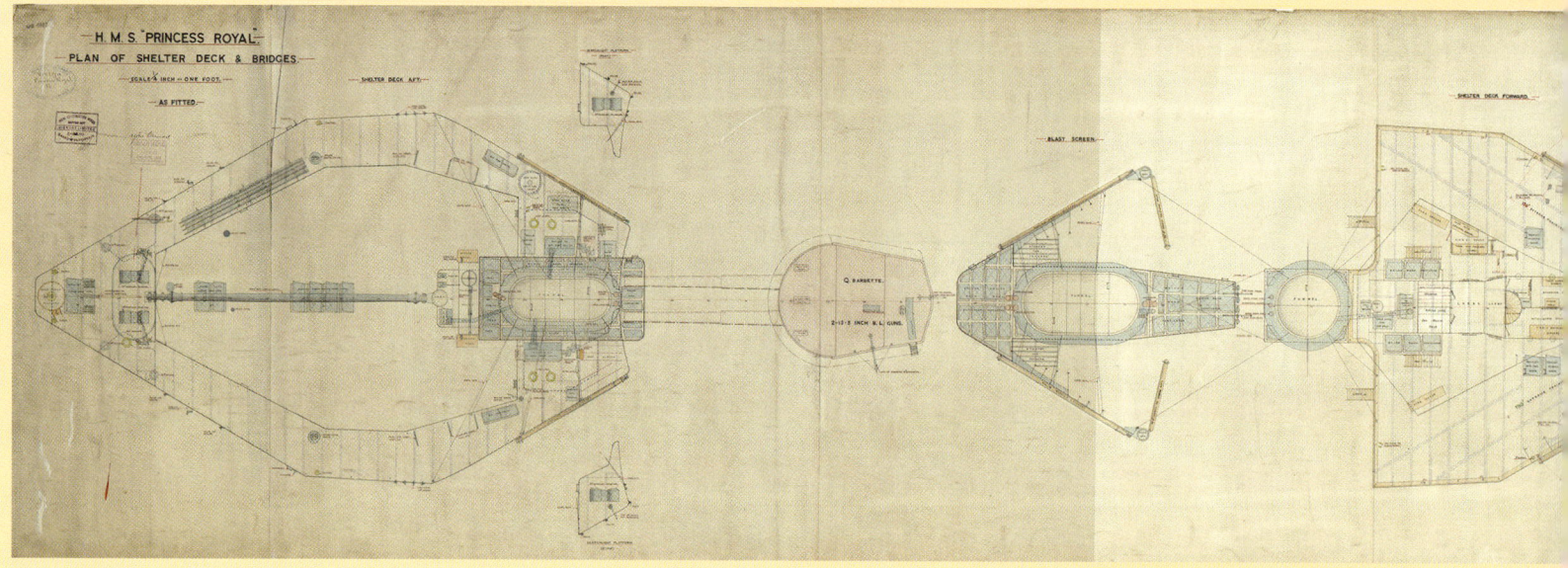

Princess Royal shelter decks and bridges 'as fitted'. The ship's primary conning positions were the bridge compass platform and, during action, the armoured conning tower. Note that the conning tower has a 'captain's' platform on each side from which a wider general view could be obtained than was possible from within the CT (particularly aft). The conning tower enclosed the base of the Argo rangefinder tower, its revolving armoured hood projecting through the roof. (© National Maritime Museum J9370).

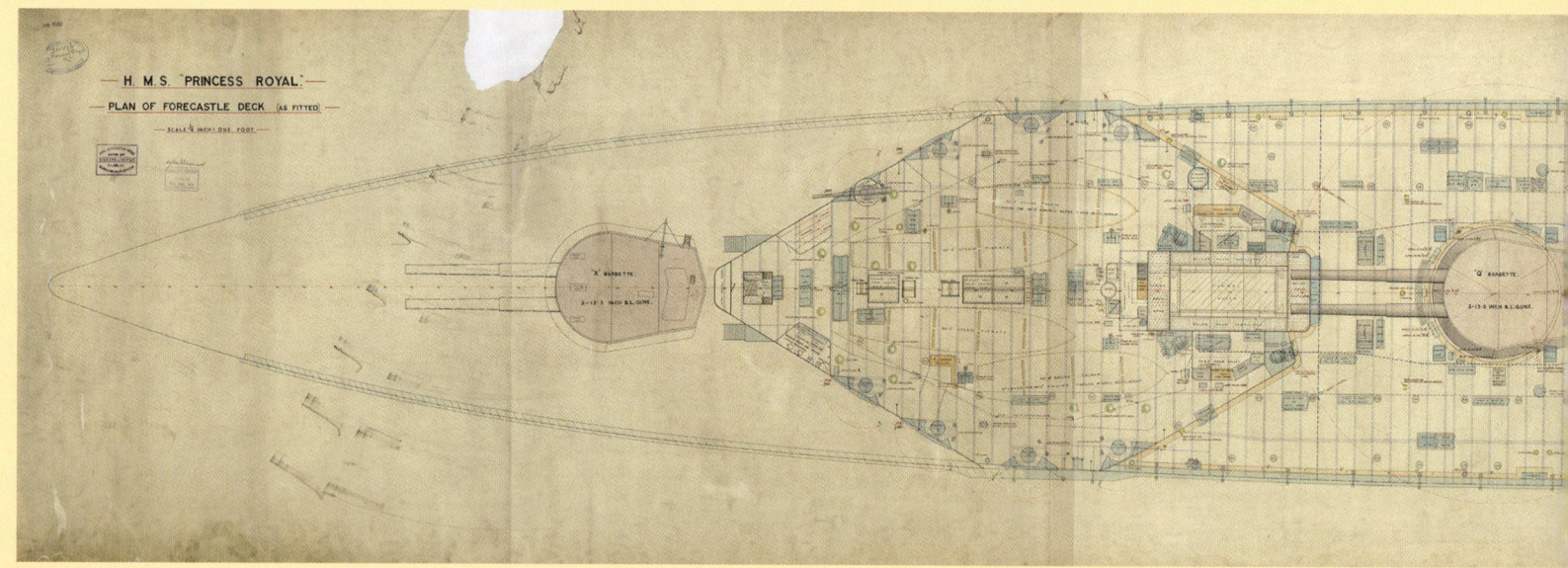

Princess Royal forecastle deck 'as fitted'. Although the secondary armament of 4in guns were protected by screens from the weather, they were unprotected in relation to action damage. The screen around the after battery also served to protect the boats from the blast of 'Q' and 'X' turrets. The forward boat stowage was similarly protected by the screen built around the second funnel. (© National Maritime Museum J9369).

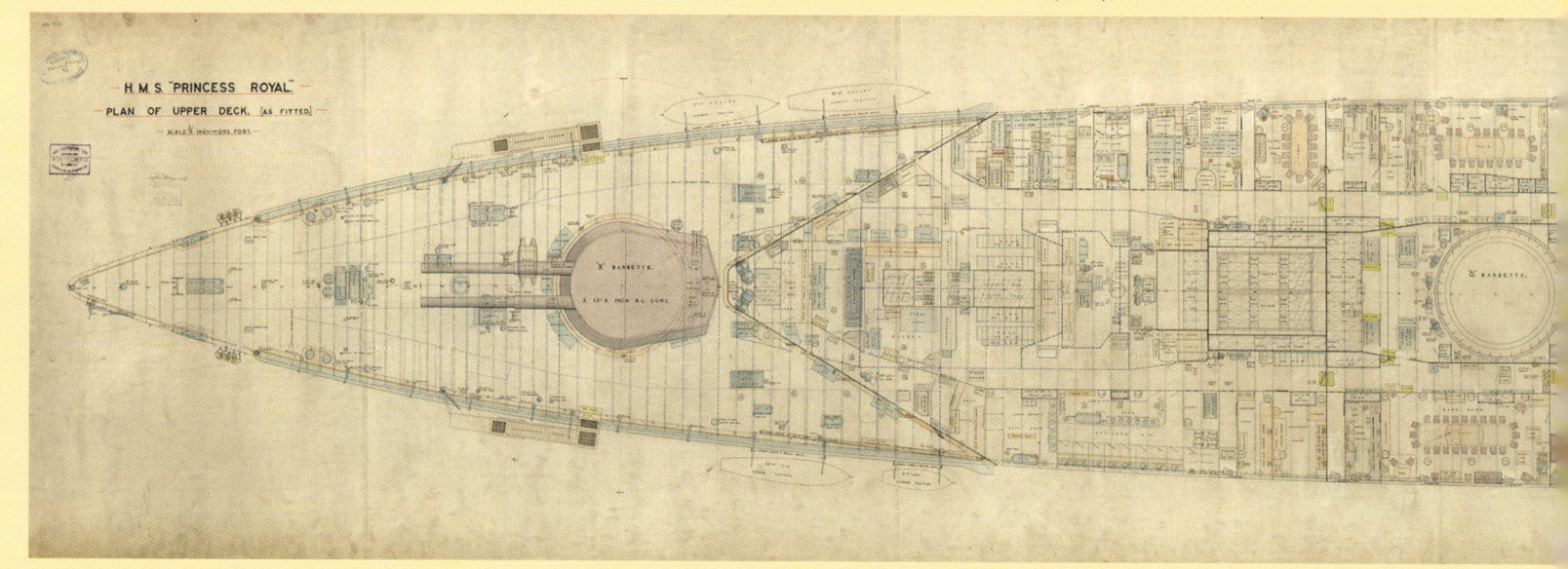

Princess Royal upper deck 'as fitted'. As in the case of *Invincible*, the area below the forecastle is largely taken up with officer accommodation, the more senior officers being located immediately below the bridge. *Princess Royal* was the last battlecruiser with this arrangement as the *Queen Mary* reverted to the traditional men forward and officers aft. Note that the after turret is designated 'X' which was the case with all the battlecruisers up to and including *Tiger*. In later battlecruisers the after turret became 'Y'. (© National Maritime Museum J9367).

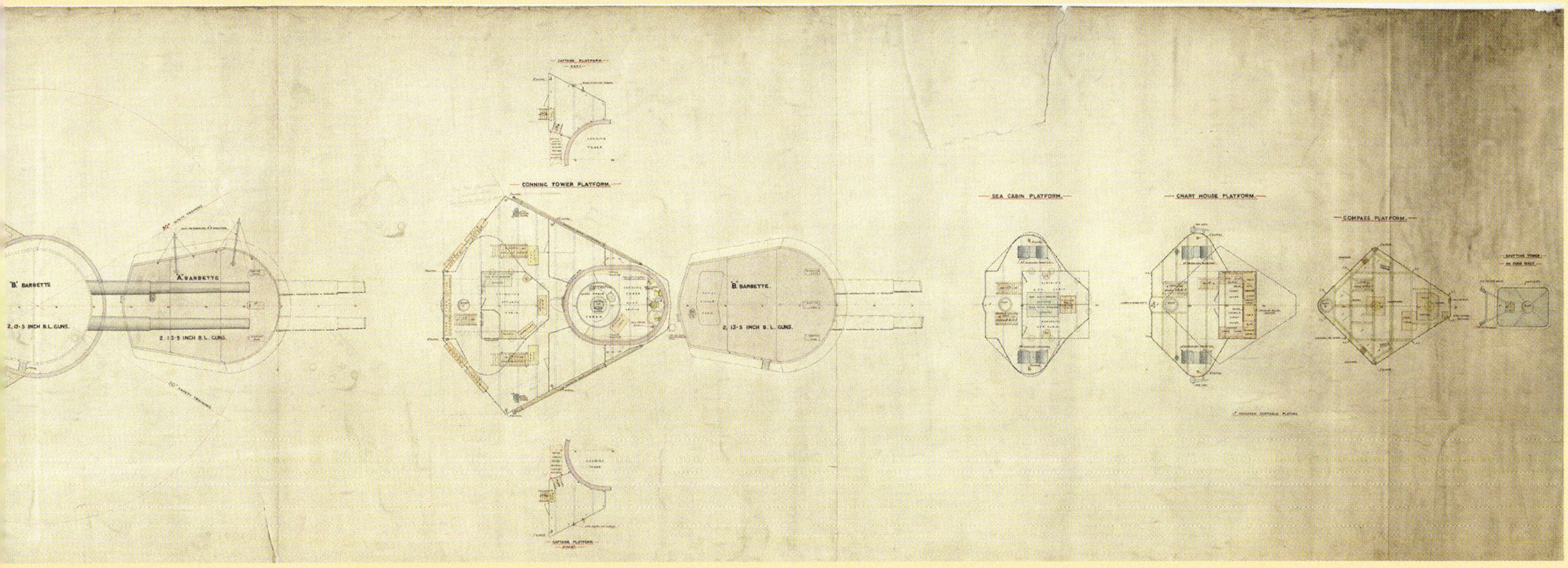

CONNING TOWER PLATFORM.
'B' BARBETTE.
'A' BARBETTE.
2-13·5 INCH B.L. GUNS.
SEA CABIN PLATFORM.
CHART HOUSE PLATFORM.
COMPASS PLATFORM.

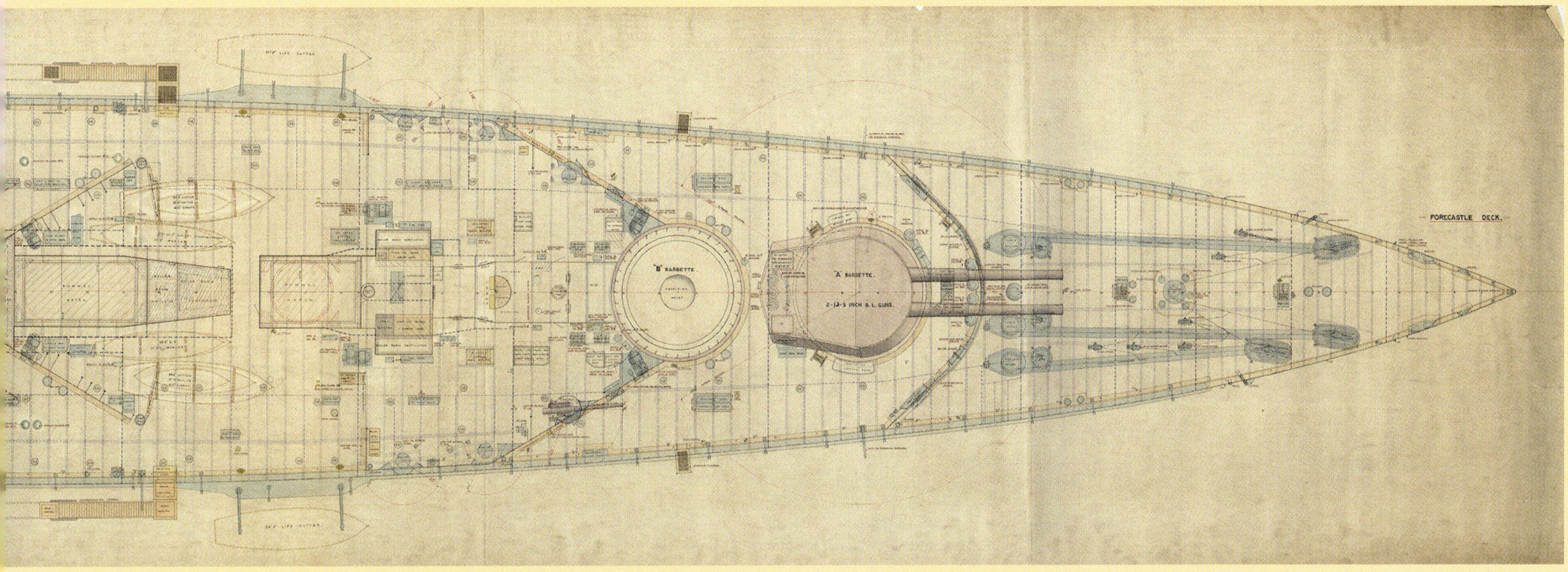

'B' BARBETTE.
'A' BARBETTE.
2-13·5 INCH B.L. GUNS.
FORECASTLE DECK.

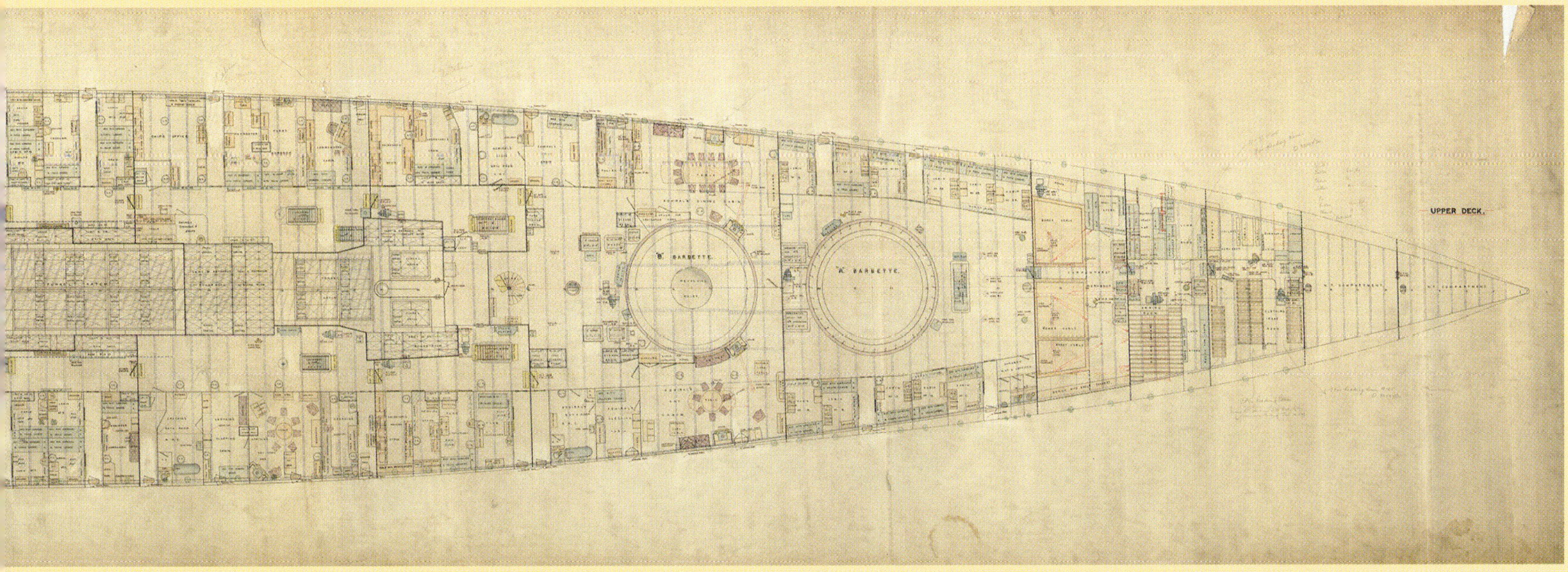

'B' BARBETTE.
'A' BARBETTE.
UPPER DECK.

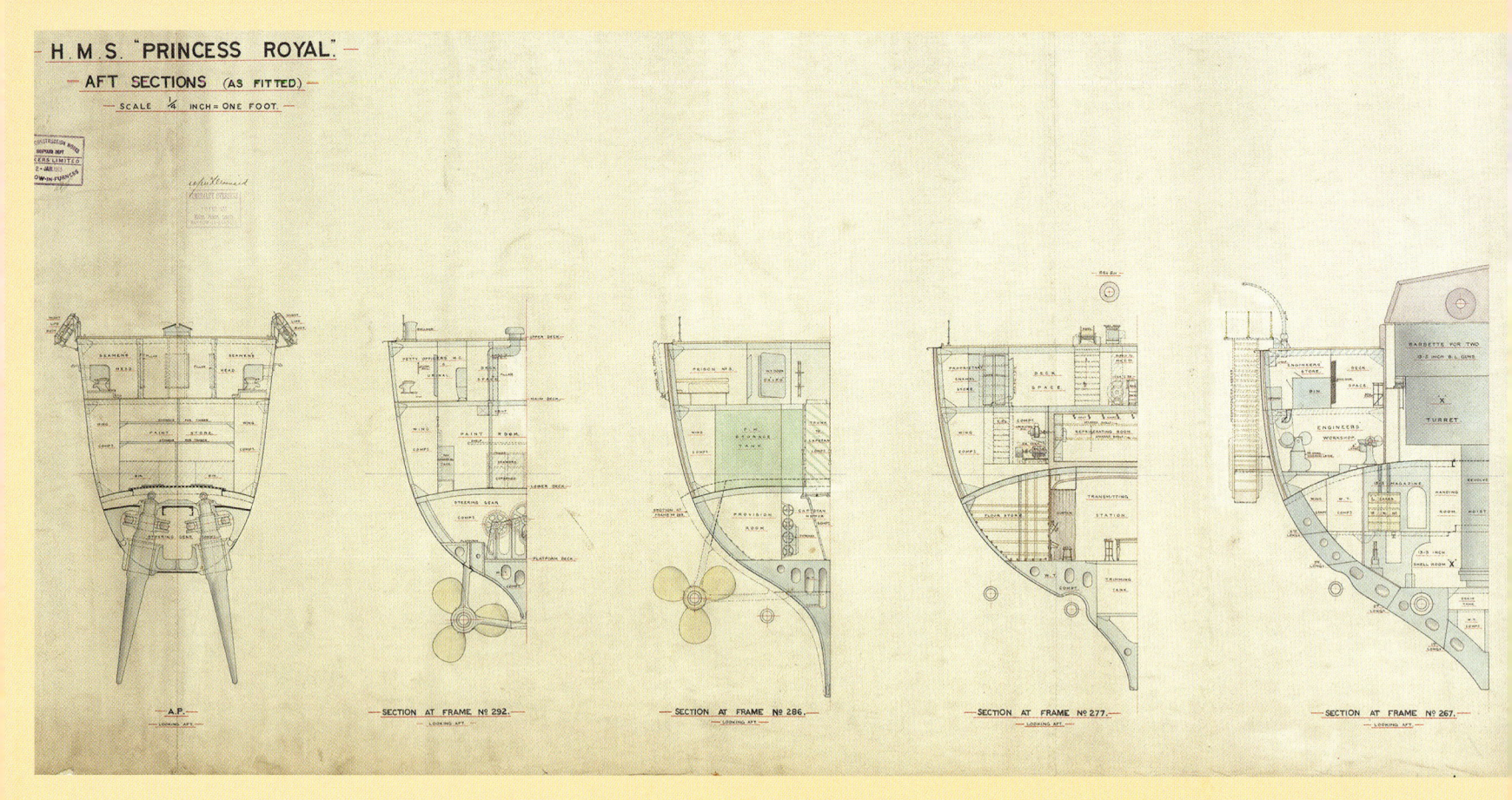

Princess Royal after sections 'as fitted'. Note that where the lower deck is raised to provide clearance over the engine rooms the central part of the main deck is omitted. (© National Maritime Museum J9366)

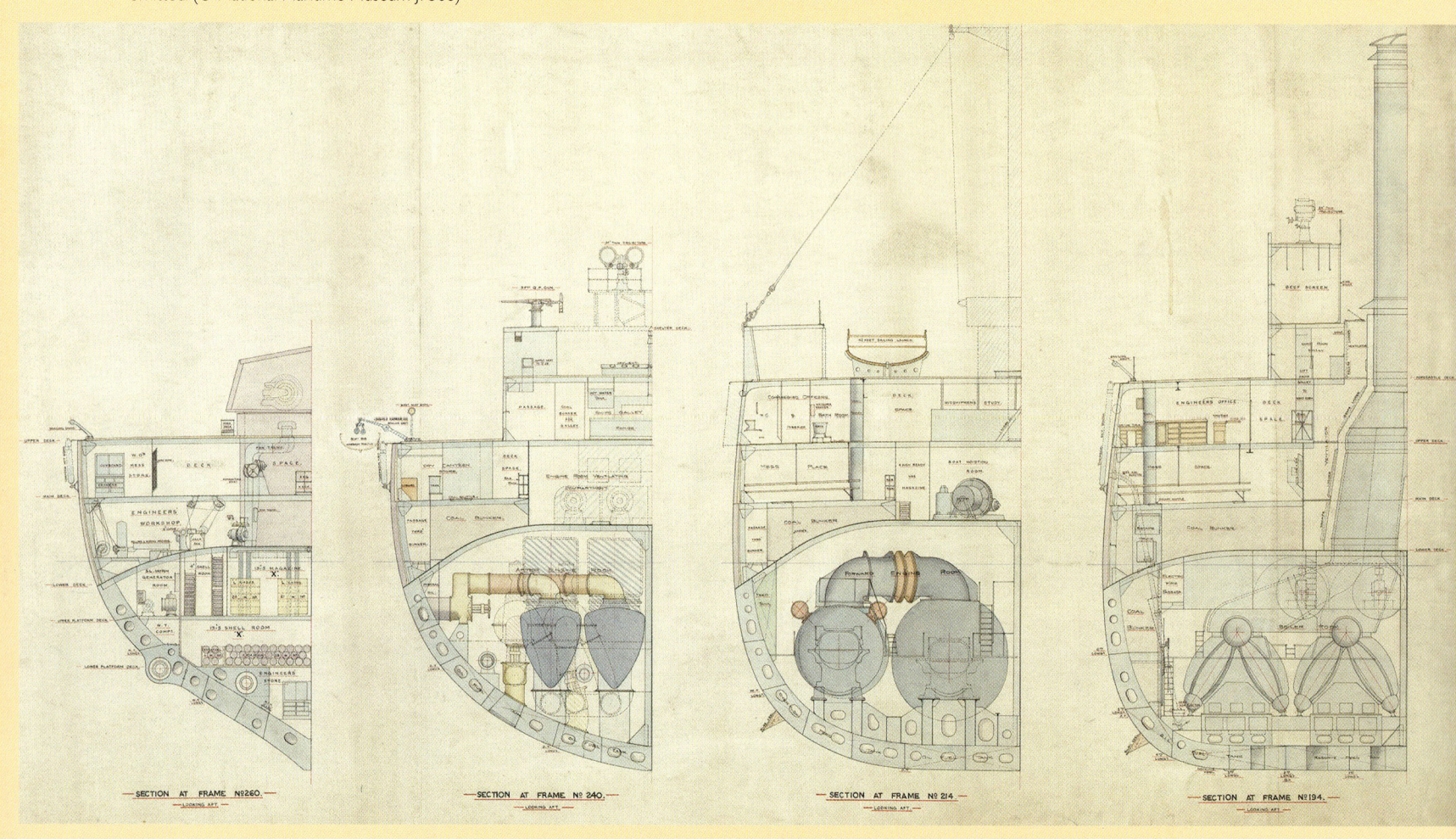

Machinery

> Both Bramwell and Siemens in the eighties of the last century visualised the use of internal combustion engines aboard ship, but the advent of the marine steam turbine was foretold by none. Yet from its earliest use the turbine proved admirably adapted for driving vessels at high speeds, and turbine vessels have now held the record for speed at sea for forty years. Used in conjunction with oil-fuel burning, the steam turbine added about 10kts to the speed of torpedo craft, and it revolutionised alike the engine-rooms of battleships and Atlantic liners; once its merits had been generally recognised its progress was phenomenal. In 1907, the total horse-power of marine steam turbines fitted was about 400,000; in 1919, the total horse-power was about 35,000,000.
>
> Engineer Captain Edgar C Smith, OBE, RN, *A Short History of Naval and Marine Engineering*, 1938

The almost total replacement of the steam piston engine by the steam turbine for the main propulsion machinery of warships as a result of the 'Dreadnought Revolution' was at least as important as the introduction of the all-big-gun armament. It was also of equal potential risk, as experience of turbine installations was limited to a few, small, comparatively low-powered vessels.[1] In the event it proved to be an outstanding success, the by-passing of the intermediate development process, which was only just beginning when the Committee on Designs first sat, having little effect on the outcome. There can be little doubt that Fisher was the prime instigator of this rapid introduction of new technology. He had after all advocated the use of turbine propulsion in his 'HMS Perfection' of 1902, but Watts, Durston and probably others were also strongly urging its adoption. It is not difficult to see why. Turbines used less steam for a given power than piston engines and therefore needed fewer boilers to achieve the same speed. This saved weight not only on the machinery but on the hull and armour (as a result of the reduced length of the machinery spaces) and greatly aided the construction department in achieving a well-balanced design. In addition, turbines were of considerably less height than the piston engine, so could be kept entirely below the waterline where they were easier to protect. For the engineer the turbine provided a rotary engine that, compared with the piston engine, had fewer moving parts and was therefore much less liable to wear and breakdowns, was cleaner, required considerably less maintenance and employed fewer staff to run. Finally there were those items which probably appealed most to Fisher – the ability to run at high speed economically and for extended periods, an increase in the ship's range for any given fuel stowage and the reduced costs of construction, maintenance and personnel. However, while the turbine had great advantages in efficiency and economy over the piston engine, it also had disadvantages in relation to fuel economy at cruising speeds and potentially dangerous limitations in handling abilities that were critical to ships intended to manoeuvre in close proximity to each other. As a result the naval members of the Committee on Designs were initially reluctant to accept the change without further investigation.

At the end of December 1904, when Whiting, the ADNC, received his first instructions for the preparation of a sketch design for an armoured cruiser to be considered by the Committee on Designs, turbines were specified for the main machinery. However, within twenty-four hours these instructions were changed to reciprocating engines and it seems possible that some resistance to the introduction of turbines was anticipated. Presenting first the reciprocating type and then, after the difficulties of keeping the size of the ships within reasonable limits had been seen,

Steaming at high speed through a North Sea swell in 1917 Fisher's 'Splendid Cats' were indeed a splendid sight. Nearest the camera is *Tiger* with, in line abreast to starboard, *Princess Royal* and *Lion*, flagship of the Battlecruiser Force throughout the First World War. (Author's collection)

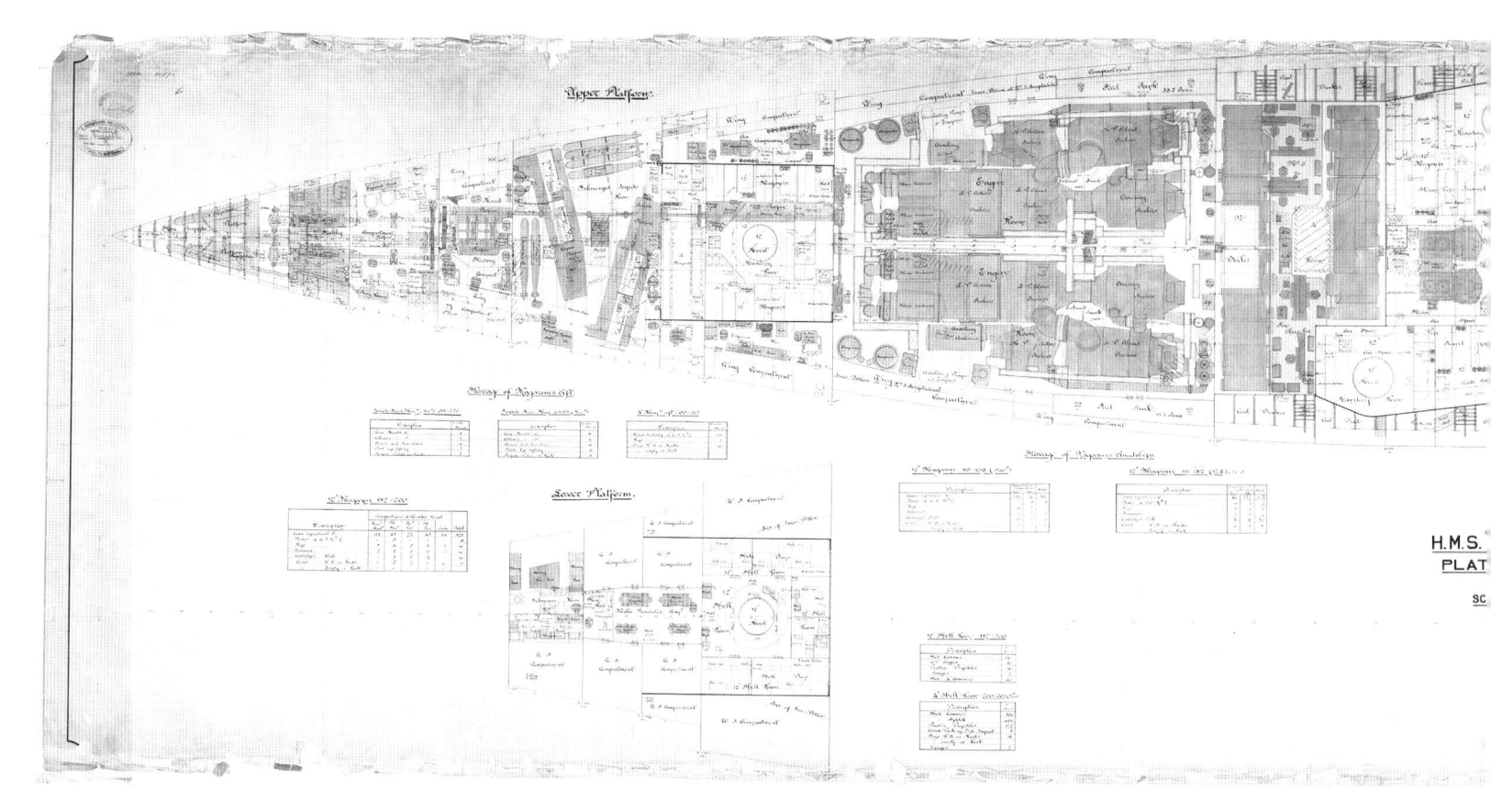

introducing the possible savings with turbines may well have been a deliberate strategy. In part this is reinforced by the fact that some of the early designs showed some rather optimistic figures for the possible savings in weight. Following a request by Whiting for figures on which to base the alternative turbine designs, Durston suggested on 12 January 1905 that 3000 tons be taken for a 275rpm turbine installation and 3700 tons for a 110rpm reciprocating installation. However, a number of the designs assumed a massive 30 per cent saving and a machinery weight of 2350 tons. By the end of February this had increased to a more realistic 3000 tons and in the final approved design to 3300 tons giving an approximate 200 tons, or 6 per cent, saving on the reciprocating engine design and a reduction in length of ship of 20ft. The legend displacement was 350 tons less but, as the reciprocating design was not worked out in detail and as weights were adjusted as the design developed (including the addition of cruising turbines and more powerful astern turbines), it is not possible to take this as a reliable indication of the overall saving made, which was certainly greater.[2]

The primary problem with the turbine was that it ran most efficiently at high speed and this necessitated the use of small diameter, fine-pitch propellers of relatively large blade area. In turn this required an increase in the number of propellers in order to transmit the required power. The overall effect was an increase in the time required for the ship to react to changes in propeller revolutions – resulting in increased time to stop, go astern or get under way and a loss of control at low speeds. Larger propellers could only be used if larger diameter, slower-running turbines were employed but this ran contrary to the desire to save weight and space. The armoured cruisers did in fact use turbines of 275rpm, exactly that suggested by Durston in December 1904, a subsequent recommendation by Parsons for 250rpm being ignored.

These matters were debated at length by the Committee on Designs during the meetings from 13 January onward. The discussions seem largely to have consisted of persuading the naval officers of the Committee that the manoeuvrability problems could either be overcome or did not exist. Charles Parsons himself attended the meeting on 17 January and later provided a written statement of his remarks and recommendations. In addition, the results of trials with the few recent turbine ships were examined and Froude was asked to conduct trials to establish the relative efficiency of large and small propellers.[3] The naval members eventually accepted that some loss of acceleration and braking power was acceptable for the gain in overall efficiency but only after an alternative arrangement for improving manoeuvrability had been adopted. This came from Parsons, who suggested fitting astern turbines on all shafts, the existing practice being to fit them on only two, and to substantially increase their power which, at some cost in added weight (about 150 tons), could provide high astern power for bringing a ship to rest, going astern or for rapid turning by reversing the turbines on one side only. This system was already in use on the 3-shaft turbine-driven passenger ferries recently built which had an astern turbine on each wing shaft. One of these, the *Queen*, was inspected by Winsloe, Jellicoe and Madden on 4 February and they were so impressed by her manoeuvrability that they 'confidently' recommended the adoption of turbines to the Committee.

Another innovation to improve manoeuvrability seems to have occurred sometime after the Committee completed its First Progress Report, as this document does not refer to it. This was the introduction of twin balanced rudders, in place of the more standard single central rudder, one being fitted directly behind each inner propeller. This greatly increased the rudder area and the effectiveness of the steering, particularly at low speed. It was as well that this innovation was introduced, as the turbine-driven ships proved less than reliable for steerage at slow speed, although once commanders had become used to the differences in handling such vessels, it caused few major problems. At moderate to high speed they proved as good if not superior in handling to piston-engined ships, in part due to the fact that turbines were easier and quicker to operate. The twin rudders had the added advantage of substantially reducing the turning circle, which in such long ships was expected to be large. This arrangement of steering remained standard in all British battleships and battlecruisers up to and including the *Queen Elizabeth* class of the 1912–13 Programme.

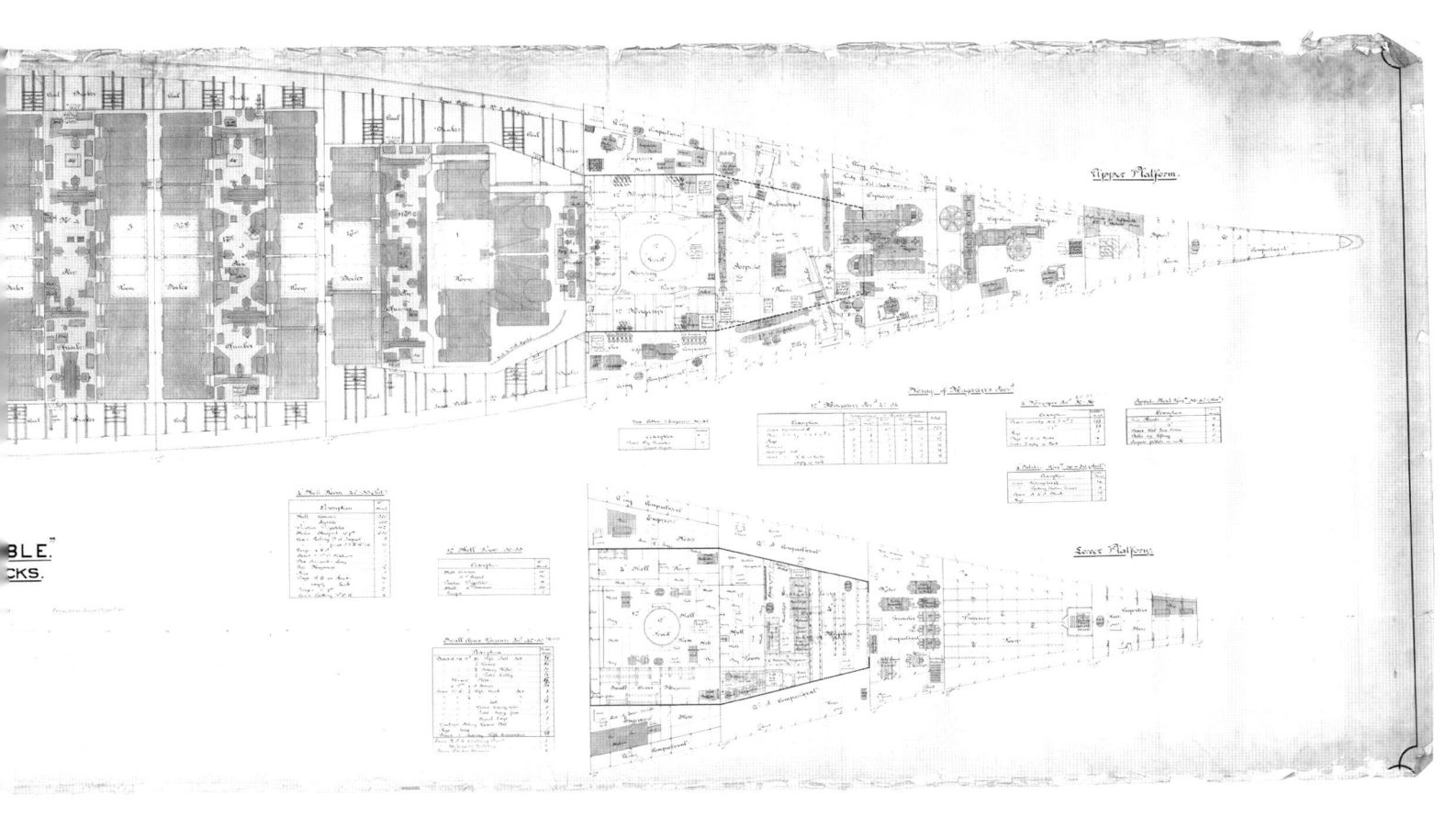

The problem of low economy at cruising speed was covered by the provision of separate cruising turbines, designed to give high economy at low power when operating in conjunction with the main turbines.

Turbine arrangements

The *Invincible* class was provided with port and starboard engine rooms of 76ft length divided by a central longitudinal watertight bulkhead. Each room contained one set of turbines, driving two shafts, and a main condenser. The wing shafts were coupled to the HP ahead and astern turbines and the inner shafts to the LP ahead and astern (in the same casing) and the cruising turbine. In normal operation the steam expanded from the HP to the LP turbine and then into the condenser. When using the cruising turbine steam was passed through this first and then followed the standard route. The cruising turbines proved to be troublesome in service due to intermittent use and they were eventually disconnected, and they were not fitted in any of the later battlecruisers with direct-drive turbines. As experience was gained in the operation of turbines other methods were found of achieving economy and in later ships cruising elements were built into the front end of the HP turbine that could be bypassed at full power.

The *Indefatigable* class employed the same design and general arrangement of turbines except for the omission of the cruising turbine and the fitting of a transverse watertight bulkhead abaft the turbines that isolated the condensers into separate rooms. The overall length of these spaces was 84ft of which just under half was occupied by the condenser rooms. These contained the main circulating pumps, evaporators, distillers, steering engine, auxiliary condensers and various other small auxiliary machines besides the main condensers. This layout was repeated in all the later battlecruisers up to and including *Renown* and *Repulse*.

In *Lion*, *Princess Royal* and *Queen Mary* the engine rooms were 62ft long and the condenser rooms 50ft long. In the *Tiger*, *Renown* and *Repulse* they were 64ft and 46ft respectively. It is not clear why these

Invincible platform deck 'as fitted'. With the exception of the submerged torpedo tube compartments and the 12in magazines, space is almost entirely taken up with main and auxiliary machinery compartments. As she was originally built with electrically powered 12in gun mountings, she required more generating capacity than was usually the case. Four of her outfit of six dynamos are located on this deck – two diesel driven in a compartment forward of the forward torpedo tube compartment and two driven by steam piston engines between 'P' and 'Q' magazines amidships. The remaining pair of steam piston driven dynamos were located in the hold amidships immediately below those on this deck. When the mountings were converted to hydraulic power the dynamos between the midships magazines were removed and two hydraulic pumping engines fitted in their place. One was located in what had been 'P' magazine and the other in the after section of the former dynamo room. The fore section of the dynamo room became the new 'P' magazine and therefore immediately adjacent to 'Q' magazine. (© National Maritime Museum J9359).

condenser rooms were so large. Equivalent German ships also had separate condenser rooms which were substantially smaller with more closely-packed machinery. Comparison of the turbine room sizes does not reveal a similar disparity in overall dimensions, although the German ships had greater subdivision within these compartments. *Moltke,* for example, had a central and two wing engine rooms, the latter being further subdivided by transverse bulkheads for a total of five rooms. There were some disadvantages, however, as apart from the possible communication difficulties all these bulkheads were pierced by steam pipes and other cross connections between the turbines, producing potential weaknesses in the watertight integrity which, to a large extent, had been avoided in the simpler British arrangement. The war, albeit with limited experience of damage to large modern ships, showed more instances of difficulties resulting from the inability to control the spread of slow flooding than to the flooding of a single large compartment. However, in the case of the British condenser rooms it is difficult to regard their palatial design as anything other than wasteful of valuable space and weight.

All the battlecruisers up to *Queen Mary* were fitted with Parsons turbines but in *Tiger* the builders, John Brown, persuaded the Admiralty to adopt their own Brown-Curtis turbines – a variation on the American Curtis turbine which they built under licence. For direct drive these proved very successful and had distinct advantages in weight-saving and efficiency over the Parsons type. Subsequently, Brown-Curtis turbines were also fitted in *Renown, Repulse, Furious* and *Hood.* The large light cruisers adopted geared turbines for the first time in a large British warship, the installation being a repeated but doubled-up version of that fitted in the light cruiser *Champion.* This arrangement had the advantage of combining high-speed turbines with lower-speed propellers, greatly improving the efficiency of both. It also saved considerable weight in the turbines but as the gears and their cases were heavy the overall saving was negligible. However, the improved efficiency of the system again achieved a reduction in steam consumption and allowed for either a saving in the weight of boilers or the achievement of higher speeds for the same machinery weight.

In the geared turbine ships one complete set of machinery was provided for each shaft. In the large light cruisers this consisted of HP and LP ahead and astern turbines (the LP sets being in one casing) driving through a single reduction gear. Each set had its own condenser. The propeller rpm, which had been a consistent 275 in the direct-drive ships, actually rose in these vessels to over 300rpm, probably because the machinery design originated in smaller vessels which employed faster-running machinery. In *Hood* this was reduced to 210rpm. There was a separate engine room for each turbine set, the

Tiger, viewed from astern, in dry dock at Rosyth. (Author's collection)

space, with a total length of 84ft, being divided into three longitudinally, with the centre space further divided into two separate rooms, by a transverse bulkhead, the forward room containing the engines for the starboard inner shaft and the after room that for the port inner shaft.

The turbine sets in *Hood* were generally similar but also had a cruising turbine clutched to the forward ends of the HP turbines on the wing shafts. She had three engine rooms of 44ft, 40ft and 42ft length separated transversely with the wing shafts driven from the forward room, the port inner from the centre room and the starboard inner from the after room.

Boilers

In the final report of the Admiralty Boiler Committee of 1901 the Yarrow and Babcock & Wilcox boilers were recommended for use in large ships. These two types were used exclusively in all British battlecruisers up to and including *Renown* and *Repulse*, orders being split evenly between the two types. The Babcock boiler had a long history, the first being produced in 1868, but it was not adapted to marine use until 1889. It was reliable, durable and comparatively easy to maintain. The Yarrow boiler was lighter than the Babcock boiler (see Table 35), more amenable to being forced, easier to clean and cheaper to repair but was less economical in fuel consumption.

In December 1908 Constructor H R Champness wrote to the E-in-C on behalf of the DNC requesting that consideration be given to fitting *Indefatigable* with Yarrow boilers as there was 'considerable advantage as regards weight and also that the centre of gravity with Yarrow boilers is more favourable as regards to trim of the ship in deep load condition. Weights taken in the design provide for Babcock and Wilcox boilers but if Yarrow boilers be accepted the saving in weight is considerable. This weight could well, it is considered, be expended in increasing the protection of the ship by increasing side armour from 6in to 7in for two thirds of the present length of the 6in armour.' The reply from the E-in-C, H J Oram, pointed out that the Admiralty gained the advantage of competitive prices by having two suppliers and he was not therefore happy about the suggested change, which would have resulted in all the ships of that year's Programme having Yarrow boilers. He suggested that the DNC consider 'reducing the amount of coal carried as, owing to the superior economy of the Babcock and Wilcox boiler, the radius of action of the ship at all speeds with these boilers, even with the reduced stowage, will be greater than if Yarrow boilers are fitted and the full stowage provided at present arranged for.'[4] Jellicoe agreed with Oram and the matter was not pursued. The estimated machinery weights for *Indefatigable* with Babcock & Wilcox boilers was 3655 tons and for Yarrow boilers 3425 tons.

This event was typical of the DNC's constant concern with means of saving weight. In the case of boilers there was available a much simpler solution, which was the adoption of the much lighter Yarrow small-tube boiler. These, which were used extensively in smaller vessels, were not considered by the Admiralty, and the E-in-C's department in particular, as suitable for large ships because their performance dropped off more rapidly with use and they required more frequent cleaning and repair. This point was critical for a battlefleet which in wartime was expected to maintain itself at maximum possible strength at all times, and to be kept at sea for extended periods. This policy resulted in one of the larger disparities between British and German ships as the latter employed small-tube boilers of the Schulz-Thornycroft type and gained considerably in weight-saving as a result. Although they did in consequence suffer the problems which the British wished to avoid, the German Navy was, for the most part, in a very different position in that their wartime strategy enabled them to dictate when and in what strength they put to sea and to arrange their maintenance programme to suit. The only German capital ship to which this did not apply was the battlecruiser *Goeben*, which was at the end of an extended period of service in the Mediterranean on the outbreak of war. At the time her boilers were in serious need of attention and her bottom was foul but she still managed to escape from *Indomitable* and *Indefatigable* (also in need of dockyard attention) by excessive forcing of her boilers (achieving 24kts for a short period).

The saving made was considerable. Comparing *Indefatigable* with *Moltke*, the length of the boiler rooms were 172ft and 134ft respectively and in the case of *Lion* and *Seydlitz*, 190ft and 152ft 6in respectively. This represented not only a saving in machinery weight but a substantial reduction in hull and armour weight which the Germans utilised to great effect to enhance the armour thickness on their ships.[5] German vessels also had their boiler rooms more closely subdivided than British ships, with fewer boilers per room and greater use of longitudinal bulkheads.

D'Eyncourt was particularly keen on adopting small-tube boilers and eventually managed to get them into large ships by employing them in the large light cruisers, which were classed, despite their size, with other light cruisers. This at least provided a precedent and when it came to the designs which led up to *Hood* he was able to convince the Board that the enormous savings possible in such large ships more than compensated for any loss in reliability. In October 1915 he wrote to the E-in-C:

> To reduce the draught by anything approaching the figure suggested by First Sea Lord is most difficult … it is therefore of great importance [that] machinery be kept as light as possible. It is also

Table 35: Comparisons of machinery weights with Yarrow and Babcock & Wilcox Boilers (tons)

Ship:	*Inflexible*	*Indomitable*
Boilers:	Yarrow	Babcock & Wilcox
Main engines:	1326.30	1295.40
Shafts and propellers:	141.90	140.70
Boilers:	1277.50	1461.00
Water:	159.60	127.00
Water in feed tanks (say):	25.00	25.00
Water in condensers:	63.10	58.50
Evaporators:	40.20	42.80
Steering gear	13.80	15.70
Total:	3047.40	3166.10

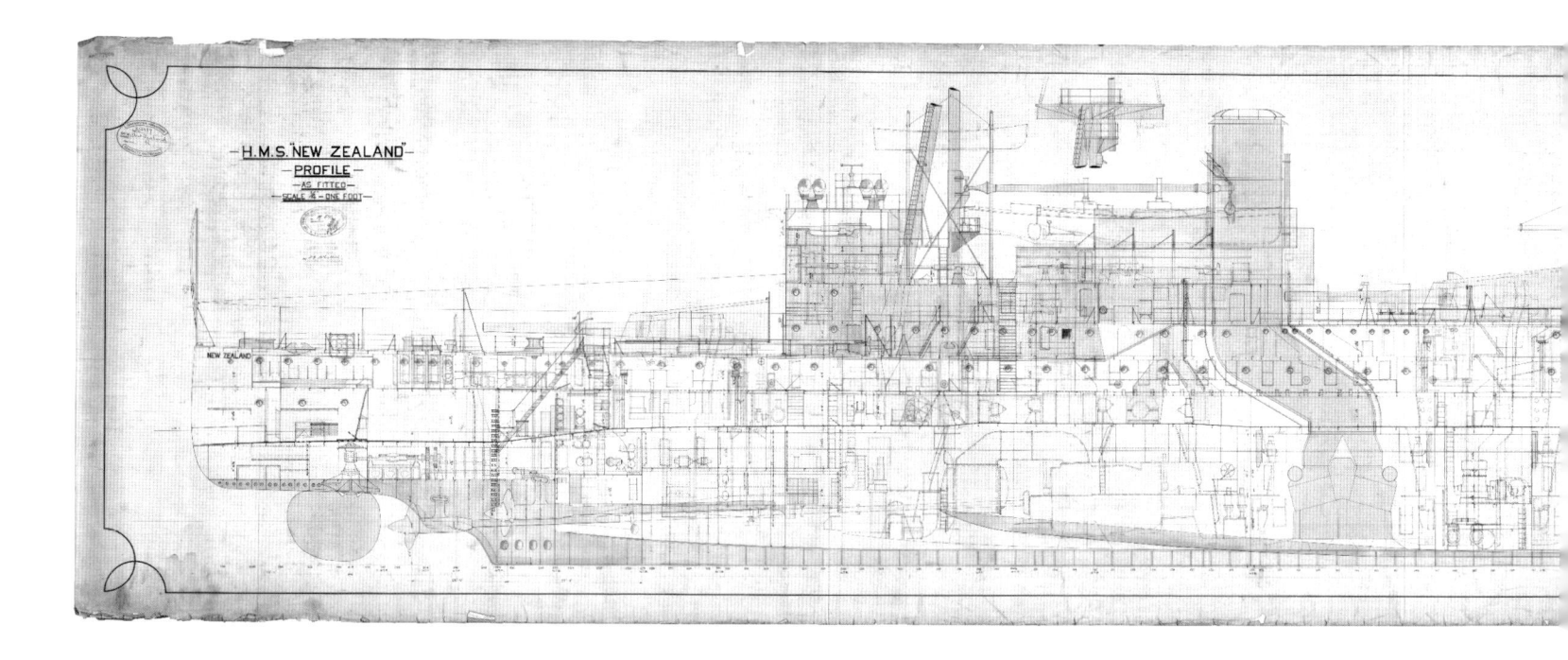

Top: The Admiralty 'as fitted' profile of *New Zealand*. Note the distribution of machinery compartments and magazines amidships and the division bulkhead between the engine and condenser rooms.
(© National Maritime Museum, London L3716)

important that the machinery take up as little space as possible, as in the large light cruisers of the *Courageous* type [where] I have found it possible to give very much better protection than in *Renown* and *Repulse* [presumably referring to torpedo protection] owing to the boilers and engines occupying much less space in the former vessels. If it is not desirable to have all the boilers in the battleship small tube as in *Courageous*, would you consider having a large proportion of them small and some of them, say 1/5th, large tube which can be used for ordinary cruising. We can also save a great deal of weight if a similar arrangement of engines to that of *Courageous* is adopted.[6]

The effect of adopting small-tube boilers can best be seen by comparing battlecruiser designs '1' and '2' of February 1916 (see Table 27 on p56). These had the same general particulars but '1' employed large- and '2' small-tube boilers which, in the case of '2' produced a reduction of almost 10 per cent in displacement and a gain in speed of 0.5kts. However, it is probable that given the great concern over limited availability of suitable docks for such large ships and the desire to retain the light draught, the Board were as much influenced by the 45ft reduction in length.

Boiler arrangements

The *Invincible* class had four boiler rooms. The foremost, being in a narrow part of the ship, was arranged with seven boilers in three rows of two, two and three and was 52ft long. The other rooms contained two equal rows of four boilers each and were each 34ft long. The magazines and shell rooms of the wing turrets were placed between the third and fourth boiler rooms. In the *Indefatigable* class the number of boiler rooms was increased to five. The first contained five boilers in two rows of two and three, the second seven boilers in two rows of three and four, the third a single row of four and the remaining pair, eight boilers in two rows of four. The third boiler room was 20ft long and the remainder 38ft each. The magazines and shell rooms of 'P' and 'Q' turrets were positioned between numbers 2 and 3, and 4 and 5 boiler rooms respectively.

In the *Lion* class and *Queen Mary* a centreline bulkhead was introduced in all but the foremost boiler room, giving them seven rooms containing six boilers each. The foremost was 34ft long and the remainder 52ft each. 'Q' turret magazine and shell room was between the last two sets of boiler rooms. In *Tiger* the centreline bulkhead was omitted and she was arranged with five boiler rooms, all forward of 'Q' magazine and all of 34ft 6in length. Seven boilers were fitted in the foremost and eight in each of the remainder. *Renown* and *Repulse* adopted the same layout but with an additional boiler room at the forward end, of 20ft length, containing an additional three boilers.

The arrangements in the small-tube boiler ships were much simpler. The large light cruisers had three boiler rooms each with six boilers and of 40ft length. In *Hood* there were four boiler rooms each of 42ft length and containing six boilers.

Steam trials

On trial the *Invincible* class were remarkably successful and confirmed experience with *Dreadnought* that the adoption of the turbine was more than justified. If anything, these three battlecruisers were even more successful than the battleship, proving to be efficient and economic steamers of high efficiency. On full power trials in 1908 all achieved over 26kts with powers about 10 per cent in excess of the designed figure. They demonstrated that the turbine was particularly suited to high-speed vessels and that they could run at high power for extended periods. In August 1908 *Indomitable* maintained an average speed of 25.3kts over a three-day period during a passage across the North Atlantic from Belleisle to Fastnet. Perhaps most remarkable of all was the efficiency of their propellers, these having coefficients of 50.2 per cent (*Indomitable*), 56.1 per cent (*Inflexible*) and an incredible 57.7 per cent (*Invincible*).[7] This set a

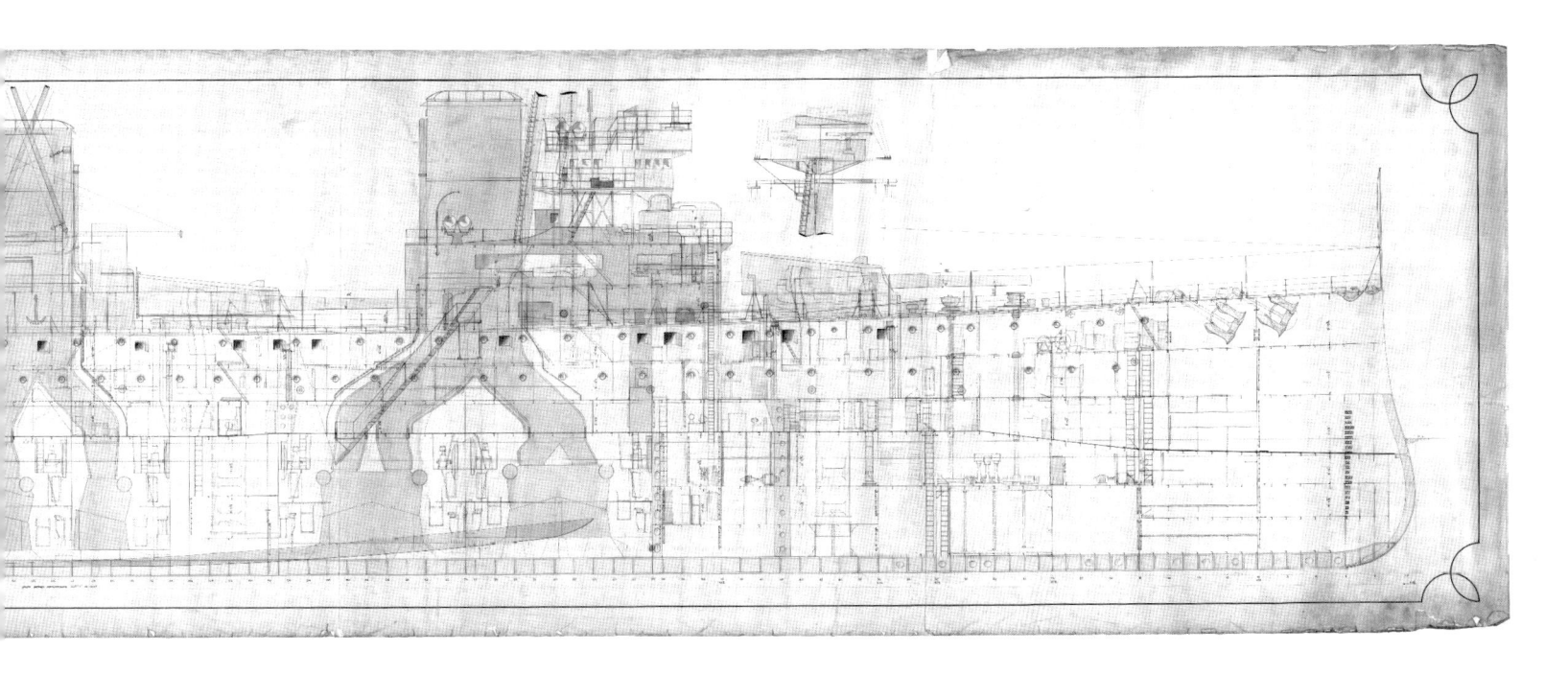

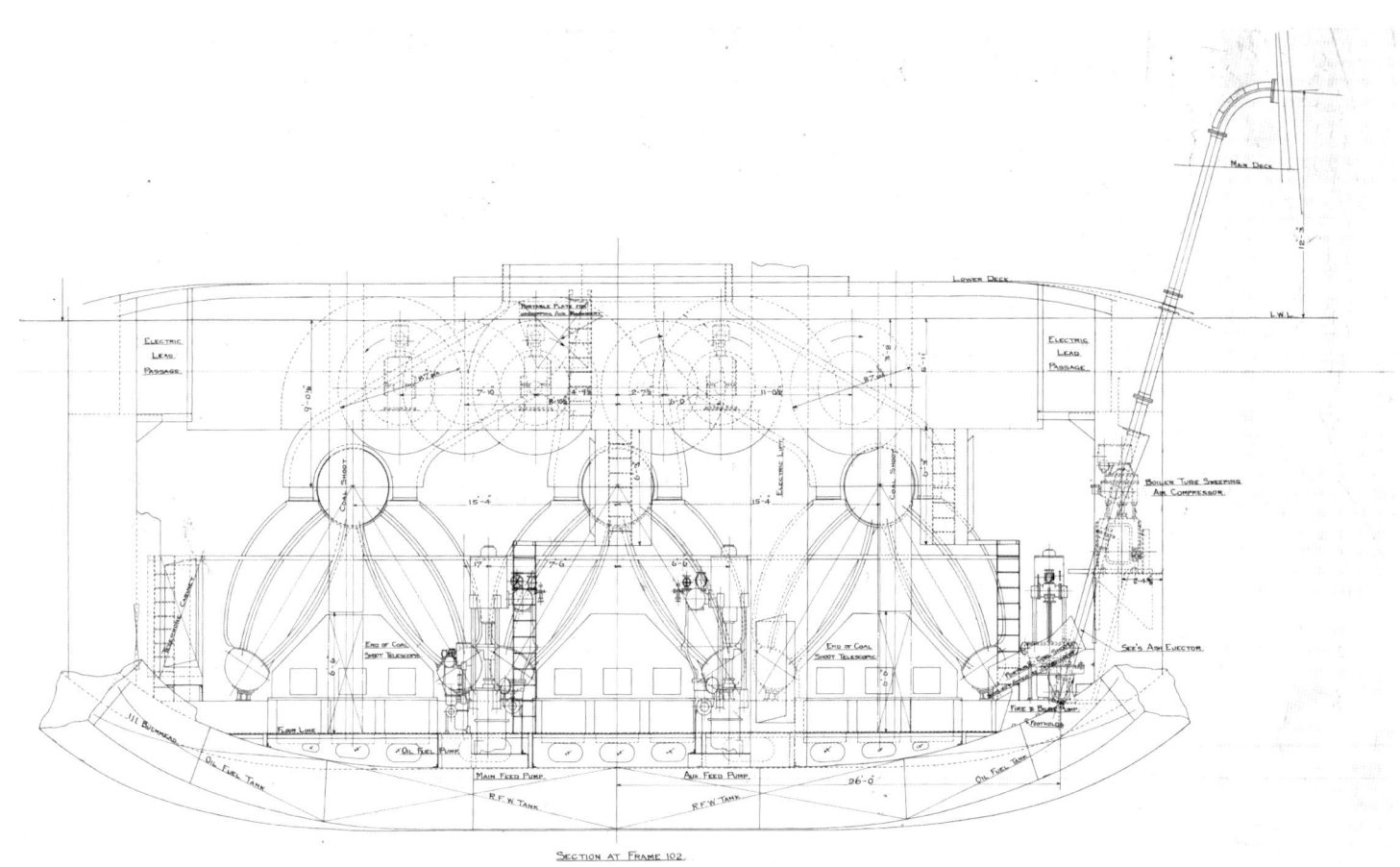

Transverse section at centre of forward boiler room of *Lion* and *Princess Royal*, looking aft, showing three of the Yarrow large-tube boilers. The fan chamber at the top was positioned centrally between the three forward and three after boilers contained within the room. It accommodated six 87in diameter fans. The ladder on the port side gave access to and from the air-lock between the boiler room and the fan chamber. Two coal chutes with telescopic extensions at the bottom allowed for the supply of coal directly from the bunkers on the lower deck to the stokehold floor while water-tight vertical sliding doors at the sides gave access to the wing bunkers. All of the boiler room's auxiliary machinery is shown – the main feed water pump with the oil fuel pump attached to its outer side; the auxiliary feed water pump (as back-up to the main pump and of identical design); the fire and bilge pump to port against the after bulkhead; the air-compressor against the port wing bulkhead (which served for boiler cleaning); and the ash ejector on the port side which served to eject ashes directly outboard from the stokehold using water pressure supplied by the fire and bilge pump. (© National Maritime Museum J9375).

standard that proved difficult to repeat in later battlecruisers but, nevertheless, it was one the DNC's and E-in-C's departments strove hard to attain.

Indefatigable ran her first steam trials in December 1910 and initially proved something of a disappointment. On her measured mile trial at full power with closed exhaust (which gave the highest power) she just made her designed speed of 25kts with 49,676shp – 13 per cent in excess of her designed power – giving a propeller coefficient of 40.2 per cent (the design calculations assumed 46.2 per cent). There were, however, extenuating circumstances. The trials were run at Polperro (as were all the trials of the pre-war battlecruisers) but,

A poor but interesting view of *Indomitable* (taken from *Inflexible*) steaming at high speed in heavy weather in the North Sea in 1915. (Author's collection)

because the weather was poor and there was a heavy sea running, it was decided to carry out the full power trials in the more sheltered waters off Chesil Beach. However, the depth of water on this course was only 17 fathoms, compared with 25 fathoms at Polperro, and shallow water has a retarding effect on large ships running at high speed (this also applied to Polperro to a lesser extent). The wind during the trial was blowing Force 6–7 and the sea was rough, which checked the ship's speed when running in one direction but did not greatly help when running in the other. The ship was yawing badly which, together with the pitch and roll, had a further retarding effect on the speed.

Although designed to give equal power on each shaft, *Indefatigable*'s machinery was found to transmit about 30–50 per cent more power on the inner shafts than the wing shafts. It was therefore decided to fit the ship with new propellers to take account of this variation and to re-run the trials. The new propellers were fitted in March, the ship's bottom being cleaned at the same time, and the second series of trials, under the observation of ADNC H R Champness, were carried out at Polperro in early April on a smooth sea and with the wind Force 2–4. Running at load displacement but trimmed 6in more by the stern than allowed for by the design, she made 25.79kts at her designed power of 43,000shp and 26.89kts when forced to 55,187shp. The propeller coefficients were 52 per cent and 50.3 per cent respectively. Similar results were achieved by *New Zealand* in October 1912, this ship making 26.39kts at 49,048shp for a propeller coefficient of 51.7 per cent. *Australia,* whose propellers were of larger area than those in her two sisters, proved slightly inferior in propeller efficiency, but on trial in March 1913 she generated a power of 55,881shp, over 25 per cent in excess of the design figure, and achieved a speed exactly equal to that of *Indefatigable* – 26.89kts.

Lion in 1918. Wartime additions thus far include aircraft platforms on 'Q' and 'X' turrets, bearing scales on 'B' and 'X' turrets, searchlight towers grouped around the after funnel, 3in AA guns on the forecastle deck abreast the fore funnel, main armament director on the foremast (just below the foretop), the addition of struts to the foremast and the removal of the torpedo net defence. (Imperial War Museum: SP1791)

Lion was much more of a problem. Apart from the difficulties encountered with her mast/funnel arrangement, her trial results of January 1912 were viewed as something of a disappointment. Although she met the design and contract requirements, it was hoped that much higher speeds would be achieved with forcing, as had been obtained in the earlier ships. The trials were attended by Constructor W T Davis, who reported that at full power, with closed exhaust, she averaged 76,623shp for a speed of 27.623kts, giving a propulsive coefficient of 43.5 per cent. Davis concluded that her performance had been adversely affected by two factors. Writing to the DNC on 15 January he stated that:

The speed was probably reduced to some extent by the state of the bottom, the composition being Moravia applied cold. It is understood the surface of this was not at all smooth ... but even allowing for this composition, the propulsive coefficient at the highest power given is very low compared with those obtained in previous battle cruisers and points to modifications in the propellers being required. [The] Propellers used in these trials were spare propellers, the dimensions of which were based on those that gave excellent results in the *Invincible* class and in the *Indefatigable*. The increase of power and in size of ship between last tried battle cruiser and the *Lion,* the power rising from 43,000 to 70,000 and the displacement from 18,750 tons to 26,350 tons, are probably the main causes of the difference in performance and it makes it desirable to carry out some special trials in the *Lion* as soon as possible with a view of deciding on the best dimensions of propeller to adopt in this ship, *Princess Royal* and *Queen Mary.*

It is not considered that the results of the present trials show any signs of cavitation. Apparently the area is too great, especially on the inner screws, and it is proposed that arrangements be made to run the ship on the Polperro course with the set of propellers originally made. These propellers are smaller in area than those tried and with them there is a possibility of cavitation occurring but, in spite of this, it is very desirable to have knowledge of what actual results would be obtained from them. After these results were known the matter could be further considered.

It appears desirable to carry out these trials under the same conditions as those obtaining during the present trials and it is a point for consideration whether they could be carried out immediately after the

Table 36: General machinery particulars

Ship	No of Boilers	Designed shp	Designed speed (kts)	Turbine Type
Invincible class	31	41,000	25	Parsons direct drive
Indefatigable	31	43,000	25	Parsons direct drive
Australia & *New Zealand*	31	44,000	25	Parsons direct drive
Lion class	42	70,000	28	Parsons direct drive
Queen Mary	42	75,000	28	Parsons direct drive
Tiger	39	85,000*	28	Brown-Curtis direct drive
Renown class	42	112,000	31.5	Brown-Curtis direct drive
Courageous class	18	90,000	32	Parsons geared drive
Furious	18	90,000	32	Brown-Curtis geared drive
Hood	24	144,000	31	Brown-Curtis geared drive

* With designed overload power of 108,000shp = 29kts.

All ships had 4 shafts. Designed propeller rpm at maximum designed speed was 300 in large light cruisers, 210 in *Hood* and 275 in remainder. *Invincible*, *Inflexible*, *Lion*, *Princess Royal* and *Queen Mary* had Yarrow large-tube boilers; the large light cruisers and *Hood* Yarrow small-tube boilers; the remainder had Babcock & Wilcox boilers.

The boiler working pressure in the *Invincible* and *Indefatigable* classes was 250psi and in the remainder 235psi.

Table 37: Fuel and water stowage (tons – maximum)

Ship	Coal	Oil fuel	Fresh water for boilers	Fresh water for crew**
Invincible	2997	738	350*	134
Inflexible	3084	725	350*	110*
Indomitable	3083	713	360	110*
Indefatigable	3300	870	502	176
Australia	3170	840	400	186*
New Zealand	3170	840	400	186*
Lion	3500	1135	650	140
Princess Royal	3500	1135	663	250*
Queen Mary	3600	1170	650	200*
Tiger	3320	3480	745	149*
Renown	112	4289	720	150*
Repulse	104	4243	720	150*
Courageous class	?	3250*	?	?
Furious	?	3393	?	?
Hood	58	3895	572	?

* As designed
** Excludes water in filler and gravity tanks (15 tons).

Table 38: Propeller dimensions

	INNER			OUTER		
Ship	Diameter (ft–in)	Pitch (ft–in)	Blade area (sq ft)	Diameter (ft–in)	Pitch (ft–in)	Blade area (sq ft)
Invincible	11–0	11–0	60	10–0	11–0	45
Indomitable & *Inflexible*	10–6	11–4	60	9–6	11–4	45
Indefatigable (1910)	10–9	11–0	42.5	10–9	11–0	42.5
Indefatigable (1911) & *New Zealand*	10–10	11–2	55.5	10–3	11–2	46
Australia	10–10	11–2	59	10–3	11–2	46.5
Lion (designed)	12–6	12–3	57	12–6	12–3	57
Lion (1911) & *Princess Royal*	12–3	12–4	75	11–8	12–2	60
Princess Royal (Sept 1912)	12–3	12–3	57	12–3	12–3	57
Tiger	13–6	12–6	90	13–6	12–6	90
Repulse	13–6	13–6	100	13–6	13–6	100
Furious	11–6	11–6	?	11–6	11–6	?

torpedo and gun trials, which take place this week, and before opening out the machinery. These trials might slightly delay the commissioning of the ship and would involve extra cost to contractors but it appears worth considering whether this could not be accepted in the case of the first ship of a new type such as this.

Before finally making proposals as to dimensions of new propellers I would suggest that it may be considered desirable for the results of the trials to be taken to Haslar and personally discussed with Mr Froude.[8]

The DNC considered that the bottom composition was the main cause of the poor performance and it was proposed to carry out another series of trials under similar conditions but with the bottom recoated with a smoother composition. However, the Controller, Rear Admiral C J Briggs, did not approve this proposal, presumably on grounds of cost, and it was decided that *Lion*'s

Princess Royal in 1918 shows modifications similar to those of *Lion* but with detail differences – there is a rangefinder tower at the after end of the after superstructure, the mainmast has no starfish and the gaff is positioned at a higher level. In addition (although not clearly visible here) the AA guns abreast the fore funnel were on small raised platforms, those in *Lion* being fitted at deck level. The black box above 'X' turret is a canvas aircraft hangar. (Imperial War Museum: Q19280)

original set of propellers should be tried. These were, however, smaller in area, which the *Indefatigable* trial had demonstrated were not likely to achieve the best results. The full trials did not materialise, it being decided to use *Princess Royal*'s results instead, but during *Lion*'s acceptance trials in June 1912, carried out at deep draught and on low powers only, the results showed little difference from the earlier trials and 'what difference there was, was in favour of the old propellers'. This was confirmed by the trials of *Princess Royal* carried out at Polperro in September 1912. At full power she achieved 28.5kts with 78,803shp at a mean draught of 28ft. She was then fitted with the smaller-area propellers and made a second series of runs but achieved only 28.05kts with 79,424shp, showing that these were less efficient, giving an estimated reduction in speed of 0.55kts at 70,000shp. In addition, as a result of a comparison of the results from *Lion* and *Princess Royal*, it was estimated that the rough bottom composition in *Lion* had resulted in a 0.8kt loss in speed. This was taken to confirm the DNC's opinion that the bottom coating was the prime problem and both *Lion* and *Princess Royal* had their larger-area propellers replaced.

On 20 September 1912 the E-in-C, J H Oram, wrote to the Controller with regard to the trials of *Princess Royal*:

Power was obtained burning coal only. Submitted, it is considered that when burning oil and coal the power developed could be increased to about 90,000shp for a short period, say four hours. It has been considered undesirable to attempt to obtain this high power in contractors trials as experience shows that results so obtained invariably find their way into the public press. The preferable course would be, as in the case of *Superb* and *Indefatigable*, to make such a trial after the vessel is in commission and when her crew are accustomed to the machinery. Such action was contemplated for *Lion* in connection with speed trials which were originally proposed to be made in that vessel after commissioning but which were not carried out as vessel was not available. Submitted that high power trial be arranged for in *Princess Royal* after vessel commissions.[9]

The new Controller, Rear Admiral A G H W Moore, agreed and it was arranged for a special high-power measured mile trial to be conducted after the *Princess Royal* had been in commission for a short time. This was carried out on 3 January 1913 but the results were far from satisfactory, for, although the machinery worked well, the maximum power obtained was much less than anticipated. For short periods 84,190shp was achieved burning coal and 84,700shp burning coal and oil. Oram concluded that the primary problem was the stokehold personnel being inexperienced in the use of oil and coal together and submitted that the trial be repeated after a three-month gap during which time 'the ship's officers should arrange for as much instruction as possible'. This second special trial was approved and was run on the Polperro mile on 8 July 1913 with 'very satisfying results'. The sea was smooth, the wind Force 3 and apart from the fact that the ship's displacement was rather high at 29,660 tons, conditions were ideal. Seven runs were made of which the first was rejected, the remaining six constituting three pairs of runs. The mean results of these runs were 27.87kts with an incredible 95,117shp (96,238shp = 27.97kts taking last four runs only). Bearing in mind the fact that the ship was running deep and that the Polperro course was comparatively shallow, the full speed of the ship at legend displacement, under ideal conditions, was probably in the region of 29kts.

Why there was such interest in the extreme performance of these ships is not clear, for while at high speeds it took a very large increase in power to obtain a comparatively modest increase in speed, it also took very little to knock it down. The primary purpose of trials was to ensure that (a) they met their contract requirements – which these ships did – and (b) to provide data for the engineering and design staffs of the Admiralty which could be used to provide performance data for existing ships and information for future machinery development. Such problems as propeller design, bottom coatings and running trials in shallow water could as easily be sorted out with normal high-power runs as they could by excessive forcing. No doubt it was useful to know how far the ships could be pushed but such performances were only possible under ideal conditions and could only be maintained for short periods of time.

Queen Mary carried out her steam trials during May and June 1913, the full-power measured mile being run on 2 June. With closed exhaust she made 28.17kts with 83,003shp as a mean of four runs.

Tiger's contract specified a high power of 85,000shp for a speed of 28kts, the builders not being held responsible for the results of the designed overload power of 108,000shp for 30kts, either in performance or mechanical failure. The trials were run after the outbreak of war in October 1914, when she made 28.38kts with 91,103shp on her contractor's measured-mile trials and 29.07kts with 104,635shp on overload. Although the latter fell short of expectations and it was thought she would do better in deep water, she did not achieve the required shaft revolutions, which it was hoped could

Looking aft from the foretop of *Renown* in 1917. Note the searchlight platform on the second funnel and the 3in AA gun at bottom right. (Author's collection)

The funnels and bridge of *Hood* viewed from the port side of the after shelter deck. (Author's collection)

be improved by fitting new propellers. It was proposed to modify her spare propellers, by cutting off 4in from the tips of each blade, reducing the area by 2sq ft and rebalancing them, orders being sent to Devonport for this to be done. There does not appear to be any record of subsequent trials and it seems likely that the delay in her joining the fleet was not considered acceptable. It is also not clear if her modified spare propellers were ever fitted.

The problems of uncertain speed figures in shallow water were avoided in the case of *Renown* and *Repulse* by laying out a special measured-mile course for them in the deep water off the Isle of Arran in the Firth of Clyde. *Repulse* was tried on this course during a four-hour full-power run in August 1916 on her way south to Portsmouth. However, while there are records of these results for the full run there do not seem to be any figures recorded for the measured mile, apart from a note to the effect that she achieved about 125,000shp. She carried out more extensive progressive measured-mile runs on the Arran course on her way north to join the fleet in September and at full power made 31.725kts with 118,913shp. Although below her designed speed of 32kts, the ship was 3400 tons in excess of her designed load displacement and the wind was blowing at Force 5–6 at the start of the trials and at Force 8 towards the end. It was estimated that at load draught and with 120,000shp the ship would achieve 32.5kts. As if to prove the point *Renown* made 32.58kts, but this was with 126,300shp and with a displacement only 1400 tons in excess of load draught.

Trials of the large light cruisers were not extensive due to war conditions and the *Furious* was not tried at all. *Courageous* ran some fairly limited trials off the Tyne on 16 November 1916 and developed 91,200shp with open exhaust. Speed was recorded by log as 30.8kts. It was estimated from these results that she was capable of 110,000shp and 33kts with closed exhaust. Further runs were abandoned due to the structural damage mentioned in the previous chapter. *Glorious* ran more extensive trials in December 1916 on the Arran course. Conditions were good, with a smooth sea, but the programme was curtailed due to poor visibility. The maximum power developed, from the mean of two runs, was 91,195shp giving a speed of 31.42kts. Both ships were run at deep displacement.

With the considerable advantage of being completed in peacetime, *Hood* by contrast enjoyed an extensive programme of trials that, for the first time, included runs at both load and deep displacement. These were highly successful, the ship achieving just over 32kts at load draught with 151,600shp.

Table 39: Steam trials data

Ship	Date	Trial type and place	No of runs	Mean Speed (kts)	Mean shp	Mean rpm	Displacement (tons)[1]	Mean draught (ft–in)[1]
Indomitable	26/4/08	7/10th power (Polperro mm)	6	22.49	26,880	248	17,620	26–3
Indomitable	27/4/08	1/5th power (Skelmorlie mm)	4	16.5	10,304	178	17,120	25–8
Indomitable	27/4/08	7/10th power (Skelmorlie mm)	6	23.67	30,920	260.5		
Indomitable	29/4/08	Full power (Skelmorlie mm)	4	26.1	47,879	296	17,435	26–0
Invincible	22–23/10/08	30 hour 1/5th power (Newcastle to Spithead)	n/a	15.9	9301	170.7		27–0.5
Invincible	23/10/08	1/5th power (Chesil Beach mm)	6	16.24	9695	174.4	17,600 (e)	26–3
Invincible	3/11/08	7/10th power (Popperro mm)	6	24.26	34,124	269.5		
Invincible	7/11/08	Full power (Polperro mm)	6	26.64	46,500	295.2	17,400 (e)	26–0
Invincible	9/11/08	3 hour high power (Polperro mm)[2]	6	20.81	21,266	225.6	17,330 (e)	25–11
Invincible	10/11/08	3 hour low power (Polperro mm)[2]		11.55	3854	122.5		
Invincible	10/11/08	3 hour intermediate power (Polperro mm)[2]		18.2	13,291	196.3		
Invincible	11/11/08	Low power (Polperro mm)		11.55	3854	122.5		
Inflexible	12/6/08	1/5th power (Polperro mm)	6	16.62	9128	169.6		
Inflexible	6/08	30 hour 1/5th power	n/a	16.53	9139	169		
Inflexible	1908	Full power (Skelmorlie mm)	6	26.48	46,947	291.3		
Inflexible	1908	High power (Skelmorlie mm)[2]		20.67	19,703	215		
Indefatigable	11/12/10	7/10 power (Chesil Beach mm)	6	22.95	31,718	256.4		
Indefatigable	14/12/10	Full power (Chesil Beach mm)[3]	4	25.01	49,676	299.1		
Indefatigable	14/12/10	Full power (Chesil Beach mm)[4]	4	24.44	44,596	288.5		
Indefatigable	10/4/11	High Power (Polperro mm)	4	25.79	43,000		18,750 (e)	26–6
Indefatigable	11/4/11	Full Power (Polperro mm)	4	26.89	55,140	315.3	18,750 (e)	26–6
New Zealand	10/12	30 hour high power	n/a		31,794			
New Zealand	14/10/12	8 hour full power (English Channel)	n/a	26	46,894	250		
New Zealand	14/10/12	Full power (Polperro mm)		26.39	49,048	300		
Australia	7–8/3/13	30 hour 3/5th power	n/a	22.98	32,094			
Australia	8/3/13	3/5th power (Polperro mm)	6	23.43	33,122	266.2		
Australia	11/3/13	Full power (Polperro mm)	6	26.89	55,881	308.6	18,750 (e)	26–6
Australia	11/3/13	8 hour full power	n/a		48,420			
Lion	8–10/1/12	8 hour full power[3]	n/a		75,685	273.5		
Lion	8–10/1/12	8 hour full power[4]	n/a		71,920			
Lion	11/1/12	Full power* (Polperro mm)[5]	2	27.62	76,121	279	26,690	28–0.5
Lion	11/1/12	Full power* (Polperro mm)[6]	4	26.35	66,156	266	26,690	28–0.5
Lion	3/1/12	3/4 power[7]*	6	24.99	54,872	251.1	26,570	28
Lion	12/1/12	35,000shp* (Polperro mm)[3]	4	23.08	41,208	228.8	26,570	28
Lion	12/1/12	20,000shp* (Polperro mm)	4	19.58	22,580	188		
Lion	12/1/12	16,000shp* (Polperro mm)[3]	2	17.18	15,461	162.2	26,690	28–05
Lion	12/1/12	10,000shp* (Polperro mm)	4	14.93	10,091	142		
Lion	12/1/12	Low power* (Polperro mm)	4	11.84	4908	107		
Princess Royal	9–12/9/12	24 hour 3/4power	n/a	25.94	53,315	253.9		
Princess Royal	9–12/9/12	3/4 power (Polperro mm)	6	25.97	53,972	254.3	26,750	28
Princess Royal	12/9/12	8 hour Full Power	n/a	28.25	76,510	282.3		
Princess Royal	12/9/12	Full power (Polperro mm)	6	28.5	78,803	284.8	26,710	28
*Princess Royal***	?/9/12	Full power (Polperro mm)[3]		28.05	79,424	290.9		
*Princess Royal***	?/9/12	Full power (Polperro mm)[4]		26.99	69,221	275.6		
*Princess Royal***	?/9/12	3/4 power (Polperro mm)		25.97	55,179	255.7		
Princess Royal	3/1/13	Special full power (Polperro mm)	4	27.82	79,462		28,440	29–7
Princess Royal	8/7/13	Special full power (Polperro mm)	6	27.97	95,117	295.7	29,660	30–7.5
Queen Mary	27/5/13	7500shp (Polperro mm)	4	14.25	7827	134.8	27,380	28–2
Queen Mary	27/5/13	15,000shp (Polperro mm)	4	18	16,420	176.6	27,380	28–2
Queen Mary	27/5/13	37,500shp (Polperro mm)	6	23.28	37,275	229.5	27,380	28–2

Ship	Date	Trial type and place	No of runs	Mean Speed (kts)	Mean shp	Mean rpm	Displacement (tons)[1]	Mean draught (ft–in)[1]
Queen Mary	30/5/13	3/4 power (Polperro mm)	4	25.13	56,719	258.5	27,200	28–0
Queen Mary	29–30/5/13	24 hour 3/4 power	n/a	25.08	57,476	258		
Queen Mary	?/6/13	8 hour full power	n/a	27.54	77,306[8]	283.9		
				27.92	81,476[9]	287		
Queen Mary	2/6/13	Full Power (Polperro mm)	4	27.58	77,113	284.3	27,180	28–0
Queen Mary	2/6/13	Full Power (Polperro mm)	4	28.17	83,003	289	27,180	28–0
Tiger	12/10/14	Full Power (Polperro mm)	6	28.38	91,103	267.2	28,990	28–10.5
Tiger	12/10/14	Full power overload (Polperro mm)	4	29.07	104,635	278.4	28,790	28–8.5
Repulse*	15/8/16	Full power (Arran mm)	2	31.73	118,913	274.7	29,900	28–2.5
Repulse*	15/8/16	(Arran mm)	2	30.4	101,550	260	29,900	28–2.5
Repulse*	15/8/16	(Arran mm)	2	25.76	55,980	217.8	29,900	28–2.5
Repulse*	15/8/16	(Arran mm)	2	21.41	28,615	176.4	29,900	28–2.5
Repulse*	15/8/16	(Arran mm)	2	15.71	12,055	130.4	29,900	28–2.5
Renown	9/16	Full power (Arran mm)	?	32.58	126,300	281.6	27,900	26–7.5
Courageous	16/11/16	Off the Tyne	by log	30.8	91,200[4]	323	22,100	25–5
Glorious*	30–31/12/16	(Arran mm)	2	20.13	20,795	205	21,670	24–11
Glorious*	30–31/12/16	(Arran mm)	2	24.43	39,350	254	21,670	24–11
Glorious*	30–31/12/16	(Arran mm)	2	29.84	76,700	313	21,670	24–11
Glorious*	1/1/17	Full power (Arran mm)	2	31.42	91,195	329.5	21,300	24–7
Hood	8/3/20	Full power (Arran mm)[3]		31.79	150,473	205		
Hood	8/3/20	Full power (Arran mm)[4]		31.35	144,984	202		
Hood *	3/20	(Arran mm)		13.53	9103	80	42,090	
Hood *	3/20	(Arran mm)		15.6	14,630	93	41,700.	
Hood *	3/20	(Arran mm)		17.2	20,050	103	41,700	
Hood *	3/20	1/5th power (Arran mm)		20.37	29,080	124	41,600	
Hood *	3/20	2/5th power (Arran mm)		25.24	58,020	154	41,850	
Hood *	3/20	3/5th power (Arran mm)		27.77	89,010	176	42,100	
Hood *	3/20	4/5th power (Arran mm)		29.71	116,150	191	42,150	
Hood *	3/20	Full power (Arran mm)		32.07	151,280	207	42,200	
Hood *	22/3/20	Deep (Arran mm)		13.17	8753	81	45,000	
Hood *	22/3/20	Deep (Arran mm)		15.8	14,020	96	45,000	
Hood *	22/3/20	Deep (Arran mm)		19.11	24,720	116	45,000	
Hood *	23/3/20	Deep (Arran mm)		22	40,780	136	44,600	
Hood *	23/3/20	Deep (Arran mm)		25.74	69,010	161	44,600	
Hood *	23/3/20	Deep (Arran mm)		28.37	112,480	185	44,600	
Hood *	23/3/20	Deep full power (Arran mm)		31.89	150,220	204	44,600	

Notes
Caution should be exercised with regard to the accuracy of the speeds given above as they imply greater exactness than was actually possible; they should, however, be within about ¼kt of the true figure. Speeds given in official documents are usually to three decimal places (rounded to two places above) but this was largely a matter of the exact recording of the measurements and not a reflection of the accuracy of those measurements.
(e) estimated.
mm = measured mile
* These trials formed a progressive series.
** With modified propellers.
1. At start of trial.
2. Cruising turbine trial.
3. With closed exhaust.
4. With open exhaust.
5. With closed exhaust and closed bypass.
6. With closed exhaust and open bypass.
7. Taken from 3 hour run during 24 hour 3/4 power trial.
8. For initial 1 hour 40 min.
9. For final 2 hours 20 min.

Twin BVIII mounting for the 12in MkX 45 cal gun

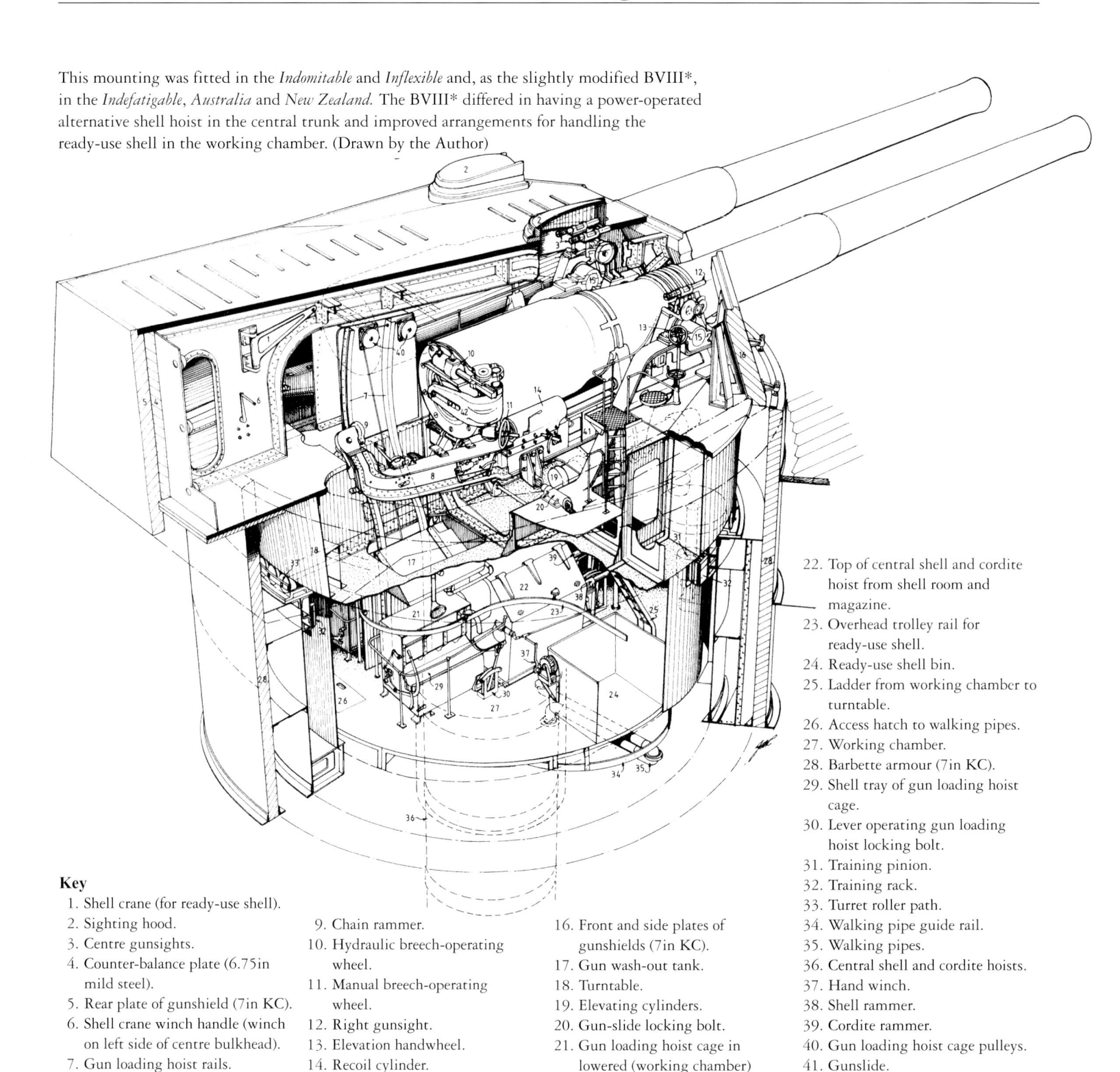

This mounting was fitted in the *Indomitable* and *Inflexible* and, as the slightly modified BVIII*, in the *Indefatigable*, *Australia* and *New Zealand*. The BVIII* differed in having a power-operated alternative shell hoist in the central trunk and improved arrangements for handling the ready-use shell in the working chamber. (Drawn by the Author)

Key
1. Shell crane (for ready-use shell).
2. Sighting hood.
3. Centre gunsights.
4. Counter-balance plate (6.75in mild steel).
5. Rear plate of gunshield (7in KC).
6. Shell crane winch handle (winch on left side of centre bulkhead).
7. Gun loading hoist rails.
8. Gun loading arm.
9. Chain rammer.
10. Hydraulic breech-operating wheel.
11. Manual breech-operating wheel.
12. Right gunsight.
13. Elevation handwheel.
14. Recoil cylinder.
15. Trunnion.
16. Front and side plates of gunshields (7in KC).
17. Gun wash-out tank.
18. Turntable.
19. Elevating cylinders.
20. Gun-slide locking bolt.
21. Gun loading hoist cage in lowered (working chamber) position.
22. Top of central shell and cordite hoist from shell room and magazine.
23. Overhead trolley rail for ready-use shell.
24. Ready-use shell bin.
25. Ladder from working chamber to turntable.
26. Access hatch to walking pipes.
27. Working chamber.
28. Barbette armour (7in KC).
29. Shell tray of gun loading hoist cage.
30. Lever operating gun loading hoist locking bolt.
31. Training pinion.
32. Training rack.
33. Turret roller path.
34. Walking pipe guide rail.
35. Walking pipes.
36. Central shell and cordite hoists.
37. Hand winch.
38. Shell rammer.
39. Cordite rammer.
40. Gun loading hoist cage pulleys.
41. Gunslide.
42. Breech block carrier.

Forward superstructure of HMS *Queen Mary* 1913

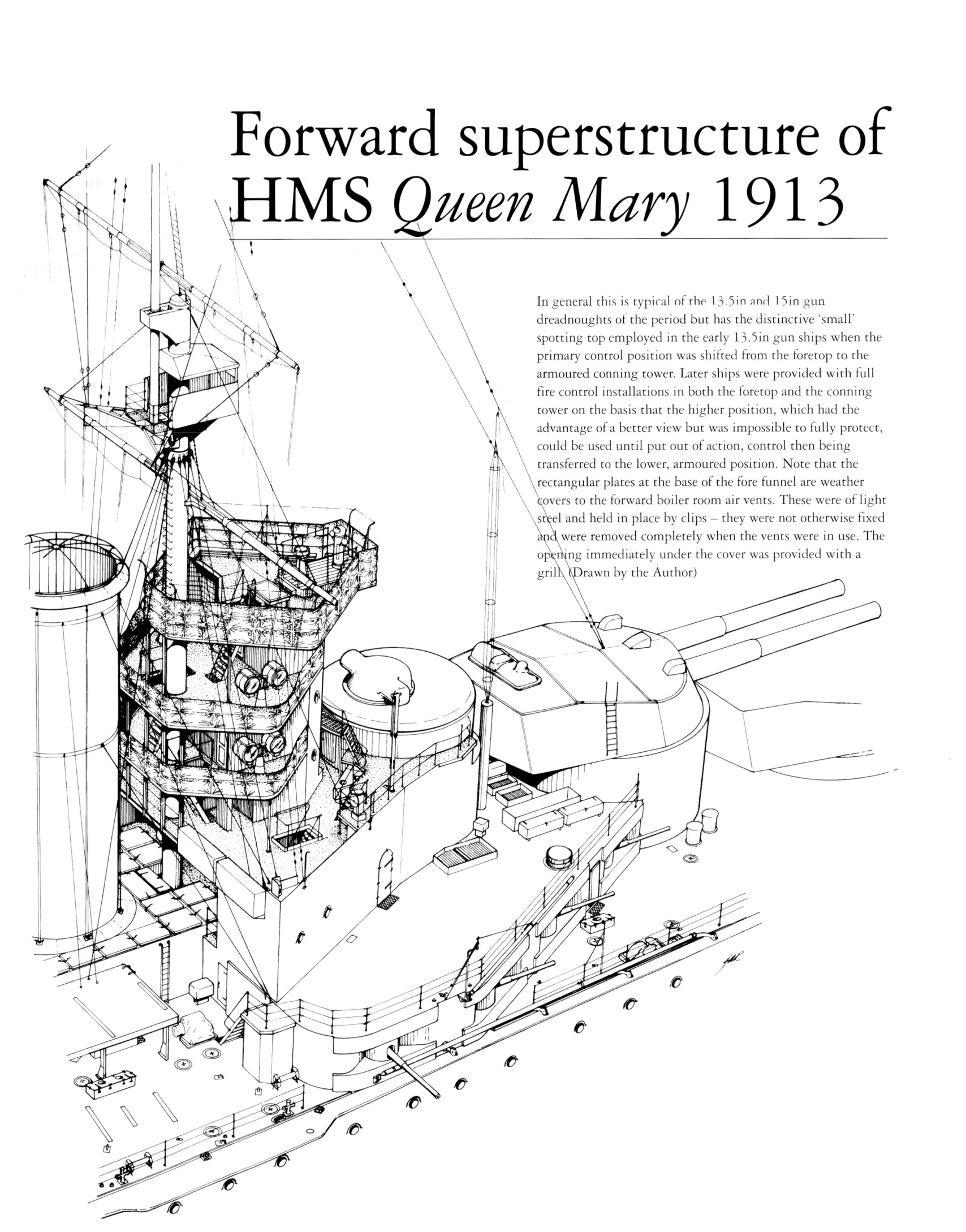

In general this is typical of the 13.5in and 15in gun dreadnoughts of the period but has the distinctive 'small' spotting top employed in the early 13.5in gun ships when the primary control position was shifted from the foretop to the armoured conning tower. Later ships were provided with full fire control installations in both the foretop and the conning tower on the basis that the higher position, which had the advantage of a better view but was impossible to fully protect, could be used until put out of action, control then being transferred to the lower, armoured position. Note that the rectangular plates at the base of the fore funnel are weather covers to the forward boiler room air vents. These were of light steel and held in place by clips – they were not otherwise fixed and were removed completely when the vents were in use. The opening immediately under the cover was provided with a grill. (Drawn by the Author)

Armament

> In the Mediterranean Lord Fisher instituted a long-range firing competition, and with it changed the faces of warships and the fates of nations. It was a go-as-you-please affair, and the results were at first lamentable. That it would be hard to score hits on a moving platform, from a moving platform which is also rolling and pitching is self-evident, but how intensely difficult the problem is at long range can only be realized by those who have tried it.
>
> Vice Admiral C V Usborne, *Blast and Counterblast* 1935

In general the armament of the battlecruisers followed closely that fitted in contemporary battleships, the primary exception being that the *Indefatigable* class mounted 45-calibre 12in guns when battleships had been stepped up to the 50-calibre gun. The only other differences were that, with the exception of *Hood*, they generally mounted fewer guns and these were more lightly protected. A number of innovations were introduced in the first few years of the century which were for the most part directly or indirectly intended to give greater accuracy and hitting power at long range. Briefly these were:

(a) The introduction of higher-velocity guns which increased the striking velocity of projectiles at long range. This also gave a flatter trajectory, which improved the chances of hitting by extending the target's danger space. This was associated with a number of other changes which included the introduction of improved steels (primarily nickel steel) for gun manufacture, which allowed for higher chamber pressures without excessive increases in weight, and the adoption of uniform, as opposed to increasing, twist rifling which was more suited to the higher velocities.

(b) The adoption of MD (Modified) cordite in place of MkI cordite that, being slower-burning, allowed for larger charges and more sustained and uniform pressure and was therefore more suited to the new, longer, high velocity guns and more conducive to accuracy. It also reduced barrel wear, increasing the guns' life.

(c) The introduction of improved training machinery in heavy turrets which allowed for more sensitive manipulation when bringing the gun onto a target – a much more critical factor at long range.

d) The development of improved elevation machinery for heavy guns, which enabled gunlayers to keep the gun aimed on a target while the ship was rolling. The earlier method of firing as the sights came on during a roll was never entirely abandoned and was later reintroduced.

(e) Improvements in the ammunition supply and loading arrangements of heavy turrets to allow of a higher sustained rate of fire.

(f) The strengthening of heavy gun mountings to accommodate the higher forces imparted by the heavier charges in high-velocity guns.

(g) The introduction of a centralised fire control system.

(h) The introduction of improved and more accurate gunsights.

The 12in gun

All the 12in gun battlecruisers carried the MkX, 45-calibre gun, which in the *Indomitable* and *Inflexible* were mounted in

'Q' turret of *Inflexible* viewed from the bridge in 1917. In the background is *Indomitable*. (Author's collection)

Table 40: Particulars of Armament

Invincible class
MAIN: Eight 12in BL MkX on four twin BVIII mountings (*Invincible* two BIX and two BX).
ATB: Sixteen 4in QF MkIII on single PI* mountings (reduced to twelve mountings in 1915 and replaced by twelve 4in BL MkVII on PVI mountings in *Indomitable* and twelve 4in MkIX on CPI mountings in *Inflexible* in 1917).
AA: *Invincible*: One 3in/20cwt MkI on HA MkII mounting (fitted Oct–Nov 1914 and April 1915 on); one 3pdr on HA MkIc mounting (fitted Nov 1914 on). *Indomitable*: One 3pdr on HA MkIc mounting (fitted Nov 1914 – Aug 1917); one 3in/20cwt MkI on HA MkII mounting (fitted July 1915); one 4in BL MkVII on HA (60deg) MkII mounting (fitted April 1917).
TT: Five 18in submerged, 14 torpedoes.

Indefatigable class
MAIN: Eight 12in BL MkX on four twin BVIII* mountings.
ATB: Sixteen 4in BL MkVII on PII* mountings (reduced to fourteen guns in late 1915 and to thirteen in *New Zealand* only in 1917).
AA: *Indefatigable*: One 3in/20cwt MkI on HA MkII mounting (fitted March 1915). *Australia*: One 3in/20cwt MkI on HA MkII mounting (fitted March 1915); one 4in BL MkVII on HA (60deg) MkII mounting (fitted June 1917). *New Zealand*: One 6pdr on HA MkIc mounting (fitted Oct 1914 – end 1915); one 3in/20cwt MkI on HA MkII mounting (fitted Oct 1914); one 4in BL MkVII on HA (60deg) MkII mounting (fitted 1917).
TT: Two 18in submerged, 12 torpedoes.

Lion class
MAIN: Eight 13.5in BL MkV on four twin BII mountings.
ATB: Sixteen 4in BL MkVII on PIV* mountings (*Lion*) and PII* mountings (*Princess Royal*) – (reduced to fifteen in 1917).
AA: *Lion*: One 6pdr on HA MkIc mounting (fitted Oct 1914 – July 1915); two 3in/20cwt MkI on HA MkII mountings (fitted one in Jan and second in July 1915). *Princess Royal*: One 6pdr on HA MkIc mounting (fitted Oct 1914 – Dec 1916); one 3in/20cwt MkI on HA MkII mounting (fitted Jan 1915 – April 1917); two 4in BL MkVII on HA (60deg) MkII mountings (fitted April 1917).
TT: Two 21in submerged, 14 torpedoes.

Queen Mary
MAIN: Eight 13.5in BL MkV on four twin BII* mountings.
ATB: Sixteen 4in BL MkVII on PVI mountings.
AA: One 3in/20cwt MkI on HA MkII mounting (fitted Oct 1914); one 6pdr on HA MkIc mounting (fitted Oct 1914).
TT: Two 21in submerged, 14 MkII torpedoes.

Tiger
MAIN: Eight 13.5in BL MkV on four twin BII** mountings.
ATB: Twelve 6in BL MkVII on PVIII mountings.
AA: Two 3in/20cwt MkI on HA MkII mountings.
TT: Four 21in submerged, 20 MkII torpedoes.

Renown class
MAIN: Six 15in BL MkI on twin MkI* mountings (two mountings in *Repulse* were MkI).
ATB: Seventeen 4in BL MkIX on five triple MkI mountings and two single PXII mountings.
AA: Two 3in/20cwt MkI on HA MkII mountings.
TT: Two 21in submerged, 10 torpedoes.

Courageous class
MAIN: Four 15in BL MkI on twin MkI* mountings.
ATB: Eighteen 4in BL MkIX on six triple MkI mountings.
AA: Two 3in/20cwt MkI on HA MkII mountings.
TT: Two 21in submerged, 10 torpedoes. (Twelve 21in above-water tubes on six twin mountings were added after completion).

Furious
MAIN: Two 18in BL MkI on single MkI mountings (only one fitted).
ATB: Eleven 5.5in BL MkI on P1* mountings.
AA: Two 3in/20cwt MkI on HA MkII mountings.
TT: Two 21in submerged, 10 torpedoes.

Hood
MAIN: Eight 15in BL MkI on twin MkII mountings.
ATB: Twelve 5.5in BL MkI on CPII mountings.
AA: Four 4in QF MkV on HA MkIII mountings.
TT: Two 21in submerged, four 21in above-water.

Notes: Main armament projectile stowage in the 12in and 13.5in gun ships was 80rpg (peace) or 110rpg (war); in the 15in gun ships it was 120rpg. The *Invincible* class completed with 2crh projectiles (replaced 1915–16 with 4crh) and the remainder had 4crh.

twin BVIII mountings and in the three ships of the *Indefatigable* class in slightly modified BVIII* mountings. The gun was a Vickers design, first ordered in 1903 and proof tested in 1905. It introduced nickel steel construction (for the 'A' and inner 'A' tubes), high velocity and the Vickers pure couple breech mechanism to the heavy naval ordnance of the Royal Navy. It was a successful weapon, of good accuracy, with an expected life of 280efc. The mountings were the same as those fitted in the *Dreadnought* with the primary exception that all, except those fitted in *Inflexible*, were equipped with 6-cylinder radial training engines that were smoother in operation than the 3-cylinder in-line training engines of the earlier mountings. The mounting represented a standardised combination of the best features of earlier Vickers and Armstrong designs, the all-angle loading system of the former being combined with the central loading trunk arrangement of the latter. In the hoist, between magazine and working chamber, the shell and cordite cages were separate, the cordite cage being left at the handing room on the way down and picked up again by the shell cage on its way up. In the working chamber these had to await the gun loading cage, into which the ammunition was rammed directly, before they could be returned, which involved some delay in the loading sequence. In the later mountings, for the 50-calibre 12in gun, a waiting position was provided in the working chamber into which the shell and cordite could be tipped, allowing the cages to be returned immediately. At the same time the shell and cordite cages were combined – the cage being loaded first at the shell room and then stopping at the magazine handing room on the way up for the charges. The 12in gun mountings of *Inflexible* and *Australia* were constructed by Vickers and those of *Indomitable*, *Indefatigable* and *New Zealand* by Armstrong. In the *Indefatigable* class the gunshields were of modified shape and structure with a view to improving their protection.

Invincible differed from her sister ships in being fitted with experimental electrically-powered mountings. This idea dated back to 1900 when the Assistant Director of Torpedoes suggested that the time had arrived for a more extensive use of electric power for auxiliary machinery – this having already been adopted with success in both US and continental European warships. By the time of *Dreadnought*'s construction this had led to the application of electric power to all auxiliaries outside the main machinery spaces except for the forward steam-powered capstan engine (the provision of electric power for a machine that was used so little was considered wasteful), the hydraulically-powered main boat hoist and, of course, those electrical generators driven by steam engines. It also included the main engine room ventilation fans. This had the effect of greatly reducing the number of steam pipes running fore and aft in ships and substantially improved watertight integrity. The application of electricity to gun mountings was, however, approached with more caution. The existing system of hydraulic power was proven and had the great advantages of simplicity, smoothness of operation and safety. On the other hand the electrical system offered some advantages in overall weight-saving (primarily due to the omission of the heavy pumping engines and their associated pipework) and in rapidity of operation. However, the DNO did not consider that there was sufficient advantage to justify a change, particularly as it 'would be in the nature of an experiment and would probably take years to perfect'.

The matter came up again at the end of 1902 when the Committee on Electrical Equipment strongly recommended the introduction of electrically-worked turrets and shortly after this preliminary designs for such mountings were called for from both Vickers and Armstrong for twin 12in and twin 9.2in mountings. The designs, which took some time to produce, were considered first for a trial in one of the *Lord Nelson* class battleships and then for a pit trial only. However, it was decided early in 1905 to fit *Invincible* with all-electric mountings, this being approved by the Board in August. Two of her twin 12in mountings were supplied by Vickers and two by Armstrong for comparative trial and general evaluation. The Vickers mountings, designated BIX, were fitted in 'A' and 'X' positions, and the Armstrong mounting, designated BX, in 'P' and 'Q' positions. The two designs were generally similar, both adopting a Ward-Leonard system of control, the primary differences being in the recoil and elevation arrangements. The Armstrong design had a recoil cylinder under the cradle, a pneumatic run-out system and an elevation bracket worked by a large screw thread. The Vickers mounting had recoil cylinders on each side of the cradle, run-out springs above and below the cradle and arc and pinion elevating gear. They also employed different gunhouse designs. Both types had two training motors, either of which could operate the mounting alone, which were mounted in the fixed structure, outside the mounting, on the lower deck – the latest hydraulic mountings all carried their training engines within the revolving structure but problems of space and balance precluded this arrangement in the electrically-powered mountings.

Even before the turrets were fitted some doubts were being expressed as to their utility. In July 1907 the DNO, Jellicoe, despite having been involved in the original decision to build the mountings stated that he was '... convinced that it would be a most fatal step to introduce electric mountings into any more new vessels until the 'Invincible' has shown by trials *in commission at sea* that the system offers sufficient advantages over our well-tried hydraulic system to warrant such a change. The hydraulic system has now been brought to great perfection, the new elevating and training arrangements give control as perfect as that of a handworked 6-inch gun, and it is difficult to see how electric control will improve on this ... In the case of the 'Invincible's' mountings, it is difficult to see what advantage has been gained by the adoption of the electrical system, since the cost of each electrical turret is about £500 greater than [the] hydraulic turrets in the sister ships, the weight is about 50 tons more, and the staff required for care and maintenance very much greater.'[1]

As it turned out Jellicoe's misgivings were more than justified. *Invincible*'s gun trials were carried out off the Isle of Wight in October 1908 and were described by the Captain of *Excellent*, Reginald Tupper as the 'most dangerous' that he had ever attended:

> Everything on board appeared to be in a very unfinished and dirty condition, but we put to sea from the Tyne with a good deal of our [turret] wiring still exposed and not all of the [electrical] gear labelled. When the order was given to train the turret, elevate or run a gun in or out, it was only necessary to push a button or move a switch, but the result was often a flash of blue flame which seemed to fill

the turret. Something had gone wrong and the fuses had burnt out, so the experts had to chase around and find out what was wrong. Smouldering cordite and red hot residue was left in the breech of the gun and the water-douche did not work. Cordite from the magazine came up with a run and narrowly escaped being rammed straight on to the red-hot residue.[2]

This initiated a series of refits and improvements intended to correct the mountings' problems – principally constant breakdowns, and slowness of operation, the Armstrong mountings being more of a headache than the Vickers ones. The mountings were subjected to major modification at Portsmouth Dockyard in August–November 1909 and March–June 1911 but continued to give an unsatisfactory performance and were plagued by breakdowns. It was finally decided that the experiment had been a costly failure and in February 1912 the First Sea Lord, Admiral Sir Francis Bridgeman, recommended that they be converted to hydraulic power at an estimated cost of £151,200 with the comment that 'the *Invincible* as a fighting unit in the Fleet can only be regarded as a gamble as far as her efficiency is concerned. She may get her guns off or she may not. Electrically worked turrets have hitherto proved themselves failures both in America and in our own Navy.' On 20 March 1912 a Conference was held at the Admiralty to discuss the details of the modifications with representatives from Armstrong and Vickers. To avoid costly complications it was decided to leave the training engines on the fixed structure, Armstrong swash plate engines being fitted in place of the electric motors. There were also two reserve mountings, one Vickers and one Armstrong, which were also to be converted to hydraulic power. The work was carried out at Portsmouth Dockyard during March–August 1914.

The 13.5in gun

When the designs for the 1907–8 Programme were under discussion in 1906, alternative main armaments were considered for twin 12in, triple 12in and twin 13.5in mountings. In the end the DNO, Jellicoe, decided to recommend the adoption of the 12in/50cal gun in twin mountings on the grounds that:

The fore turret and bridge of *Australia* in 1918. (Imperial War Museum: Q18740)

The forward 13.5in gun turrets of *Queen Mary* on 14 July 1914. (Author's collection)

(a) The adoption of the 13.5in gun without manufacturing and testing a trial gun was rather risky.
(b) The increase in calibre was unnecessary since the Germans had adopted the 11in gun for their new ships.
(c) To provide a substantial gain in performance over the 12in/50cal gun it was necessary that the 13.5in be capable of using its greater striking power to penetrate heavy armour at a range beyond that at which the 12in gun was effective. To do this required a reasonable prospect of a fair percentage of hits at very long range and the existing system of fire control was not up to this standard.
(d) As it was required that the existing size of ships should not be greatly exceeded, the number of guns carried would have to be reduced to compensate for the greater weight of the 13.5in gun mounting.

The 13.5in guns of *Queen Mary*'s 'X' turret trained to port while she takes on ammunition in 1913. Note the after torpedo control tower at the after end of the superstructure. (Author's collection)

The idea of adopting a larger calibre gun remained dormant until the naval scare of 1908, which both generated a desire to outclass the German adoption of the 12in gun and allowed for the necessary increase in the size of ships to make it a more attractive proposition. In October 1908 Vickers was asked to produce designs for 13in, 13.5in and 14in guns that would give the same velocity to a projectile at 8000yds as the 12in MkX (1639fps). In January 1909 the DNO, Bacon, invited Vickers to tender for the manufacture

ARMAMENT | 87

'Q' turret of *Lion* in April/May 1918 with a Sopwith 2F.1 Camel on the flying-off ramp. The first of these platforms were fitted in the *Renown* and *Repulse* and tested in October 1917; by the spring of 1918 all the battlecruisers, including *Courageous* and *Glorious* had been similarly fitted. The designs and positions varied slightly – in this case the platform is offset to the left side of the turret. Note the Carley rafts on the turret side and against the blast screen and the searchlight towers around the after funnel. (Author's collection)

Another view of *Lion*'s 'Q' turret and aircraft flying-off ramp, this time looking forward. The offset of the ramp is clearly visible in this view. (Author's collection)

The forward turrets and bridge of Princess Royal in December 1917. (Author's collection)

of a trial gun to the 13.5in design and this was duly submitted on 2 February. The price, including delivery to Woolwich, was £11,400 for the gun and £1250 for the breech mechanism, which was accepted by Admiralty letter dated 22 February 1909. The first 13.5in MkV gun was proof tested at Shoeburyness late in 1909 and gave very satisfactory results. Designed for a chamber pressure of 18 tons/sq in, it had a considerable margin of strength and subsequent firings revealed that it also had an exceptionally low wear rate – estimated to give a barrel life of about 450efc. It was decided to utilise these features to increase the power of the gun by raising the chamber pressure to 20 tons/sq in, using a larger charge. This was employed firstly to raise the muzzle velocity of the 1250lb projectile but in later ships a heavier 1400lb projectile was introduced that reduced the muzzle velocity but greatly increased the hitting power of the shell. Naturally these changes reduced the barrel life but this was still estimated to be a very acceptable 300–350efc. The success of the 13.5in gun was particularly welcome as the earlier attempt to increase gun power by raising muzzle velocity in the 12in/50cal MkXI was not an unqualified success, the gun suffering from serious accuracy problems as a result of insufficient stiffness of the barrel and irregular combustion of the propellant charge.

The design of the twin 13.5in mounting, again by Vickers, was based on that of the twin 12in for the MkXI, 50cal gun and, to keep the weight of mounting and armour down, the overall dimensions of the latter were not greatly exceeded, the internal barbette diameter being kept the same at 28ft. The increased weight of each turntable was only about 60 tons. The principal differences between the two, apart from the necessary increase in the strength of the mounting for the larger gun, were as follows.

(a) The dimensions of the loading trunk, being only a few inches larger in diameter than that of the 12in mounting, made it necessary to tip the projectile tray of the combined shell and cordite cage to an angle of 38° during its passage from the shell room to the working chamber in order to fit the longer shell into the available space. The tray was automatically brought to the horizontal at the top of the hoist and at the shell room. Similar arrangements were adopted for the gun loading cage, operating between the working chamber and the gunhouse.

(b) The introduction of a 7-cylinder swash plate training engine (two per mounting) which was more efficient, more compact and lighter than the radial type and gave excellent control, particularly at slow speeds. The design of the swash plate engine was the same as that already adopted in the battleships *Hercules* and *Colossus*. The first experimental version of this engine, with 10 cylinders, had been tried earlier in 'Q' turret of the battleship *Superb*.

(c) Each gun had only a single elevating ram instead of two (back-to-back) in order to accommodate the increase in elevation to 20°.

(d) Owing to the limited space between the guns, the auxiliary cordite supply was moved from a central position to outside the guns and combined with the auxiliary shell supply.

The mountings for *Lion* and *Queen Mary* were constructed by Armstrong and those for the *Princess Royal* and *Tiger* by Vickers. The original mounting, employing the 1250lb

The forward turrets of *Repulse* viewed from the bridge in the latter part of 1918. The aircraft on 'B' turret's flying-off ramp is a Sopwith 1½ Strutter. The portable platforms that extend the turret ramp over the 15in guns are in the process of either being fitted or removed. (Author's collection)

projectile, fitted in *Lion* and *Princess Royal* was designated MkII while the later mountings, with the 1400lb projectile became MkII* (*Queen Mary*) and the MkII** (*Tiger*); the additional star on the latter mounting indicated changes to the elevating gear which increased the speed of operation from 3°/sec to 5°/sec. *Lion* was fitted with on-mounting dynamos for the gun firing circuits driven by Pelton wheels (water-turbines) supplied directly off the hydraulic main. This innovation was also provided in *Queen Mary* and *Tiger* (and the later 15in gun mounting), but in the latter ships the position of the dynamos was altered from one on each side of the turntable to the centre girder.

Some consideration was given to abandoning the all-angle loading system in the 13.5in mounting, which would have saved weight, increased the amount of floor space in the gunhouse and improved the mounting's structural strength. There would have been a slight increase in the loading cycle time, which was not considered significant, but more important was the loss of the ability for continuous aim as the guns would have had to come off-target each time they were loaded. It was eventually decided that the gains with fixed loading were not sufficient to counter the loss in flexibility allowed by all-angle loading.

The 15in gun

By the time the 15in MkI had been installed in a battlecruiser it was already fully established as a battleship weapon, having previously been installed in the *Queen Elizabeth* and *Royal Sovereign* classes. It was essentially an enlarged version of the 13.5in MkV that continued the Royal Navy's move away from high-velocity heavy guns and towards increased projectile weight. The gun was shorter in calibre terms than the 13.5in, had a slightly lower muzzle velocity and a minimal increase in maximum range. Its advantage was almost entirely concentrated in the greater energy and destructive effect of its 1920lb projectile. It was again a very

Table 41: Particulars of main armament guns

Calibre:	12in	13.5in	15in	18in
Mark:	X	V	I	I
Weight excl. bm (tons):	56.81	74.91	97.15	146.2
Weight of bm (tons):	0.85	1.21	2.85	2.8
Total length (ins):	556.5	625.9	650.4	744.15
Length of bore (cal/ins):	45/540.9	45/607.5	42/630	40/720.2
Chamber dia x length (ins):	13 min, 19 max x 81	15 min, 16.85 max x 92.13	20 x 107.5	23.85 x 127.05
Chamber capacity (cu-in):	18,000	19,650	30,590	51,310
Length of rifling, (ins):	453.193	509.57	516.33	585.42
Number of rifling grooves:	60	68	76	88
Charge type:	MD45	MD45	MD45	MD45
Charge weight (lbs):	258	297 (293*)	428	630
Projectile weight (lbs):	850	1400 (1250*)	1920	3320
Designed chamber pressure (tons/sq ins):	18	20	19.5	18
Muzzle velocity (fps):	2725	2500 (2582*)	2450	2270
Muzzle energy (foot-tons):	44,431	60,674 (56,361*)	79,914	118,592
Max range (yards/elevation):	18,850/ 13.5deg**	23,800/20deg	23,734/20deg 29,000/30deg	28,800/30deg

Notes:
In all cases rifling was Plain Section, polygroove MkI with a uniform twist of one turn in 30 calibres.
* These figures apply to the 1250lbs, 13.5in projectile fitted in the *Lion* class.
** This applies to the 4crh projectile – the 2crh projectiles of the *Invincible* class gave a maximum range of 16,450yds.

The forward turrets and bridge of Hood seen from the forecastle. Note the 'squarer' form of the 15in MkII gunhouse. (Author's collection)

The forward 15in turret of Courageous in mid-1918. (Author's collection)

successful gun with good accuracy and low barrel wear (350efc) which was to see continuous service with the Royal Navy to the end of the Second World War and beyond.

The 15in MkI mountings were again an expansion of the 13.5in twin mounting with the internal barbette diameter increased to 30ft 6in and the mounting strengthened to take the extra weight and greater recoil forces of the 15in guns. All the mountings in *Renown, Courageous* and *Glorious*, but only 'Y' turret in *Repulse* were MkI*. These were generally similar to MkI apart from a reduction in the thickness of the gunhouse armour, a curved (rather than faceted) front shield to the gunhouse and modified shell-handling arrangements for the lower hoist; however, these differences were inconsistent in their application.[3]

For *Hood* the mountings were redesigned to increase the maximum elevation of the guns from 20° to 30° in recognition of the greater ranges at which actions were being fought. This involved increasing the depth of the mounting to give sufficient clearance for the breech on recoil at full elevation, which increased the height from the base of the barbette to the gun axis from 21ft 2in to 23ft 11in. The front of the gunhouse was also increased in height, again to provide the necessary clearance to the guns at full elevation, which coincidentally – or possibly deliberately – had the effect of producing a flatter roof which presented a more acute angle of impact to plunging shell. The mounting still had all-angle loading but, as this was still of essentially the same design as the MkI, it was only available up to 20° elevation.

Hydraulic power

Power for the main armament mountings was supplied by large steam-driven hydraulic pumping engines which supplied pressure into a common ring main. In all the 12in gun battlecruisers two pumping engines were fitted, which was just adequate for normal operations but gave little reserve power in case of breakdown or action damage. In 1909 the DNO, Bacon, concluded that as no problems had been encountered with earlier ships the provision of two engines, of slightly increased capacity (110 cub ft/min as against 98 cub ft/min) would be adequate for the *Lion* and *Princess Royal*. Following *Lion's* gunnery trials in January 1912, her Captain recorded that:

> Assuming that for 5 turrets three hydraulic pumps are sufficient, which they are not, more than two pumps are necessary for four turrets but this ship has only two pumps. Again with three pumps the breakdown of one pump reduces the capacity by 33% whereas with only two pumps the capacity is reduced by 50%. The pump capacity is a matter of vital importance and it should be raised so as to provide ample margin for contingency. If possible this should be done in existing ships.[4]

In April 1912 it was approved to fit a third hydraulic pump in *Lion, Princess Royal* and *Queen Mary*, at the cost of an additional 30 tons per ship, an arrangement that became standard in the later battlecruisers. This decision was also influenced by the introduction of director firing which, because it resulted in the gun mountings working in unison, showed that the existing pumping system could not cope with simultaneous loading operations. There were also problems with guns being run-out together, particularly at high elevations. This was solved in *Hood* by the fitting of pneumatic run-out gear, a system first tried in the Armstrong electric-powered mountings of *Invincible*, and it was later approved to convert other mountings to this arrangement as soon as it was conveniently possible.

Blast

The problems of blast which so exercised the members of the Committee on Designs in 1905 were very real but, with hindsight, it is difficult to see why more effort was not put into attempts to solve the difficulties at a detail level, as occurred later, rather than simply moving the gun mountings as far apart as possible. The latter had serious effects on the designs produced, in particular by making the superimposed turret unacceptable when such an arrangement would have greatly eased the difficulties of producing a compact and workable superstructure layout. In addition, the positioning of the wing turrets, while reducing the interference with other gun mountings, actually increased the blast effects on the conning towers, ship's boats and the secondary armament. The primary problem with the superimposed turret was the fact that the blast pressure would enter through the lower turret's sighting hoods and gun ports causing both disruption to the turret's operation and possible injury to its crew – particularly those at the gunsights, who stood a good chance of suffering serious concussion or head injury from being thrown back against the sighting hood. These difficulties had been solved to a large extent by the time superimposed turrets were adopted by the introduction of periscope type gunsights (which kept the operator's head below the turret roof) and blast excluders in the sighting ports. In addition the gun ports were closed-up by the fitting of blast-bags – heavy canvas strengthened with twine – which enclosed the area between the gun ports and the chase of the gun. In *Tiger* experimental horizontal periscope sights were fitted in 'A' turret for the side sighting positions, which meant that this gunhouse had only one sighting hood on the roof – in the centre position – as opposed to the usual three. The new sights projected through the side walls and were protected by small armoured hoods. The idea was not pursued in later ships but, so far as is known, the only objection was the early wooding of the sights because they were that much further from the centre of rotation of the turret. The idea reappeared post-war in the 16in triple mountings of the battleships *Nelson* and *Rodney*. A somewhat simpler approach was employed in *Hood* where turret sighting hoods were abandoned altogether in favour of straight telescopic sights fitted lower down and sighting through small rectangular ports in the front shield armour.

Fire control

The fire control system in the *Invincible* class was controlled from the spotting tops at the heads of the fore- and mainmasts. These communicated with two transmitting stations (TSs) immediately below them on the lower deck, via electrical transmission instruments, giving range, deflection and order information, and by direct voice communication in the form of navy-phones and voice pipes. The principle equipment in each top was a 9ft Barr and Stroud rangefinder, and two Dumaresq instruments that provided information on the target's rate of change of bearing and range relative to the firing ship. The information supplied from these was processed in the TS, principally by the range clocks, which constantly updated the predicted future range of the target, and then transmitted to the guns as range and deflection. At the same time a record was kept of the target's position, using the information received, on a plotting table in the TS, which allowed a visual representation of the target's movements to be constructed upon which advice could be offered to the control officer as to how the action was developing. Each gun mounting had its own group of transmission instruments and navy-phones and a separate wiring system. Both control positions and each gun mounting could be connected to either TS via change-over switches which allowed for all the guns being controlled from either top via either TS or divided control with two turrets operated from the fore TS and two from the after TS. In practice the foretop became the principle control position, the after control serving as a back-up – it was in any case more liable to smoke interference from the funnels than that forward.

This arrangement was repeated in *Indefatigable* except that a combined armoured spotting and signal tower was fitted low down under the bridge and abaft the main conning tower (CT). This decision resulted from concerns about the survivability of the control tops and their communications during an action. In firing trials against the old battleship *Hero* in 1907, the control top was hit twice, once by a splinter and once by a shell, and the mast supporting it by a large splinter which severed the voice pipe and all the electric leads from the top. It was, therefore, envisaged that the masthead position would most probably only be used in the opening phases of an action and that control would be transferred to the lower position when either the higher position became untenable or the ships had closed to a decisive range. In addition to these alterations the after CT in

The bridge and forward turrets of *Tiger* viewed from the forecastle in the mid-1920s. Note the gunsight ports of 'A' turret in the sidewalls on each side – an arrangement unique to this turret in *Tiger*. There are two 3in AA guns on each side of the forward shelter deck. (Authors collection)

Indefatigable was dropped in favour of a lightly-protected torpedo director tower, which was adopted partly to compensate for the added weight of the combined spotting and signal tower. The *Indefatigable* layout was an interim measure adopted at a time when discussions on the fire control arrangements for future ships were in the early stages of an extended debate. As a result *Australia* and *New Zealand*, completed that much later than their sister, incorporated changes decided upon after the *Indefatigable* design had been settled. In these ships the armoured spotting tower was incorporated into the CT where it was better protected, had a much-improved field of vision and direct access, for communication, with the primary conning position. This and the foretop were to be the two primary control positions, the control top on the mainmast and the after TS being omitted, while the fore TS was enlarged as a result of complaints that these compartments were too cramped. At the same time 'A' turret was fitted with a 9ft rangefinder, which projected through a hole in the roof at the rear of the gunhouse and was protected by a large cast-steel armoured hood. This last modification, approved in 1909, was also applied to *Indefatigable* and the three ships of the *Invincible* class during refits from 1911 to 1914. The turrets so fitted did not simply provide a protected rangefinder position as they were also equipped with the necessary instruments to serve as secondary control positions for the entire main armament. In *Lion and Princess Royal* this was taken a stage further in that both 'B' and 'X' turrets were fitted with 9ft rangefinders and equipped to serve as secondary control positions. The *Lion* and *Princess Royal* were the last of the battlecruisers to have a second main TS.

Queen Mary's initial design differed from that in *Lion* in that the proposed primary control positions were the foretop and the after torpedo director tower. The latter was increased in size, to accommodate the necessary fire control equipment, including a revolving 9ft rangefinder with an armoured hood, and provided with substantially heavier protection than that fitted in earlier ships. Also included were a spotting tower forward and 'B' and 'X' turrets equipped for secondary control. However, following the problems of smoke and heat interference encountered in 1911 with the first ships of the 1909–10 Programme it was decided to modify her mast/funnel arrangement and to abolish the control top altogether. The aft control position in the torpedo control tower and the forward spotting position were also omitted. The new primary control position was shifted to the armoured CT and the 9ft Argo rangefinder, which was to have been fitted in the foretop, was moved to a revolving armoured tower in the roof of the CT. The problems encountered in *Lion* during her steam trials in January 1912 led to this same arrangement being adopted in both that ship and *Princess Royal*, with some variations in detail due to the fact that these two ships were virtually complete and the alterations had to be adapted to the existing structure. Thus all three ships ended up with no aloft control position, apart from a light top for a spotter, and all the main controls low down and behind armour.

In 1910, the battleship *Vanguard* was employed in trials to establish whether individual gun mountings could provide for their own 'local' fire control if communication to the main control system was cut off or the main control was destroyed. As a result of these trials it was decided that all the turrets in all dreadnought battleships and battlecruisers should be fitted with a 9ft rangefinder and the necessary instruments to allow for local control. The first battlecruiser to benefit from this change was *Queen Mary*, the fitting of earlier ships being deferred pending the results of initial experience with the single turret rangefinder installations already approved. The earlier battlecruisers were not, therefore, provided with the full outfit of turret rangefinders until 1914–15.

The *Tiger* installation was identical to that of *Queen Mary* except that the control top, complete with 9ft rangefinder, was restored and she was provided with a second TS for her 6in gun armament.

Two major fire control innovations were introduced in the years immediately preceding the First World War. The first was the introduction of a mechanical fire control computer that in essence combined the functions of the range clock and Dumaresq with various ballistic and other corrections to provide a continuous read-out of range and deflection for transmission to the guns. Two such pieces of equipment were initially available – the Dreyer Fire Control Table developed by Captain (later Admiral) F C Dreyer and the Argo Clock, a commercial invention by A H Pollen. Five sets of each were ordered for comparative trials in 1912, and of these, two of the Dreyer Tables were supplied to *Lion* and *Princess Royal* and one Argo Clock MkIV to *Queen Mary*. The Dreyer Table, unlike its rival, incorporated a plotting system but in other respects the purpose of the rival equipment was much the same.[5] One of the major claims for the Argo system was that it was 'helm-free' – in other words, it would continue to accurately track a target regardless of any changes of course by the firing ship. In fact, this was a feature of the 1912 Dreyer Table which was directly connected to the ship's gyro compass to provide automatic correction for changes to own ship's alterations of course and of yaw. By contrast, the Argo Clock required manual intervention when own ship changed course, in which condition it was no longer running automatically with regard to target bearing.[6]

The Admiralty chose to adopt the Dreyer Table because it was cheaper, less complex and just as capable, even though it was less sophisticated in mechanical design. It is also probable that the Dreyer Table was adopted because it was a Service-originated device. The failure to adopt the Argo system has been the subject of much criticism but, even assuming that it had some substantial advantage over that of Dreyer Table as an instrument, this author doubts that any loss resulting from this was as great as has been supposed. These devices formed only part of a much larger system, which was more dependent on the input of accurate information from observation of the target than on the machinery which processed it. Moreover, constant adjustment of the input was required to feed-in spotting corrections and to keep track of changes of course and speed by the target. This adjustment meant that any solution was unlikely to produce a constant output for any length of time, which rather negated any advantage resulting from improved mechanical accuracy – just as over a limited period it is as easy to obtain an acceptably accurate measure of the passing of time with a domestic alarm clock as with a chronometer.

The prototype Dreyer Table was installed in the pre-dreadnought *Prince of Wales* in 1911 and then relocated in the dreadnought *Hercules* in 1912. The first production Dreyer Tables were the five ordered for comparative trials in 1912. In addition, Dreyer developed a small table for use in turrets to provide local control, the first version being fitted in 'B' turret of *Queen Mary* in 1913. To 'avoid confusion' it was decided early in 1914 to provide the Dreyer Tables with mark numbers. This was promulgated in Admiralty Weekly Order 972 of March 1914. At this time MkI was allocated to the turret table installed in *Queen Mary*, MkII to the prototype in *Hercules*, MkIII to the first production version and MkIII* to the Dreyer plotters used in conjunction with the Argo Clock. The next iteration of the Table, with more fully integrated electric motor drives, appeared later in 1914 as the MkIV, and was fitted in *Tiger*. The *Tiger* was also provided a 'Local Control Table' in each turret.

A simplified, hand-operated, version of the Dreyer Table, introduced in 1915, adopted the MkI designation previously applied to the turret table in *Queen Mary*, the latter losing its mark and simply becoming the 'Local Control Table' (assuming she still had it, see footnote 7). The MkI had probably been installed in the *Australia*, *New Zealand*, *Inflexible* and *Invincible* by April 1916.

As built the *Repulse*, *Renown*, *Courageous*, *Glorious* and *Furious* were fitted with MkIV* Tables and a 'Local Control Table' in each turret. The MkIII Tables in *Lion* and *Princess Royal* were replaced sometime during the latter half of the war with MkIV* Tables (these are listed for these ships in the 1918 Dreyer Table Handbook). The final version of the Dreyer Table, the MkV, was fitted in *Hood* together with 'Local Control Tables' in each turret, which by 1918 had been re-designated as 'Turret Control Tables'.[7]

The second, and the most important, addition to the fire control equipment of British ships was the director firing system. This consisted of a remote gunsight, positioned high in the ship, connected by electric transmission instruments to elevation and training receivers at the guns. Up until the post-Jutland period director control and gun layer control were both regarded as primary systems, the choice of which to use being dependent on conditions, principally visibility and weather. Director control replaced the local aiming of the turrets completely as all the trainers and layers had to do was keep the elevation and training pointers worked from their guns' machinery in line with pointers worked from the director. Thus all the guns were under the control of the director layer who also fired the guns of a salvo simultaneously from a trigger fitted to the director sight. The system made it unnecessary to 'hunt the roll' and eliminated the problem of a wild shot which could confuse the spotting system. The simultaneous discharge of the guns also avoided the problem of the spread of the fall of shot being affected by the ship's roll due to slight variations in the firing times by the gun layers of each turret. Training of the director, to maintain target bearing, was required to remain steady for one or two seconds before firing to allow turret training to settle. War experience modified these methods in that gunnery officers adapted the operation of the director according to their personal preferences and prevailing weather conditions. This was formalised later in the war by requirements to keep the director sight consistently on for elevation and bearing. The one or two seconds of keeping the sight steady before firing being applied to elevation while training was to be constant but with the proviso that it should not be reversed immediately before firing.

The first battlecruiser to be fitted with the director was *Invincible* during her refit of April–August 1914. However, the work was not completed and her director was not brought to a fully working state until after the Battle of the Falkland Islands. *Tiger* was completed with a director system installed, while all the other pre-war battlecruisers were fitted between mid-1915 and May 1916, the last to be so equipped being *Indomitable* and *Inflexible* immediately before the Battle of Jutland. Because of the late fitting in the latter pair it is possible that their director systems were not fully operational at the time of Jutland due to either incomplete fitting-out or lack of time to train the personnel in their use. The *Renown* class and the three light battlecruisers were completed with two directors – one in the usual aloft position and the second in the armoured revolving hood on top of the gun control tower in the forward CT. The latter incorporated a rangefinder and represented a first step towards the 'director control towers' adopted post-war. *Hood* had a similar but more extensive arrangement in which the aloft director position also included an integral rangefinder.

Secondary armament directors were provided in all the wartime-built battlecruisers while they were under construction. The *Tiger* was fitted with secondary directors for her 6in guns in 1917. In late 1918 it was decided to fit secondary directors in some of the earlier battlecruisers but this was cancelled following the end of the war.

All the fire control systems produced, up to the introduction of radar in the Second World War, relied entirely on direct observation of the target, and particularly on observation of the fall of shot. While the complex fire control instruments developed were invaluable, particularly in calculating the future position of the target, and in processing information more rapidly than would otherwise have been possible, the most important aspect of the fire control system as a whole was the *method* adopted for the control of fire. The British, although ahead of the German Navy in the development of fire control equipment, *appear* to have been somewhat less successful in the implementation of an organisation designed to achieve early and sustained hitting. This assumption is primarily based on the poor quality of fire control demonstrated by most, but not all, of the British battlecruisers during The Battle of Jutland, particularly during the Run to the South. At this time visibility conditions greatly favoured the German squadron as did the use of stereoscopic rangefinders, which were particularly suited to obtaining ranges in conditions of visibility that did not suit the coincidence type used by the British. Even with these qualifications it has to be admitted that the general quality of fire control in several of the British battlecruisers was well below what it should have been.

Top left: The flying-off ramp and canvas aircraft hangar fitted to the roof of *Tiger*'s 'Q' turret in late 1917. The aircraft is a 2F.1 Camel. The aircraft in this case was launched over the rear of the turret, the wood frame at the right end of the ramp being the tail support. Similar arrangements were provided for in 'Y' turret of *Repulse, Renown, Glorious* and *Courageous* and 'X' turret of *Lion* and *Princess* Royal. In all other cases aircraft were launched over the fore end of the turret. *Tiger* only carried a ramp on 'Q' turret but all the other battlecruisers had two ('Q' and 'X' in *Lion* and *Princess Royal;* 'B' and 'Y' in *Renown and Repulse;* 'A' and 'Y' in *Courageous* and *Glorious* and 'P' and 'Q' in the surviving 12in gun ships). (Author's collection)

Above: Another view of *Tiger*'s 'Q' turret showing the aircraft ramp and canvas hangar. (Author's collection)

The after turret of Courageous *in mid-1918. Note the range clock on the after control position on the mainmast and the remains of the supports for the mine rails on the quarterdeck. (Author's collection)*

This is generally blamed on inadequate opportunities for gunnery practice for the ships based at Rosyth, which at best seems a half-truth. Later in the battle several British ships (in particular the battleship *Iron Duke* and the *Invincible*) demonstrated excellent control of fire despite poor visibility and limited opportunity to use either rangefinders or their fire control tables.

The basic system of spotting developed by the Royal Navy before the war was employed up to and including the Battle of Dogger Bank and in slightly modified form until after Jutland. It was assumed that an action in good visibility would begin at very long range, which in 1914, was envisaged as 15,000yds for the 13.5in gun and 13,000yds for the 12in gun. Fire was to be opened using salvos consisting of half the number of guns (with the left and right guns of each turret alternating). After waiting to spot the fall of shot of the first salvo, the second would be fired with whatever correction for range and/or line was deemed necessary, and continued in this way until the salvos were observed to have bracketed the target. Following this the correction was halved and so on until a straddle or hit was obtained, at which point the guns went into rapid fire without waiting for the fall of shot. It should be noted that if a straddle showed too many or too few short shots further small corrections were made to bring the mean point of impact (MPI) onto the centre of the target (this method of observing the number of shorts in a salvo could also, given good visibility, be used for tracking errors in range rate). If the target was lost the procedure began all over again. As a result of the Battle of the Dogger Bank greater emphasis was placed on the value of shorts at long range, due to the fact that overs and hits could rarely be seen.[8]

Barring a lucky straddle early in the process, this method was slow but worked well in peacetime practices where the target was slow and on a steady course and the visibility and weather conditions were, at the least, reasonable. The war was to demonstrate that actual action conditions could not be reproduced artificially in battle practice. After Jutland some attempt was made to improve this state of affairs by introducing throw-off shoots (that is, firing with the control aimed at a ship but with the guns offset). Post-war developments in this direction included the employment of a radio-controlled target ship and introducing high-speed battle practice targets, but even with these the results could not entirely match action conditions. Attempting to do so to the maximum extent would in any case have made the practice procedure expensive and difficult to evaluate.

British observation of the German Navy's fire control led to a number of conclusions which are probably invalid, in particular the assumed employment of a 'ladder' system (see below) which greatly influenced the future development of the British system of control. When first experienced by the British at the Battle of Dogger Bank the German system was taken simply as an indication of the enemy's ability to sustain a more rapid rate of fire. This made some impression on the Battlecruiser Force and resulted in an excessive concentration on the training of gun crews for rapid loading, which in turn led to some dangerous practices with regard to the by-passing of normal safety procedures in the handling of ammunition. Another item noticed about German fire, both at Dogger Bank and Jutland, was the very small spread of their salvos. The British encouraged the use of a fairly wide spread to facilitate straddling the target but this could actually result in no hits occurring from a straddle. Conversely, the German fall of shot, while more reliant on accuracy, could, once the target was found, produce two or possibly three hits from a single salvo. Combining this with the rapid fire that occurred once the target was found often produced devastating effects from a series of hits in rapid succession. This actually occurred during the Battle of Dogger Bank when *Lion* received ten hits or damaging near misses within fifteen minutes and was put out of action as a result. The effects at Jutland were even more severe.

It was following the Battle of Jutland that the British actually took serious note of what they assumed was the operation of the German fire control system. On 7 June 1916 Rear Admiral Pakenham, second-in-command of the Battlecruiser Fleet, with his flag in *New Zealand*, wrote to Beatty:

1. I have the honour to bring to your notice the advisability of considering without delay the relative values of the British system of obtaining hits as compared with that apparently used by the Germans.
2. The part to which I particularly refer is the 'straddle' as opposed to the concentrated salvo. Observation of the almost irresistible effect of two or three shots striking together has impressed me with the view that without adequate reason we may now be denying ourselves the benefit of a very powerful weapon.
3. I also think the principle of the straddle has been abused. Of late gunnery practice has not exacted hits. Gunnery officers have been pressed only to straddle, and this has acted as a premium on increase of longitudinal spread. Hence spreads of over three hundred yards have been accepted as satisfactory. Great longitudinal spread has obtained so much sanction, indeed, that it has been stated 'Barham' was actually ordered to increase a spread which she had reduced to 70 yards, because so moderate a spread diminished prospects of straddling.
4. It appears to me that when we have done everything possible to obtain concentrated fall and to eliminate every error, we shall still have a spread sufficient for all gunnery purposes. Concentrated fall would facilitate spotting. The principle on which ranging is done would have to be changed; but Lieutenant-Commander Smith of 'New Zealand' has a proposal which promises well and no doubt discussion would elicit many other instructive suggestions.[9]

The proposals from Lieutenant-Commander Smith referred to by Pakenham were based on the former's observation of German fire at Jutland, which he describes as follows:

The Germans appear to fire about three salvoes in rapid succession without waiting for the fall of shot. These salvoes appear to fall about 400yds apart, each successive salvo falling beyond the one before it.

It is assumed that the second or middle salvo was fired with the mean RF [rangefinder] Range on the sights ... The result is a ladder of salvoes about 1000yds [*sic*] in length with three steps, and by watching the fall of each step in turn a very close estimate of the true range is obtained, and far more rapidly than [with] our bracket system. The difficulty of getting the first salvo correct for line of course arises, but this affects both systems.

As there was no opportunity of timing the German salvoes, it is not known whether the third salvo was fired before the first pitched (if so the loading must be very rapid), but it certainly did not appear to be corrected for the fall of shot of the first salvo.

If the ladder straddles, the enemy has a very approximate range within a minute and a half of opening fire. If the ladder fails to straddle another ladder is probably fired with a mean range of 500 to 600 [yards] more or less than the original ladder.[10]

Smith then went on to describe a slight variation on this arrangement for adoption by the British. These were subsequently reworked by the Grand Fleet's post-Jutland Gunnery Committee and emerged as the '1916 Spotting Rules'. These followed the principle outlined above but adopted double rather than triple salvos and included an initial deflection step for line before commencing the spread for range. This system was designed to obtain rapid and early hitting which the old bracket system could not provide. When targets might be only intermittently visible this was particularly critical and the war demonstrated that interference with the line of sight was the normal situation rather than the exception. If the fall of shot was missed then that salvo was wasted so far as control was concerned. Apart from interference from gun smoke and funnel smoke, sighting instruments were affected by sea spray (particularly with ships running at high speed as at Dogger Bank), enemy hits and shorts and, of course, the prevailing weather conditions. Add to this the fact that, particularly at long range, 'overs' and hits with APC shell were almost impossible to see and it is not difficult to see why the pre-war desire for a low protected control position was abandoned in favour of the original spotting top (and director position) high on the foremast where the chances of clear observation were that much greater. A very clear idea of the difficulties involved, particularly from a low position, can be gathered from the following passage describing the experiences of the officer in

Courageous in the spring of 1917 fitted as a minelayer – the mines are just visible as a row abaft 'Y' turret. She could carry over 200 mines on rails on the quarterdeck but was so fitted for only a short time and was never used operationally in this role. (Author's collection)

charge of 'A' turret of the *New Zealand* at the Battle of the Dogger Bank:

> For approximately the first two hours after the chase had commenced, the spray from the forecastle caused the greatest possible inconvenience to the gunlayers, trainer, rangefinder operators and myself. It was found to be almost useless to wipe over any of the glasses, as the spray came over practically continuously ... The spray being driven through my observation slit made my eyes extremely sore, and the blast from my own guns firing made this soreness worse. In a very short time I was wet through to the skin and very cold ...
>
> My rangefinder operator did not obtain one good reading the whole time.
>
> The water from the hoses ran forward and over the side, where the wind caught it and immediately blew it back over the turret. I sent one man out to shut off all the forecastle hoses.
>
> At one period, after a lull and slight alteration of course, the fire gongs were rung and one of my guns fired at the fourth cloud of smoke on the right. I then noticed that there was yet another cloud of smoke to the left of this one, and immediately asked the conning tower which was our target. They replied: 'The left-hand cloud of smoke – the fifth cloud.' ...
>
> I was unable to use my glasses (except at the very end), and my field of view was interrupted by the muzzles of both guns. Consequently I never obtained a detailed view of the enemy; in fact, during the chase, I never saw the ships, but only clouds of smoke. (A description of the target would have been useless to me.)[11]

Torpedoes

The *Invincible* class was fitted with five 18in torpedo tubes, two on each broadside and one astern. The broadside tubes were regarded as 'offensive' and the stern tube as 'defensive'. Subsequent development of long-range gunnery made it appear that there would be little opportunity to use these weapons except in the closing phases of an action and the number of torpedo tubes fitted in *Indefatigable,* and later ships up to and including the *Queen Mary,* was therefore reduced to two, one being fitted on each side forward. However, during 1908–9 substantial advances were made in the development of the Royal Navy's torpedoes with the introduction of the more powerful 21in type and an enhancement of the propulsion system in the shape of the 'Hardcastle' heater. The last, in very simple terms, increased the range and/or speed of the torpedo by heating the compressed air used to drive its engine. The heater could also be retrofitted to the 18in torpedo and by 1910 the standard long-range settings for these had increased to about 6500yds, while the new 21in could reach over 10,000yds at 30kts.

In 1910 another innovation was introduced in the shape of the 'angled gyro', a device that could also be fitted to existing as well as new torpedoes. This allowed the torpedo to be set to run at a different angle from that at which it was discharged, moving to its new course shortly after being launched. This obviated the need for the firing ship to be in exactly the right relationship to the target before the torpedo could be fired and added greatly to the flexibility of the system as a whole. Fixed settings were provided in 100 steps from 40° abaft to 40° before the tube's line of sight.

These innovations produced a reconsideration of the role of the torpedo as it was anticipated that good opportunities would occur for the capital ships of the fleet to fire them at a much earlier stage in an action. In June 1910 the C-in-C Home Fleet, Admiral W H May, recommended a reinstatement of the after broadside tubes to increase the possible volume of fire. Commenting on the C-in-C's recommendation, the Assistant Director of Torpedoes, S Nicholson, stated that 'In the early stages of an action, when opportunities for firing torpedoes may be few and brief, it is very important to fire as many torpedoes as possible when the chances occur and for this reason more than one tube on each broadside is extremely desirable.'[12] Consideration was given to carrying out this alteration in *Queen Mary* but it would have meant a 10ft increase in length and a 400-ton increase in displacement and it was decided to defer the change to the ships of the next year's Programme. Thus *Tiger,* completed in 1914, was the first and only battlecruiser to benefit from changes discussed four years earlier. The difficulties involved in fitting a submerged room aft required a substantial reworking of the arrangement of compartments in this area and led to her markedly changed appearance with 'Q' turret moved aft of all the boiler rooms. The wartime-built battlecruisers, including *Hood,* did not have an after room and although this was requested for *Hood* the difficulties of fitting it into an area already crowded with magazines, shell rooms and propeller shafts led to the adoption of above-water tubes instead. There were, however, concerns about the vulnerability of torpedoes carried above water due to the danger of their warheads being detonated by direct hits or near misses which led to *Hood*'s above-water tubes being provided, initially, with armour 'box' protection to the front ends of the tubes.

Despite the potential offered by the torpedo it did not prove a decisive weapon in heavy ships either during the First or Second World Wars. Of the battlecruisers only *Lion* ever fired any number in action. This was at Jutland where she fired two at the van of the enemy battlecruisers during the Run to the North, one at a light cruiser (probably *Wiesbaden*) that was claimed to hit, and a further three at some German battleships. The latter were fired with extended range settings, by which the torpedo could reach about 18,000yds but at a much-reduced speed of about 18kts. As this gave a running time of around 30 minutes the chances of achieving a hit were slim. The only other battlecruiser to fire a torpedo at Jutland was *Princess Royal*, which fired a single torpedo at around 8.30pm, late in the day action, at one of the German battleships at a range of 10,000yds. Apart from the possible hit on the cruiser none of these torpedoes are believed to have hit their targets.

Anti-torpedo-boat guns

The Committee on Designs initially favoured an ATB armament of 4in guns but the development of a new high-velocity 12pdr gun of improved accuracy caused a modification of this view on the basis that more such guns could be mounted and they offered a higher rate of fire. However, in 1906 firing trials against the old destroyer *Skate* with 3pdr, 12pdr and 4in guns led to a reversal of this decision as the latter calibre was shown as the only one of the three tried that stood a good chance of stopping a destroyer before she got close enough to deliver a torpedo attack. In consequence the ATB armament of the *Invincible* design was altered from eighteen 12pdr guns to sixteen 4in. These were mounted in open positions on the superstructure and the roofs of the

12in turrets. At the time it was envisaged that a serious torpedo craft attack would only take place at night, probably after the end of a day action, or possibly when the ships were at anchor in harbour. The guns were not expected to be manned in a ship-to-ship action as both the guns and their crews would be excessively vulnerable to the enemy's heavy shells and subject to the blast of the main armament. Conversely the heavy guns were not expected to take part in a night action against torpedo craft as their chances of obtaining a hit at night on such a small high-speed target was limited, while the blast and flash from the guns would interfere with the ATB armament proper. However, in 1909 it was approved to provide 6rpg of shrapnel shell for heavy guns for this purpose, the requirement of accuracy with such projectiles being substantially less.

The arrangement in *Invincible* was not popular as there was a good chance that a high percentage of the ATB guns would not survive a day action and the guns' crews had little protection from the blast of adjacent guns and the weather. In addition the guns on the turret roofs were considered dangerous as they could serve to detonate heavy shells that might otherwise have passed harmlessly over the gunhouse. The latter point was dealt with in the *Indefatigable* class by placing all the guns in the superstructure, an arrangement also adopted in the *Invincible* class when the turret roof mountings were moved to the superstructure during refits in 1914–15. At the same time, in both this class and in the *Indefatigables*, the 4in gun positions were enclosed in light casemates and provided with light shields to give weather and blast protection to the guns and their crews.

In *Lion* and *Princess Royal* the 4in guns were grouped in batteries, one forward and one aft, which provided blast protection and shelter from the weather. They also had a single open 4in gun fitted on each side of the forward shelter deck above the forward battery. Following the trials of *Lion* in January 1912 it was decided to enclose these latter guns in unarmoured casemates. In *Queen Mary* the latter guns were moved down into the forward battery, this being provided with armour protection against splinters and light shellfire. However, the after battery, which was open-backed, remained unarmoured.

By 1910 the increasing range and power of the torpedo meant that torpedo attack by destroyers in a daylight action was a much more likely possibility. In addition, the size of destroyers had increased and the need to stop these vessels at much greater range soon led to demands for an increase in the power and range of the ATB armament. There was, moreover, a strong body of opinion in the Navy that considered the abandonment of the intermediate gun to be a serious error. Fisher, however, was very much against any increase in the calibre of this armament and it was not until after he left the Admiralty that anything positive was done. In this respect the German Navy adopted a quite different policy, all their battleships and battlecruisers being equipped with a substantial secondary battery of 5.9in guns fitted in a well-protected central battery. Much the same arrangement was adopted by the British in the armoured ships of the 1911–12 Programme, the battlecruiser (*Tiger*) being fitted with six 6in guns on each side, protected by 6in armour. However, while the German Navy appears to have considered their 5.9in armament as an important support to the main armament as well as for ATB defence, the Royal Navy, while accepting that the 6in gun might have some minor advantages in the closing phases of an

A poor but interesting view of *Inflexible*'s 'A' turret in early 1915. The two 4in guns on the turret roof were converted to high-angle fire by her gunnery officer and employed for bombardment purposes at the Dardanelles. (Author's collection)

Table 42: Particulars of ATB guns

Calibre:	4in	4in	6in	4in	5.5in
Mark:	QF MkIII	BL MkVII	BL MkVII	BL MkIX	BL MkI
Weight incl bm (tons):	1.318	2.092	7.398	2.125	6.05
Total length (ins):	165.35	208.45	279.23	184.6	284.728
Length of bore (cal/ins):	40/160	50.3/201.25	44.9/269.5	44.35/177.4	50/275
Chamber capacity (cu in):	213	600	1715	468.3	1500
Length of rifling (ins):	143.456	171.6	233.602	149.725	235.92
Number of rifling grooves:	24	32	24	32	40
Charge type:	MD16	MD16	MD26	MD16	MD19
Charge weight (lbs):	5.11	9.37	28.625	7.688	22.25
Projectile weight (lbs):	31	31	100	31	82
Muzzle velocity (fps):	2300	2832	2772	2642	2725
Muzzle energy (foot-tons):	1135	1937	5349	1500	4222
Max range (yards/elev):	9600/20deg	11,600/15deg	14,600/20deg	13,840/30deg	17,770/30deg

Inflexible in early 1915 showing the unusual camouflage pattern adopted during her time in the Mediterranean and the two 4in guns on the roof of 'A' turret converted to HA fire. (Author's collection)

action, saw them primarily as ATB weapons. For this reason it appears that the 6in gun was often seen as excessively large for the purpose intended. However, the Royal Navy possessed no modern guns with a calibre between 4in and 6in and there was an inbuilt reluctance to introduce a new-calibre gun that would add yet another type of ammunition and further complicate the supply problem. It was, nevertheless, proposed to introduce a 5in gun in 1907 and again in 1914 but neither project progressed beyond the early design stage.

With Fisher back at the Admiralty there was no question of anything other than the 4in gun being provided in *Renown, Repulse, Glorious* and *Courageous* but in the case of *Furious* a somewhat different circumstance arose. With only two 18in guns this ship was likely to encounter difficulties in dealing with light high-speed craft – cruisers as well as destroyers – as her huge weapons stood little chance of either tracking or hitting such targets. It was suggested by the DNO in April 1915 that 6in guns should be fitted for this purpose but Fisher, while agreeing that a more powerful secondary battery was required, regarded these guns as too heavy and began searching for something that would be easier to handle. Disappointed to find that the 5in gun had not progressed beyond the drawing board stage he came across the 5.5in gun, which had been introduced into British service recently in the cruisers *Birkenhead* and *Chester*. These two vessels were being built by Cammell Laird for Greece and were purchased by the Admiralty shortly after the outbreak of war. Their guns were manufactured by the Coventry Ordnance Works who were also contracted to build twenty-two 5.5in guns and mountings for the secondary armament of a Greek battleship under construction in France. In addition to these, a further sixteen 5.5in guns and mountings were in an advanced state of manufacture and Fisher suggested that some of these be completed for use in *Furious*.[13]

The 6in gun had a 100lb shell and was just on the edge of being a hand-loadable gun, but crews were likely to tire quickly if in action for an extended period. The proposed 5in gun would have had a 60lb shell while the adopted 5.5in gun used an 82lb projectile – a reasonable compromise but still somewhat on the heavy side. Although used in a number of other vessels, including *Hood*, the calibre never really established itself in the Royal Navy in the way that the 5in gun did in the US Navy.

Looking forward from the starboard side of the quarterdeck of *Inflexible* in 1915–16. Note the 3in AA gun mounted at the after end of the superstructure. (Author's collection)

Armour

From the trials with AP shell with cap so far carried out by the Ordnance Board against 4in KC armour, it is clear that when striking at angles greater than 20deg to the normal there is very little chance of any AP shell in the service carrying its burster through such armour at any fighting range, as the shell would break up in passing through the armour. Generally speaking capped AP shell, even when filled salt, may be expected to break up when striking KC armour of half calibre thickness at approx 30deg to the normal.

It is submitted that this tendency of AP shell to break up on striking 4in KC armour at angles over 20deg to the normal may be an important factor in determining the distribution of armour in future ships as when AP shell, filled Lyddite, break up on striking such armour, explosion and not detonation takes place with very much smaller all-round effect.

Remarks of Ordnance Board, quoted by DNO in Memorandum to the Controller dated 24 October 1910. ADM138/413
Iron Duke class Ship's Cover

The distribution of the armour provided in the battlecruisers can best be understood by referring to the accompanying diagrams but some explanatory comment is appropriate. The general system did not provide for immunity from damage but was intended to limit the effects of shellfire by restricting the extent of such damage and by reducing the risks to the more important areas of the ship, namely the motive power, the main armament, the steering gear and the control positions. Two particular factors of importance controlled the chosen arrangement. The first was that the distribution assumed the fighting range current at the time the ships were designed, and the second that the British used their own trial results of shells against armour (plus an analysis of the damage received by ships in the Russo-Japanese War) as a basis on which to draw conclusions.

In the case of the first point, the *Invincible* class ships were expected to face action at a maximum range of 8000yds but it was not until the range came down to about 6000yds that any substantial amount of hitting was expected to take place. At this range, with high-velocity guns, a shell's trajectory is fairly flat so the thickness of decks and the height of side armour was assumed sufficient to limit the effects of medium calibre and lighter shells – as related earlier they were not expected to expose themselves to the fire of a battleship's heavy guns. The main

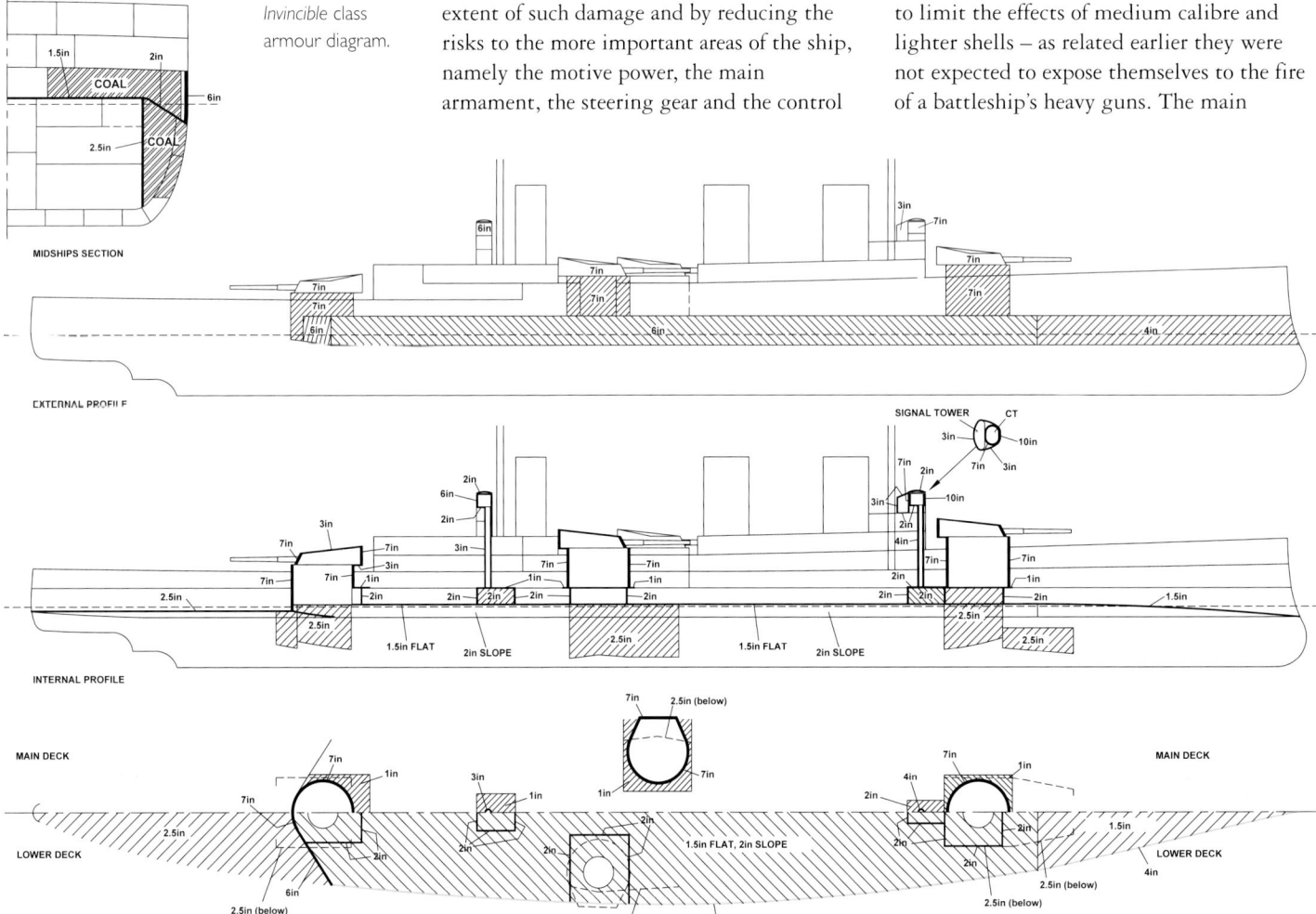

Invincible class armour diagram.

protective deck (the lower deck) provided defence against shells that penetrated the side armour, and was intended to keep out splinters, pieces of dislodged side armour and the shell itself if it hit the deck. The latter was a limited possibility as there was a good chance that the shell would detonate before reaching the deck and the strong possibility that it would break up while penetrating the side armour. The protective deck also served to stop splinters from shells that exploded in the unprotected upperworks of the ship – particularly aft where there was no side armour. The important areas behind the belt, between the main and lower decks – the bases of the barbettes and the fore and after lower conning positions – were locally strengthened against splinter damage with 1in plating (2in over the forward conning position) on the main deck and 2in bulkheads.

In the case of the second point, there was a considerable amount of development of new projectiles between 1900 and 1909 that directly affected the expected performance of armour and protective plating. Most of this work took place during the periods that Bacon and Jellicoe were at the Admiralty, the former as DNO during 1907–9 and the latter as DNO during 1905–7 and as Controller during 1908–10. Unfortunately these developments were not pursued with any vigour by later DNOs or Controllers, a fact best illustrated by the much-quoted fact that shortly before leaving the Admiralty Jellicoe asked the Ordnance Board to investigate the production of an armour-piercing shell which would remain intact after perforating armour at an oblique angle of attack – a request that was considered but not pursued.

Projectile development had two main purposes: the first to improve the shell's penetrating power and the second to increase its explosive effect. The capped AP projectile (APC) was introduced during 1903 and was expected to be able to perforate armour of calibre thickness, given a reasonable striking velocity, at up to 20° from the normal (that is with the axis of the shell at 90° to the plate's surface). However, its powder burster was only 2.5 per cent (by weight), which limited its destructive effect and the shell, having a relatively insensitive base fuse, would often fail to explode when striking unarmoured structures. In 1906 experiments were carried out with a view to increasing the bursting charge to 5.3 per cent but, although these were reasonably successful, it was found that the shells broke up into fragments that were too small to travel the same sort of distances as the larger and more damaging fragments produced by a standard service APC projectile. It was therefore decided to improve the penetration capabilities of the common pointed (CP) shell instead. These shells had been introduced in about 1901 for attack on medium to light armour and were capable of perforating thicknesses about 60 per cent of that which the AP shell could perforate. They were similar to the standard common shell but had their fuses in the base instead of the nose (hence Common *Pointed*), which, obviously, considerably increased their powers of penetration. It did, however, have the disadvantage that a time fuse could not be used as the British had no design for a base time fuse, nor did they attempt to introduce one until after Jutland! As the 12in common shell had a burster of 80lbs its destructive effects on lightly armoured or unprotected areas was considerably greater than that of the AP shell and it could also have considerable disruptive effects on armour if it burst either on impact or during penetration. A successful design for the new CP shell was produced by the Sheffield projectile manufacturers Hadfields in 1907 and was adopted by the service in the following year. Having a cap they were designated CPC (Common Pointed Capped) and were theoretically capable of perforating armour of about 75 per cent of the thickness that an equivalent APC shell could perforate. Their primary disadvantage was cost – £24 10s each for a 12in projectile compared with £14 10s for the CP shell, although the APC was actually more at £30. The CPC had sharper points than earlier shell – 4crh (calibre radius head)[1] instead of 2crh – which reduced their resistance to movement through the air and hence substantially increased their range and remaining velocity. Thus for any given range their striking velocity, and therefore penetrating powers, were also increased, together with the target's danger space. This modification was also extended to the APC shell in 1908 but in both this case and that of the CPC, the form was achieved in the shape of the cap, the underlying shell remaining at 2crh.

In addition to the above a new type of nose-fused common shell was introduced for heavy-calibre guns in 1908. These were filled with the high explosive Lyddite instead of powder and were generally referred to as either Lyddite Common or HE. They had relatively thin walls, just strong enough to stand the stresses of discharge from a gun and, in the case of the 12in, a burster of around 112lbs. Lyddite was a powerful picric acid explosive which had substantially greater destructive effects than powder. These shells were intended for use against lightly-armoured or unprotected areas although they could cause some disruption to protected structures when exploding on impact. Their blast effects on the interior of a

A perfect example of armour piercing – a neat 12in diameter hole in Tiger's *6in armour. (Imperial War Museum: SP1600)*

ship were considerable and would seriously damage decks and bulkheads in the immediate vicinity. In addition Lyddite produced dense clouds of smoke, which would interrupt the view from the target's turrets and control positions and cause considerable difficulties to the crew as the fumes produced made it almost impossible to breath, making conditions between decks and in enclosed positions very difficult.

In 1909 experiments began with APC shell filled with Lyddite instead of powder in order to enhance their destructive effects. This was not without problems as Lyddite was much more sensitive than powder and inclined to detonate while the shell passed though a plate rather than after perforation. In addition, the tendency for shells to break-up during penetration at oblique attack greatly limited the effect of Lyddite since under these circumstances it would explode rather than detonate, greatly reducing its destructive effect. Nevertheless, this filling was introduced for heavy shell in 1910 despite the fact that it had been shown that the explosive (as opposed to detonation) effect was no greater than that of powder. The effects of explosion or detonation while passing through a plate could still be severe but would obviously be largely to the exterior structure rather than deep inside a ship, except for any splinters being projected forward from the explosion. In the case of Lyddite such fragments would be small and not likely to carry far or penetrate anything at any great distance from the centre of detonation. Finally it should be said that Lyddite filled APC did not invariably fail to perforate armour, their reliability depending a great deal on both the angle of impact and the quality of the shell.

Another possible problem created by the sensitiveness of Lyddite was that it could detonate on impact with armour, resulting in the majority of its energy being expended exterior to the target. It was hoped that this would be solved by replacing Lyddite with TNT, which was sufficiently insensitive to avoid premature detonation both on impact and when passing through an armour plate. However, this in turn created another problem in that the lower sensitivity greatly increased the chance of blinds (failure to detonate). Despite considerable efforts to development an acceptable solution this was not solved until the introduction of reliable detonating fuse in the 1920s.

From the above it can be seen that the British did not expect great things from APC shell, particularly at long ranges, but were much impressed by the power of large-capacity shells and high explosives to cause extensive damage to ships' structures. As the unprotected and lightly-protected areas of a ship represented a much larger proportion of the target than those areas protected by heavy armour there was good reason to believe that CPC and to a lesser extent HE projectiles could cause sufficient damage in themselves to substantially reduce the effectiveness of an enemy vessel. The breaking-up of the ship's structure could cause substantial problems with flooding and affect a ship's speed; it might well disrupt the operation of the armament and would certainly cause problems in the command and control positions. The general philosophy appears to have been one of causing maximum disruptive damage and to so reduce an enemy's fighting efficiency as to seriously weaken his power of accurate reply. This idea was valid enough as far as it went but it placed a premium on early and continuous hitting rather than on obtaining a few seriously damaging hits from shells that perforated the armour and detonated well inside a ship.

One of the more surprising problems

Damage to the 9in barbette armour of *Tiger*'s 'X' turret at Jutland. From the top this shows the gunhouse, the 9in barbette armour between gunhouse and upper deck, the holed upper deck and the 3in barbette armour below. The shell hit the lower edge of the 9in armour near the deck, broke off a section and entered the gun mounting but fortunately failed to detonate properly. The turret was back in action after a few minutes but at reduced efficiency. One of the primary lessons of the Jutland damage was that the edges of armour plates needed better support. (Imperial War Museum: SP3159)

created by the limited performance of APC shell was that the Admiralty made no effort to fully inform the fleet. General publications, such as the Gunnery Manual and Gunnery Memoranda, gave the general impression that these projectiles were, within reasonable limits of range and obliquity, expected to pass through armour and detonate beyond it. This impression was not corrected until after Jutland when, as a result of questions being asked, some more qualified statements of APC shell performance were issued.

As a result of the pre-war developments of HE filled shell there was a strong emphasis in British ships on splinter protection and medium thicknesses of armour. In *Indefatigable* the armour, while similar to that of *Invincible*, was thinned and spread out to a greater extent. The belt armour was extended to the full length of the ship, which gave better security to the after end, and in particular the steering gear, but its thickness was reduced abreast 'A' and 'X' turrets from 6in to 4in, emphasising a preference for defence of the ship's motive power and buoyancy over that of her armament that was to continue throughout the pre-war battlecruiser designs. In addition, the forward section of the side armour was reduced from 4in to 2.5in and increased in height by about 5ft. Splinter protection was provided for the funnel uptakes between the main and upper decks and, to a height of 2ft from the main deck, for the ventilation trunks to the main and auxiliary machinery compartments. This was also provided in all subsequent battlecruisers and was to remain a consistent thickness of 1.5in on the sides and 1in on the ends throughout. In the *Invincible* class KNC quality plating (similar to the armour of that type but with the face-hardening process omitted) had been used for the upper layers of the protective deck plating. In *Indefatigable* this was improved further by the adoption of nickel steel for the protective plating which had the desirable combination of both toughness and the ability to except considerable deformation without splitting. This continued to be used until *Queen Mary* was designed when HT steel, which was of equal quality but considerably cheaper, was substituted.

The *Lion* design saw a substantial increase in the level of protection but this was again largely directed towards the defence of the ship's motive power and bouyancy and in other respects the resulting ship was little better than the earlier 12in-gun battlecruisers. The principal changes were an increase in the main belt to 9in over the length of the machinery spaces (and coincidentally the midships magazines) and the addition of a 6in upper belt between the main and upper decks. In addition a second, 1in, protective deck was provided across the top of the citadel and the lower deck thinned to a uniform 1in in the same area, thus forming a closed box. The upper protective deck was intended to stop shells that passed over the side armour and fragments of shell which burst in the upperworks of the ship. The lower protective deck, besides its usual functions, served as a secondary line of defence if the upper deck was penetrated. While the increase in the height of the side armour recognised the increasing ranges and steeper angles of descent likely in future actions, the weakening of the main protective

Indefatigable armour diagram.

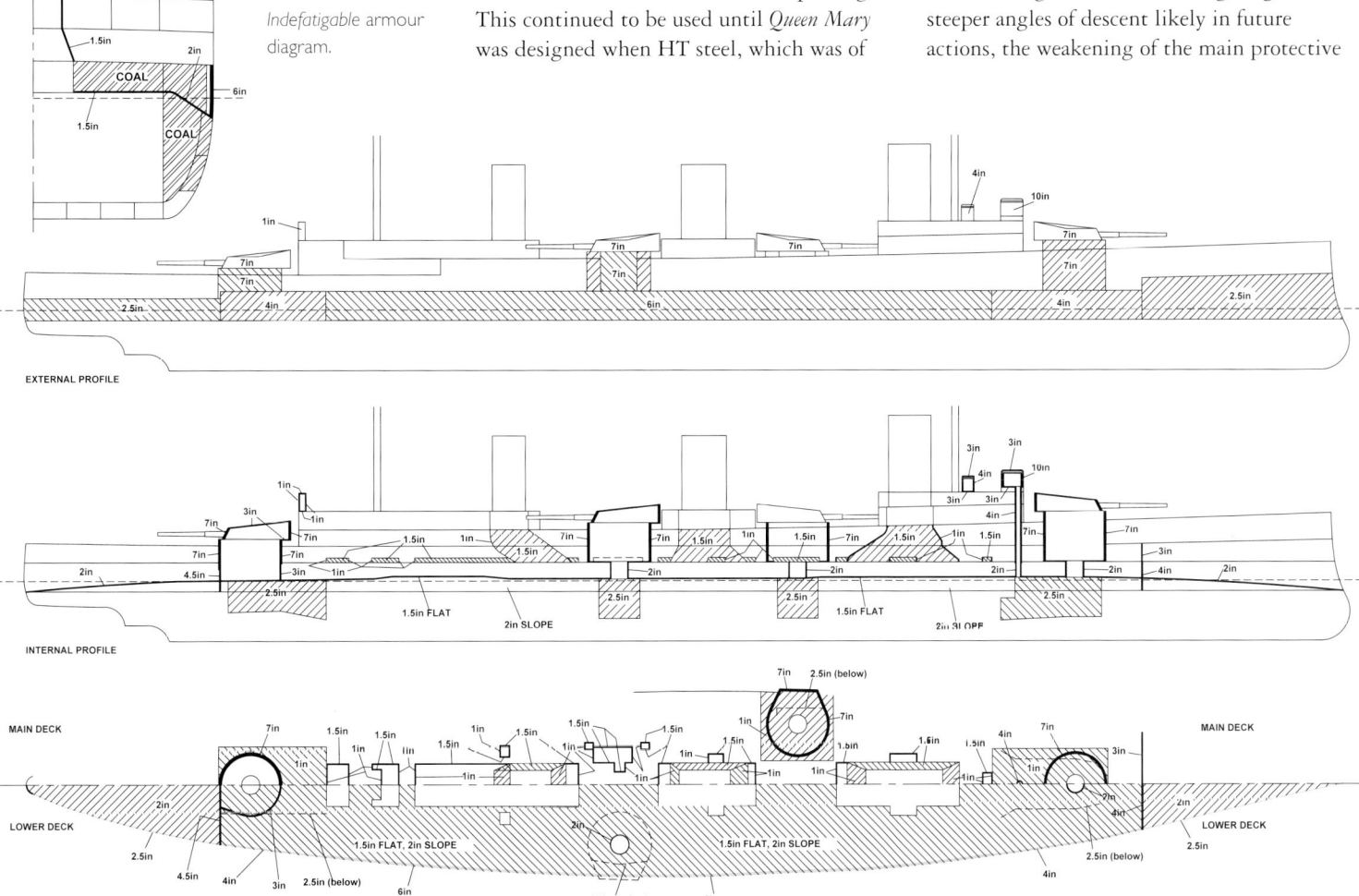

deck and the fact that the barbettes were reduced in thickness between the main and upper decks considerably reduced the effectiveness of the scheme, especially as the ranges at which actions were eventually to be fought were much greater than anticipated. In the original design the side armour did not extend much beyond the end barbettes where it was closed by 5in bulkheads. However, in 1910 it was decided to extend the side armour both fore and aft (although still not to the ends of the ship) with 4in armour, the ends being closed with 4in bulkheads. The original 5in bulkheads were omitted and the side armour and deck protection rearranged to suit. The belt abreast the forward and after barbettes gave little better protection than that provided in the *Indefatigable* (5in instead of 4in) but was enhanced to a slight extent by the provision of a 6in main belt abreast 'B' barbette only and an increase in the thickness of the splinter protection to the lower parts of the barbettes. The advantages of the higher side armour in this area were largely negated by the thinner barbettes. The modifications made to *Lion* with regard to the arrangement of the armour at the ends of the citadel and the provision of a second protective deck were also adopted in *Australia* and *New Zealand* and the pattern of *Lion*'s armour was followed, with only minor variation, in *Queen Mary* and *Tiger*. The latter ship gained a further increase in the height of the side armour by courtesy of the armoured battery for the secondary armament. However, even in the latter case the barbette armour was thinned to 3in between the upper and forecastle decks where they were behind the battery armour.

This progressively improved but flawed development of the battlecruisers' protective system came to an abrupt halt with the *Renown* class. In these ships the scheme of defence varied little from that originally provided in the *Invincible* class and one cannot help but conclude that Fisher specifically requested that this should be the case. In fact the protection was if anything slightly inferior to that of the *Invincibles*, because unlike the earlier ships, they carried only oil and therefore lost the added protection provided by the coal bunkers which in the pre-war ships were regarded as an important part of the defensive system – particularly in the case of the upper bunkers which were immediately behind the side armour. In addition to this, the flat of the protective deck amidships was at the same level as the top of the belt so a shell could easily have passed just over the top of the belt and entered the vitals of the ship through the 2in slope of the protective deck. After Jutland some piecemeal additions were made to the protective plating (as detailed in the armour tables) but these were little more than temporary expedients and both *Renown* and *Repulse* were subject to substantial reconstruction and re-armouring during 1918–21 and 1923–6 respectively.

In the large light cruisers a very odd arrangement of protection was adopted in that while the gun positions and conning tower were armoured on the same scale as that of a battlecruiser, the hull protection was equal to that of a light cruiser. This author, at least, can think of no logic in this arrangement as it implies defence against

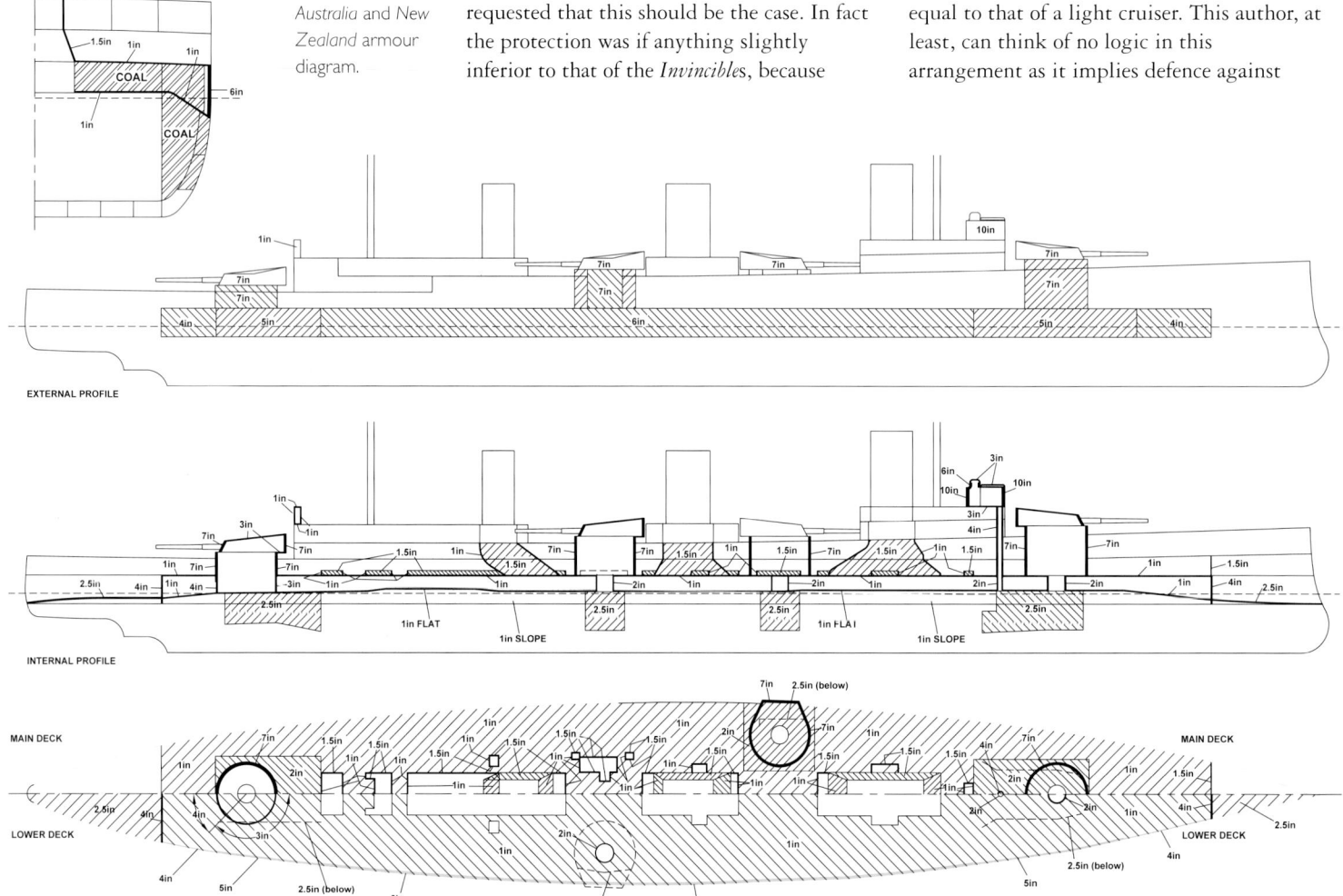

Australia and *New Zealand* armour diagram.

ARMOUR | 105

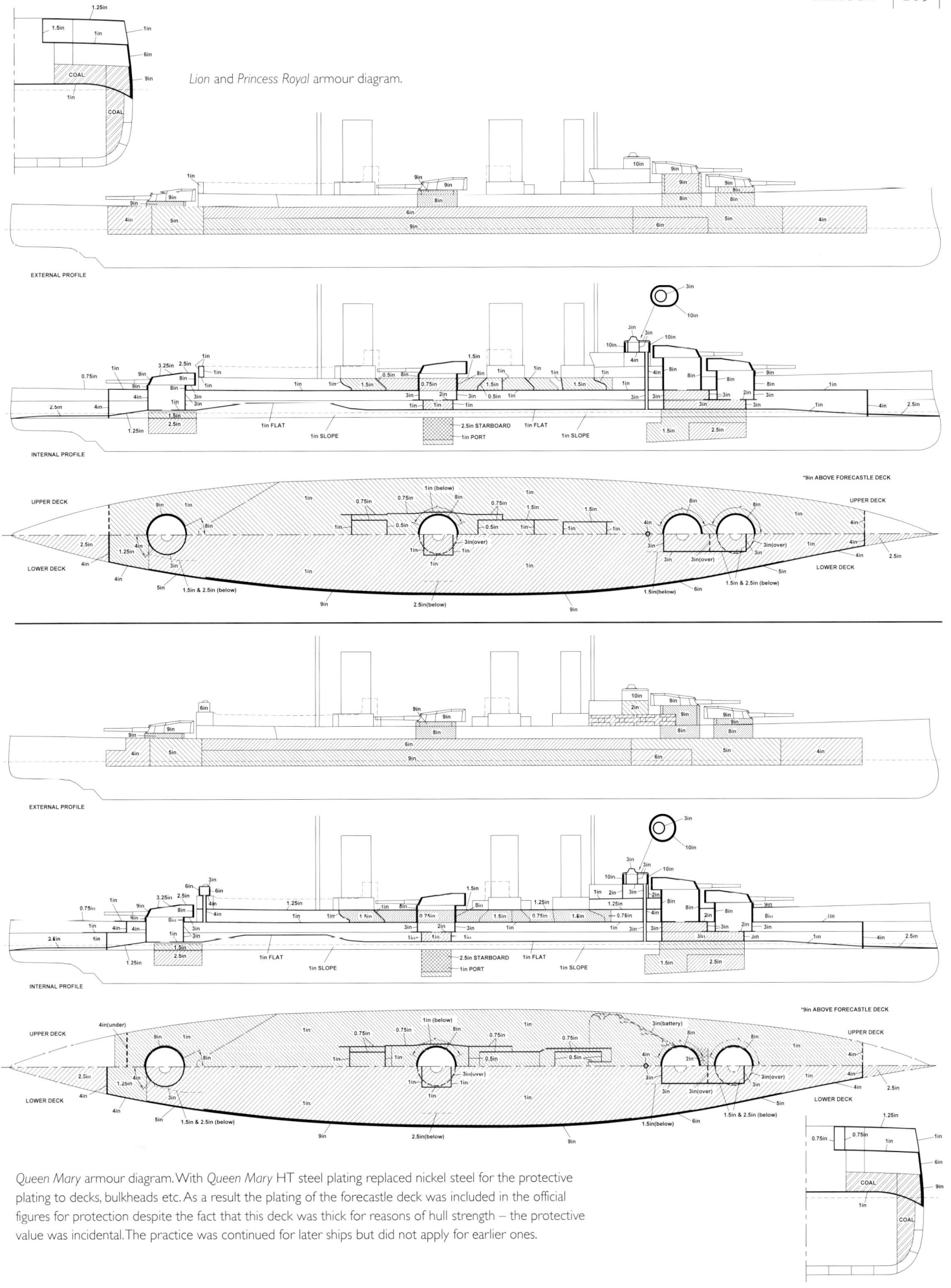

Lion and *Princess Royal* armour diagram.

Queen Mary armour diagram. With *Queen Mary* HT steel plating replaced nickel steel for the protective plating to decks, bulkheads etc. As a result the plating of the forecastle deck was included in the official figures for protection despite the fact that this deck was thick for reasons of hull strength – the protective value was incidental. The practice was continued for later ships but did not apply for earlier ones.

106 | BRITISH BATTLECRUISERS

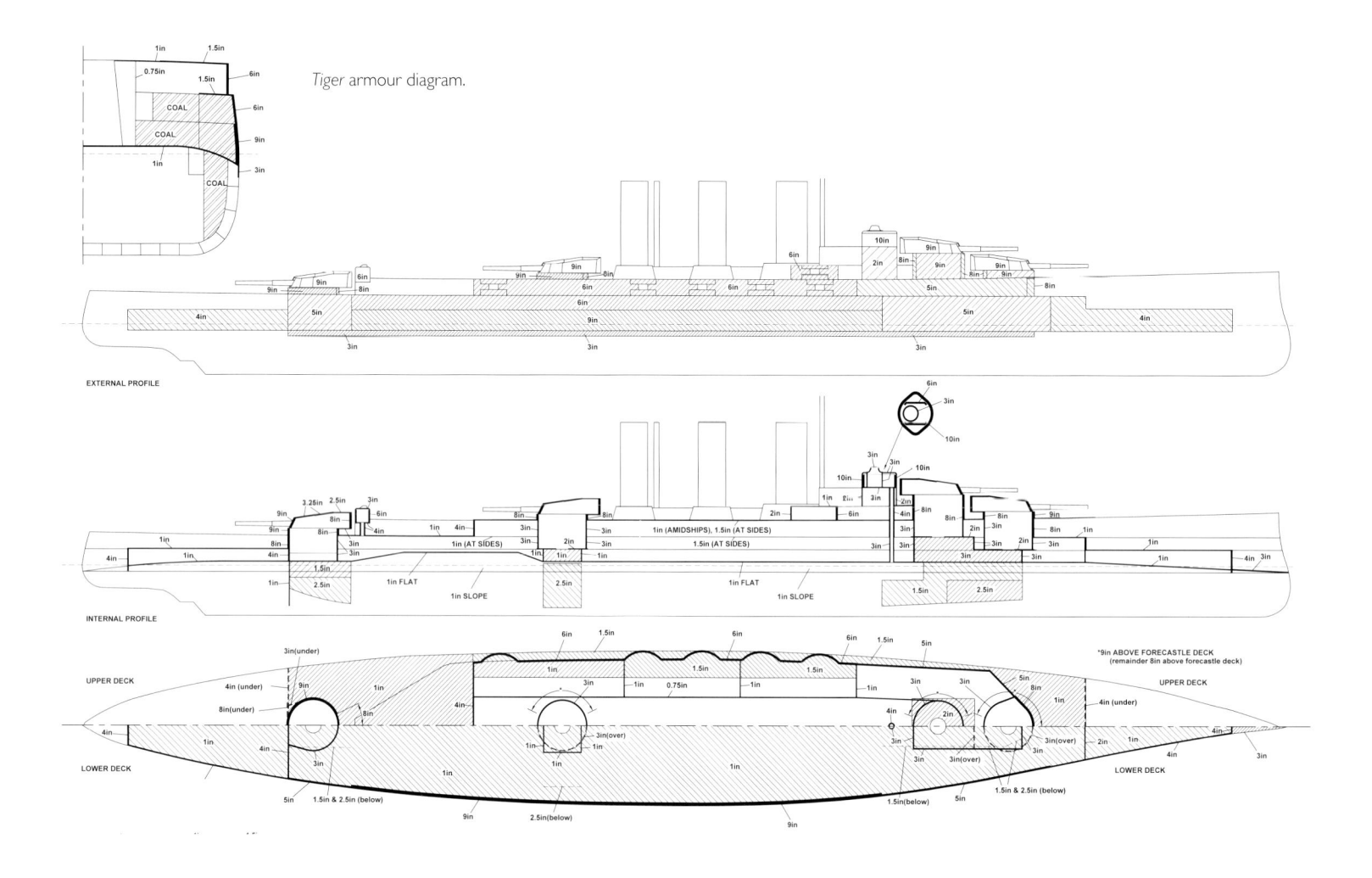

Tiger armour diagram.

Tiger in 1917 with *Lion* in the background. (Author's collection)

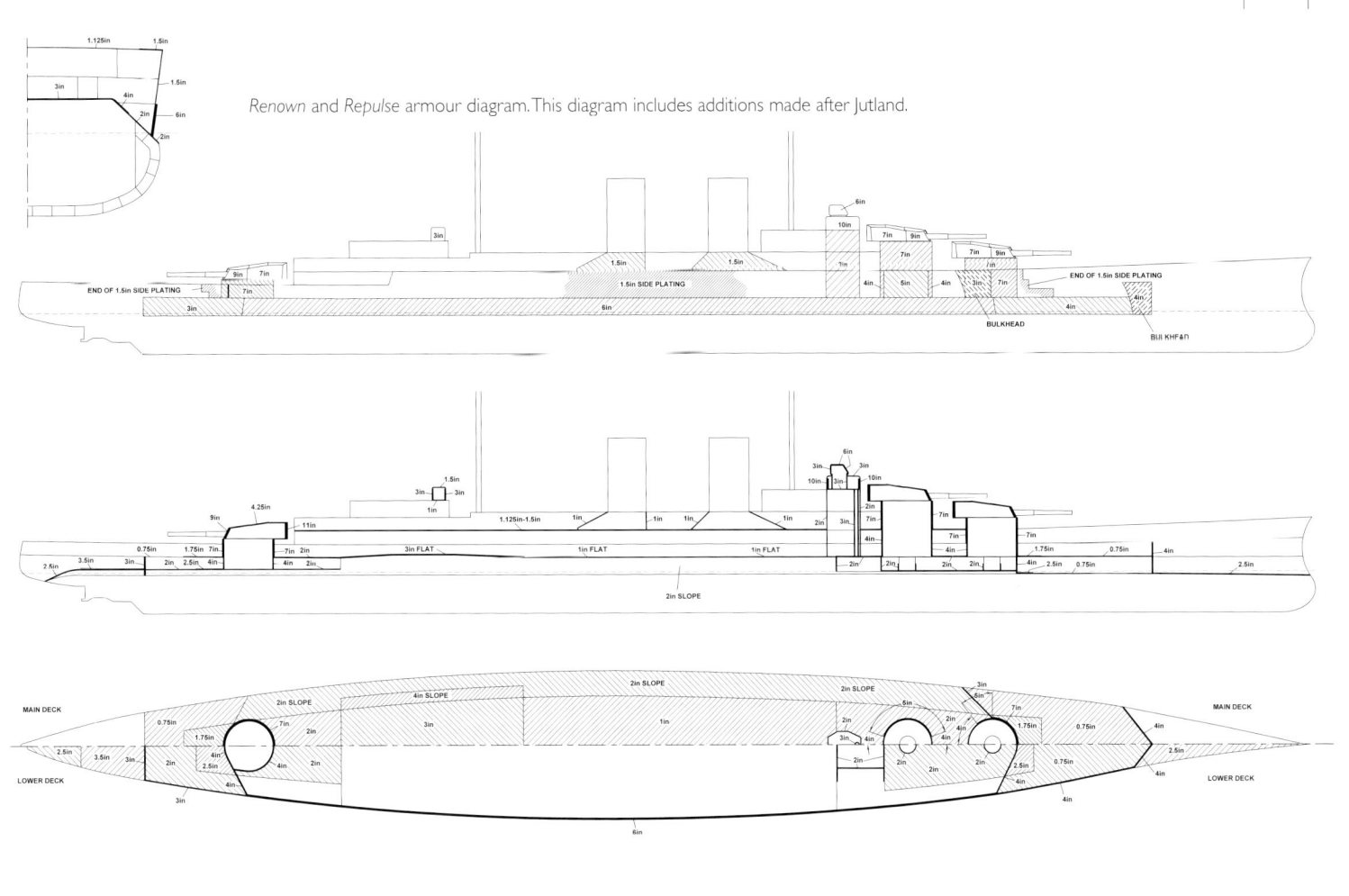

ARMOUR | 107

Renown and *Repulse* armour diagram. This diagram includes additions made after Jutland.

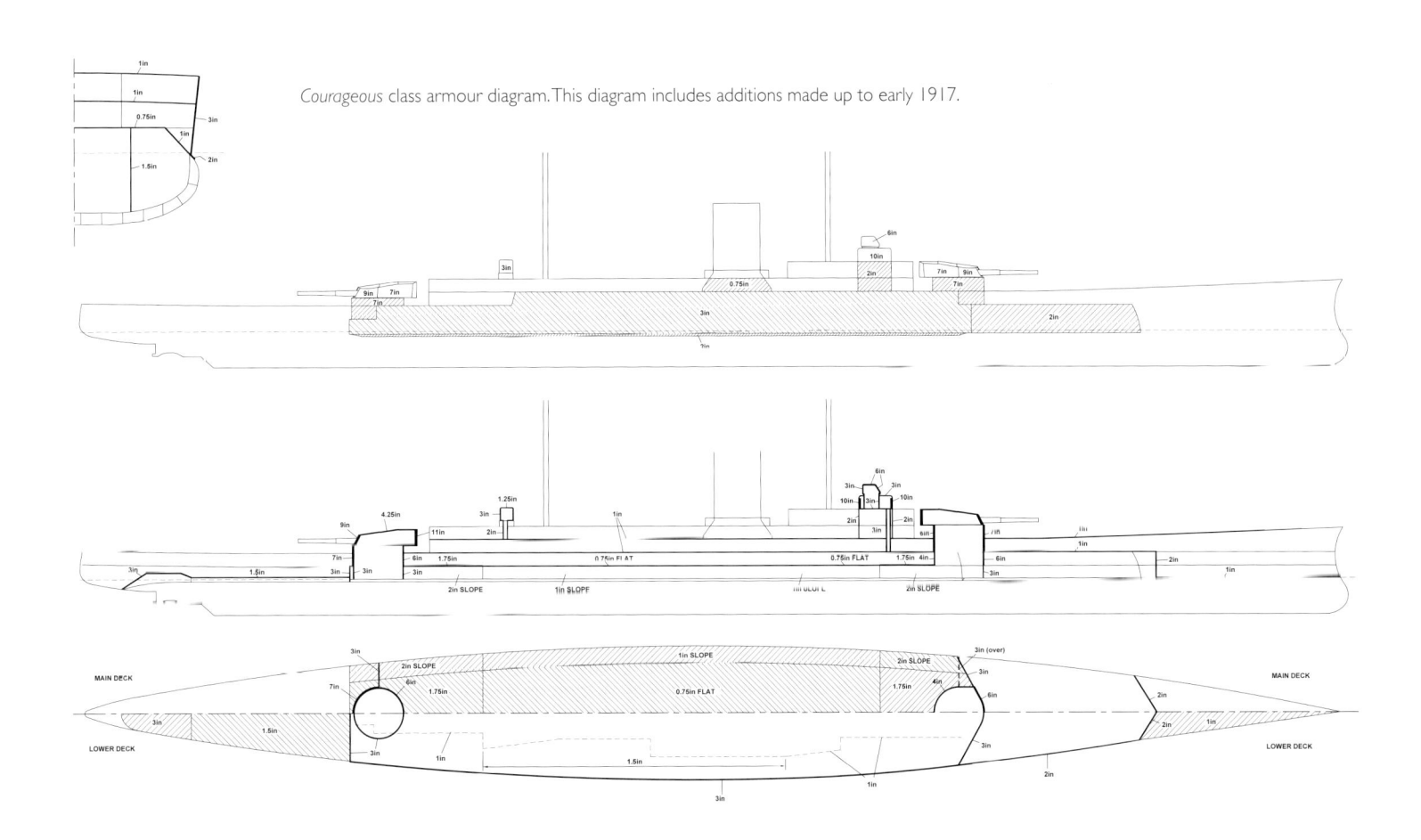

Courageous class armour diagram. This diagram includes additions made up to early 1917.

Hood armour diagram.

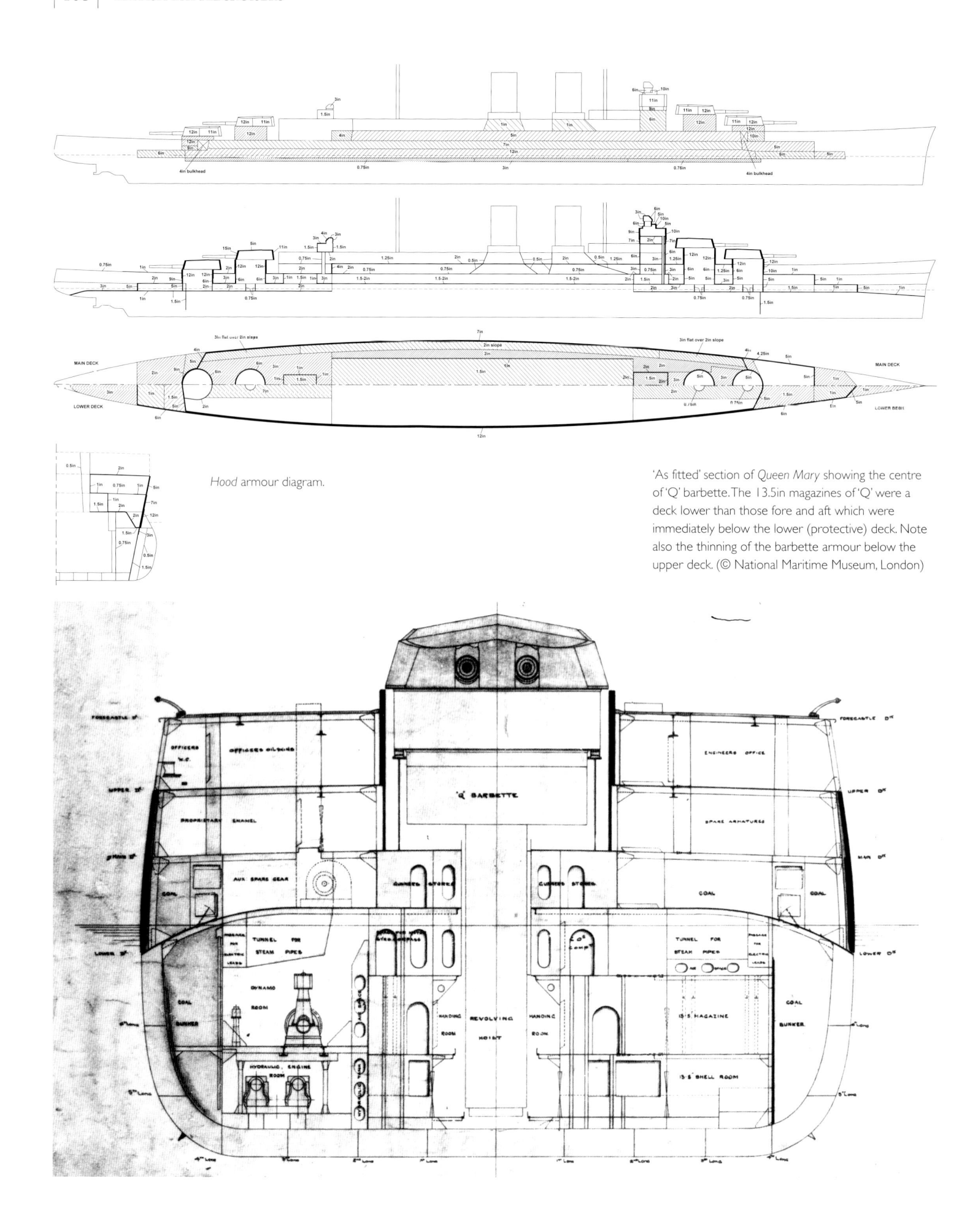

'As fitted' section of *Queen Mary* showing the centre of 'Q' barbette. The 13.5in magazines of 'Q' were a deck lower than those fore and aft which were immediately below the lower (protective) deck. Note also the thinning of the barbette armour below the upper deck. (© National Maritime Museum, London)

heavy guns in the former case and medium to light guns in the latter. The most likely explanation would seem to be that they were intended to engage only with light forces and that the heavy armour on the gun positions was partly because the gunhouses were standard and partly a continuation of the original battlecruiser idea of giving maximum defence to the barbettes and conning tower.

Hood, of course, was a very different proposition. By the standards of 1914 she was armoured on the scale of a battleship but this had been achieved by a gradual enhancement of her design rather than being planned from the start. In effect she managed to fall between the pre-war and post-war standards of protection, being advanced for the former but inadequate for the latter. In particular, the post-war standard required the use of armour rather than protective plating for decks and there was substantially less emphasis on splinter protection. The overall scheme adopted by the British in the 1920s was based on the all-or-nothing principle, standard in US Navy battleship designs since before the war, in which there was a heavily protected central citadel and very little protection outside it.

Turrets

War experience showed that British gunhouse protection was far from adequate and, in addition, the form of the structure itself contained a number of weaknesses. Foremost amongst these was the design of the roof and front plate, which sloped in such a way as to be more likely to be struck by a projectile at a shallower angle of impact than might otherwise have been the case. The problem was addressed in the design of *Hood*'s gunhouses, which were much squarer than those of earlier designs. British gunhouses also had a considerable number of detail weaknesses, which are summarised below:

(a) The gunports, although unavoidable, were weak areas and could allow splinters to enter the gunhouse. In the earlier 12in mountings these were completely open but in later designs a splinter shield was fitted to the gun on the inside of the port to limit such effects – they also served to improve the blast protection.

(b) In the earlier 12in mountings there were substantial gaps between the base of the gunhouse and the top of the barbette which, if a shell hit the gunhouse wall, could allow splinters access to the interior of the mounting.

(c) The sighting ports on the turret roofs both provided a projection above the roof which could initiate a shell's fuse and openings which weakened the roof and could allow splinters and shells to enter. During the war there were several instances of shells removing sighting hoods and of shell detonations in or near the openings.

(d) The addition of raised rangefinder hoods at the rear of turrets again provided a point of impact for shells which was more vulnerable to penetration than the roof proper. The later designs for these were improved to some extent. In the converted 12in gunhouses the hood had to be adapted to the existing structure and were relatively high, while those fitted in the 13.5in and 15in gunhouses had a flatter profile.

Torpedo protection

Fisher always regarded the danger of underwater damage from the torpedo and mine with the utmost concern, particularly after the Russo-Japanese war in which these weapons demonstrated clearly their ability to sink large vessels very rapidly. In fact this was the only area of passive defence for which Fisher seems to have been willing to accept the addition of weight to a design even if it meant a loss in speed. In his introduction to the first meeting of the Committee on Designs he pointed out that:

> The first-class Russian battleship *Petropavlovsk* sank in two minutes from the effects of the explosion of a submarine mine combined with the explosion of her magazine. The first-class Japanese battleship *Hatsuse* occupied ninety seconds in sinking from the same causes. In the new designs of battleship and armoured cruiser it is hoped to minimise the danger of such catastrophes by having inviolate main bulkheads, so that the watertight compartments *shall* be watertight, and by having a magazine under each pair of guns so situated as to be as far as possible from a mine explosion. It is proposed to place the magazines as near as possible to the middle line plane of the ship high up from the bottom, and to armour the bottom and sides.[2]

Before the Committee on Designs sat, Andrew Noble had suggested to Fisher that protective plates of soft steel (to allow the maximum of distortion before the plate split) might be used to protect magazines below the waterline. He also offered to test the theory by experiment and these duly took place about late 1904. These tests employed 5in mild steel plates, which were out of the question from a practical point of view because of the great weight involved. However, the effect of an explosion falls off rapidly with distance and it was realised that thinner plates placed well inboard could provide a good level of defence against explosions on a ship's side. These matters were discussed at the Committee meeting on 21 February 1905 during which it was pointed out that the addition of 2in plates at

The roof of *Tiger*'s 'Q' turret showing damage received at Jutland. The indent at the left of the opening is the point of contact of a shell which detonated on impact blowing off the centre sighting hood, the rectangular opening of which is at the right with the remains of the sighting gear at its centre. There was a good deal of detail damage inside the gunhouse but the guns were soon back in action. (Imperial War Museum: SP1597)

the sides and bottoms of the magazines would still add a substantial amount of weight. In the end a compromise was reached in that it was decided that the bottom protection could be omitted, as torpedoes and mines would almost certainly explode against the side of a ship rather than underneath it, and that defence need only be provided for torpedoes and small mines. The scheme eventually adopted in the *Invincible* class was to fit 2.5in-thick screen bulkheads abreast the magazines and shell rooms extending from the inner bottom to the protective deck. These bulkheads were not a great distance from the ship's side – about 8ft for the midships magazines and an average 10ft for those fore and aft (there was no consistent distance because of the curves of the hull). This arrangement and thickness of bulkhead continued to be used in all the battlecruisers up to and including *Tiger*. In the later ships there was some improvement in the distance inboard of the bulkheads of the forward and after magazines but this was generally used as an excuse for thinning them – in the 13.5in gun ships the bulkheads abreast 'B' magazine were reduced to 1.75in and the port bulkhead to 'Q' magazine to 1in (it was further inboard than that to starboard as the magazine was offset from the middle line). Despite the fact that between 1905 and 1914 the torpedo had increased in size and power, little effort seems to have been made to improve on this arrangement until after the outbreak of war, when the effects of underwater weapons became all too clear.

Renown, Repulse and the large light cruisers adopted a form of integral bulge that projected beyond the ship's side and was intended to allow an underwater explosion free access to vent upwards, experiments having shown that this was a natural tendency. However, the depth of the protection was still shallow and there was no thick torpedo bulkhead, the internal bulkhead being only 0.75in thick. As related in Chapter 3, these bulkheads were actually strengthened in the large light cruisers on Fisher's instructions but it was too late to carry out this modification in *Renown* and *Repulse*.

'As fitted' midship section of *Courageous* showing the form of the hull with its integral 'bulge' which was intended to allow torpedo explosions greater scope to vent upwards outside the hull. (© National Maritime Museum, London)

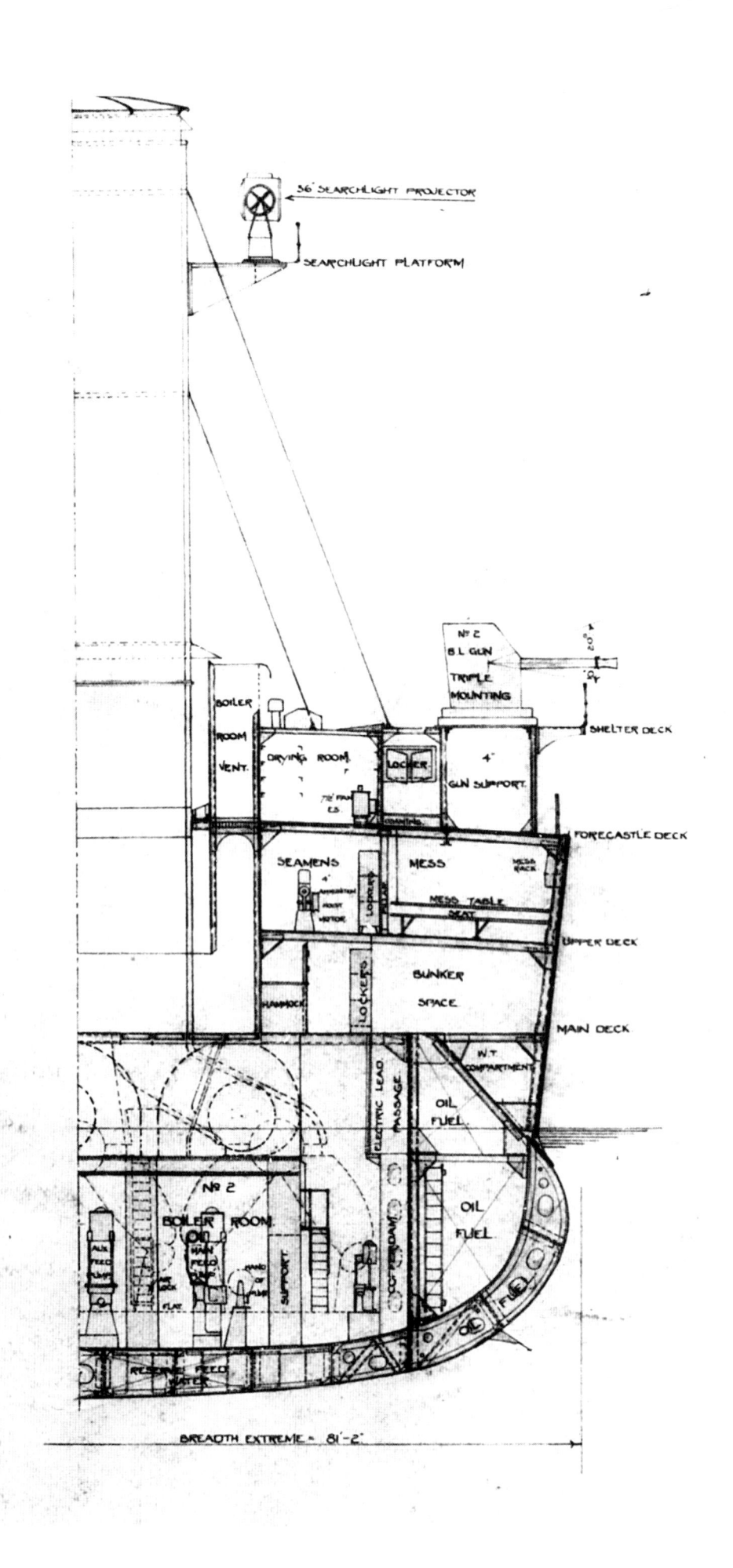

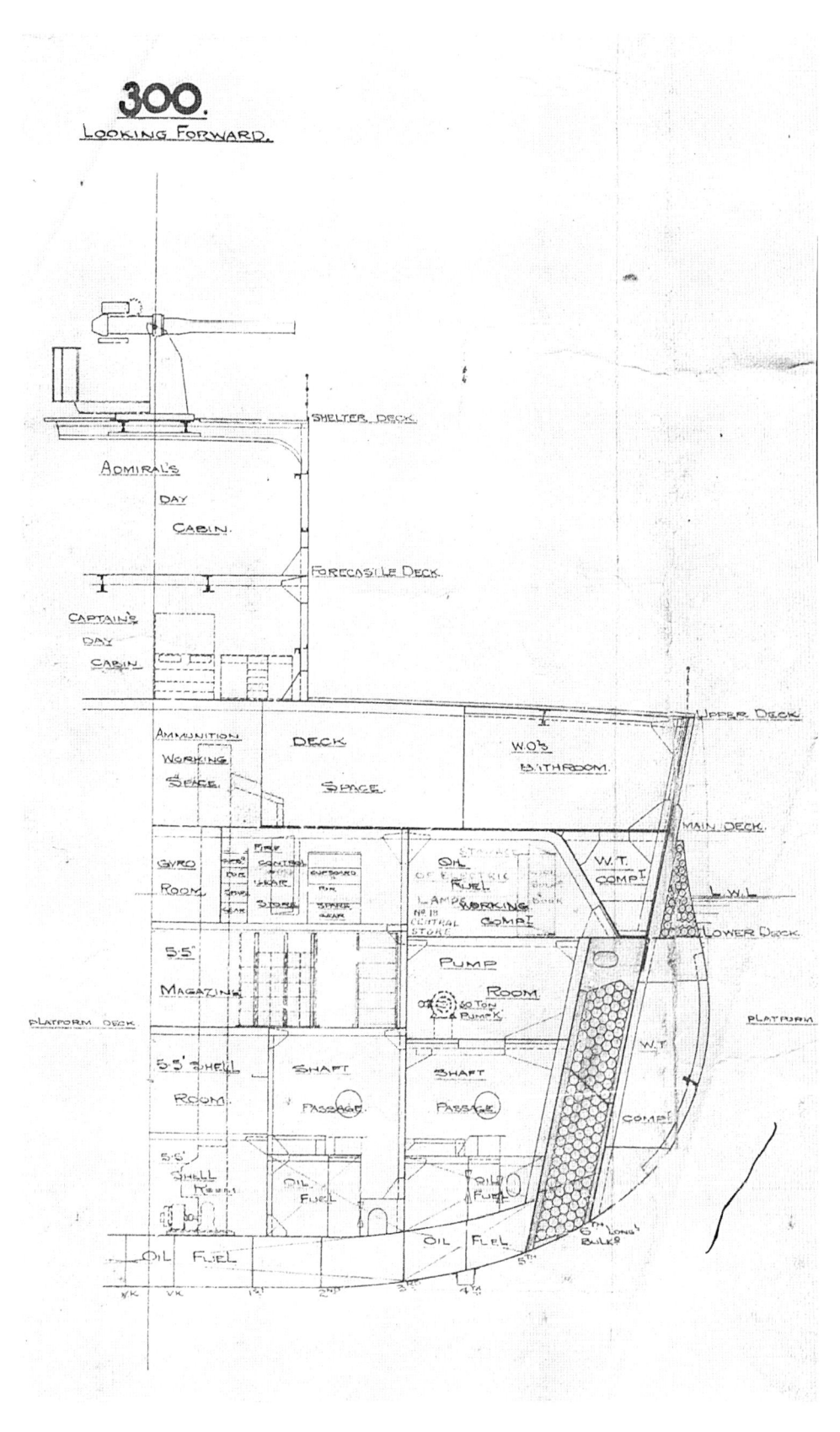

'Half section at *Hood*'s after 5.5in magazines just forward of 'X' mounting showing the crushing tubes fitted in both the buoyancy space (between the void outer bulge compartment and the torpedo bulkhead) and in the triangular space at the top of the external bulge. Note that here, and forward, the buoyancy space was internal to the hull proper whereas amidships it was external. (© National Maritime Museum, London)

In *Hood* the design of the underwater protection system received much more serious consideration. The arrangement was chosen on the basis of a series of experiments begun in 1914 that culminated in large-scale tests against the Chatham Float in late 1915. These were intended to test various ideas and provide information as to the best form for the underwater defence within the limits imposed by available docking facilities and the space required for the main machinery compartments etc. As in *Renown* a bulge integral with the hull was adopted but in this case entirely exterior to the hull proper. The bulge was divided into an outer air space and an inner tube space – the latter filled with steel 'crushing' tubes, sealed at both ends and intended to absorb (and distribute more widely) much of the energy produced by an underwater explosion and to reduce the momentum of the splinters produced. The inner wall of the tube space, which was in effect the true outer skin of the ship, consisted of a 1.5in-thick torpedo bulkhead strongly supported by 12in 'I' girders. Although by no means perfect the arrangement was far better than any of those in earlier ships, battleships included, and provided a basis for the future development of underwater protection systems that continued into the Second World War.

A secondary line of underwater defence was provided in the pre-war battlecruisers by the adoption of torpedo net defence. However, this could only be used in harbour or when moving at very low speed and once torpedoes were fitted with net cutters their utility was highly questionable. The abolition of these nets was discussed in 1912 and it was approved to omit them from all new construction ships in the following year, on the basis that their limited value did not balance the disadvantages – additional weight, danger that damaged nets or booms would foul the propellers and the fact that the heel fittings for the booms locally weakened the belt armour. Despite this they were retained in the earlier battlecruisers well into 1916, probably because the anti-submarine defences at Rosyth were not considered sufficient. It would seem more than likely that this was also the reason for deciding that *Renown* and *Repulse* should be fitted with torpedo net defence, although this idea was dropped before their construction had progressed far. The defences at Scapa Flow were much better and the battleships of the Grand Fleet abandoned their net defences much earlier.

Table 43: Particulars of Armour

Invincible class
BELT: 6in KC amidships, 4in KC forward, none aft.
BULKHEADS: 6in KC between 'X' barbette and after ends of main belt.
BARBETTES: 7in KC above main belt and on 'X' barbette between 6in bulkheads.
FORWARD CT: 10in KC front and sides, 7in KC rear, 3in KNC signal tower, 2in KNC roof and floor, 4in KNC communication tube.
AFTER CT: 6in KC walls, 2in KNC roof and floor, 3in KNC communication tube.
GUNSHIELDS: 7in KC walls, 3in KNC roof, 3in rear floor.
MAIN DECK: 1in to base of 'A', 'P' and 'Q' barbettes and crown of after lower CT, 2 in to crown of forward lower CT.
LOWER DECK: 1.5in on flat and 2in on slope amidships, 1.5in forward, 2.5in aft.
SPLINTER BULKHEADS: (Main to upper deck) 2in KNC to bases of barbettes, forward and after lower CTs.
TORPEDO BULKHEADS: (abreast magazines) 2.5in MS.

Indefatigable
BELT: 6in KC amidships, 4in KC abreast 'A' and 'X' barbettes, 2.5in KNC forward and aft.
BULKHEADS: 4in and 3in KC forward, 4.5in KC aft.
BARBETTES: 7in KC above main belt, 2in splinter protection to hoist between main and lower deck. ('X' barbette 4in KC between main and lower deck.)
FORWARD CT: 10in KC walls, 3in KNC floor and roof, 4in KNC communication tube.
SIGNAL AND SPOTTING TOWER: 4in KC walls, 3in KNC floor and roof.
TORPEDO DIRECTOR TOWER: 1in NS walls, floor and roof.
GUNSHIELDS: 7in KC walls, 3in KNC roof, 3in floor plate at rear.
MAIN DECK: 2in NS under barbettes.
LOWER DECK: 1.5in NS flat and 2in NS slope amidships, 2in NS forward, 2.5in NS aft.
FUNNEL UPTAKES: (main to forecastle deck) 1.5in NS sides, 1in NS ends. (Also fitted to machinery ventilation trunks etc for 2ft above main deck)
TORPEDO BULKHEADS: 2.5in NS abreast magazines.

Australia and *New Zealand* as *Indefatigable* except:
BELT: 6in KC amidships, 5in KC abreast 'A' and 'X' barbettes, 4in KC at ends.
BULKHEADS: 4in KC fore and aft, 1.5in NS splinter bulkhead between main and upper deck above forward 4in bulkhead.
FORWARD CT: 10in KC walls, 3in KNC roof, 6in cast steel spotting tower with 3in roof (note this was integral with CT and not separate as in *Indefatigable*), 4in KNC communication tube.
MAIN DECK: 1in NS, 2in NS under barbettes.
LOWER DECK: 1in NS amidships, 2in NS forward, 2.5in NS aft.

Lion class
MAIN BELT: 9in KC amidships, 6in KC abreast 'B' turret, 5in KC abreast 'A' and 'X' turrets, 4in forward and aft.
UPPER BELT: 6in KC amidships, 5in KC abreast 'A', 'B' and 'X' turrets, 4in forward and aft.
BULKHEADS: 4in KC forward and aft.
BARBETTES: 9in and 8in KC above upper deck, 3in and 4in KC below upper deck.
FORWARD CT: 10in KC walls, 3in KNC roof, 4in KNC floor, 4in and 3in KNC communication tube.
TORPEDO DIRECTOR TOWER: 1in NS walls, floor and roof.
GUNSHIELDS: 9in KC front and sides, 8in KC rear, 3.25in roof (front plates), 2.5in roof (rear plate), 3in rear floor.
UPPER DECK: 1in NS over citadel.
LOWER DECK: 1.25in–1in NS amidships, 2.5in at ends.
FUNNEL UPTAKES: 1.5in NS sides, 1in NS ends between upper deck and forecastle deck.
TORPEDO BULKHEADS: 2.5in–1.5in NS abreast magazines (port bulkhead to 'Q' magazine 1in NS).

Queen Mary as *Lion* class except:
AFTER TORPEDO CT: 6in KC walls, 3in cast steel roof, 4in KNC floor, 4in KNC communication tube.
FORWARD 4IN GUN BATTERY: 3in KC sides, 2in HT deck over.
FORECASTLE DECK: 1.25–1in HT.
PROTECTIVE PLATING: torpedo bulkheads, decks, funnel uptakes etc all of HT steel.
FORWARD CT: 2in KNC protection to base.

Tiger
MAIN BELT: 9in KC amidships, 5in KC abreast 'A', 'B' and 'X' turrets, 4in KC forward and aft.
UPPER BELT: 6in KC amidships, 5in KC abreast 'A', 'B' and 'X' turrets, 4in KC forward.
LOWER BELT: 3in KC.
6IN GUN BATTERY: 6in KC side amidships, 5in KC sides and bulkheads forward, 4in KC bulkhead aft.
BULKHEADS: 4in KC and 2in KNC forward, 4in KC aft.

BARBETTES: 9in and 8in KC outside citadel, 4in and 3in KC inside citadel, 3in KNC sides and bulkheads to base of 'A' and 'B' barbettes between lower and main decks.
FORWARD CT: 10in KC walls, 3in KNC roof, 3in cast steel rangefinder hood, 3in KNC GCT, 4in KNC floor, 2in KNC base to CT, 4in and 3in KNC communication tube.
AFTER TORPEDO CT: 6in KC walls, 3in cast steel roof, 4in KNC floor, 4in KNC communicating tube.
SIGHTING HOODS: (for 6in guns) 6in.
6IN CASEMATES (forecastle deck): 6in KC sides, 2in KNC rear, 1in HT roof.
GUNSHIELDS: 9in KC face and sides, 8in KC rear, 3.25in roof (front plate), 2.5in roof (rear plate).
FORECASTLE DECK: 1in (amidships) and 1.5in (sides) HT over 6in battery.
UPPER DECK: 1in and 1.5in HT fore and aft.
MAIN DECK: 1in HT.
LOWER DECK: 1in (amidships) and 3in (forward) HT.
TORPEDO BULKHEADS: (abreast magazines) 2.5in and 1.5in HT (1in HT transverse bulkhead abaft 'X' magazine).

Renown and *Repulse*
MAIN BELT: 6in KC amidships, 4in KC forward, 3in KC aft.
BULKHEADS: 4in and 3in KC fore and aft.
BARBETTES: 7in, 5in and 4in KC.
FORWARD CT: 10in KC walls, 3in KNC roof, 6in–3in cast steel hood, 2in base, 3in KNC floor, 3in and 2in KNC communication tube.
GUNSHIELDS: 9in KC front, 9in KC forward side plates, 7in KC rear side plates, 11in rear, 4.25in KNC roof.
TORPEDO CT: 3in KC.
FORECASTLE DECK: 0.75in–1.5in HT.
MAIN DECK: 1in HT (2in HT over magazines) flat, 2in HT slope (increased to 3in flat and 4in slope over engine rooms in 1917).
LOWER DECK: 2.5in HT fore and aft (increased to 3.5in over steering gear in 1917), 1.75in HT amidships (1.75in HT over 'A' and 'Y' magazines).
FUNNEL UPTAKES: 1.5in HT sides, 1in HT ends between forecastle and shelter decks.

Courageous class
BELT: 2in HT on 1in HT shell plating amidships, 1in HT on 1in HT shell plating forward.
BULKHEADS: 2in and 3in forward, 3in aft.
BARBETTES: 7in and 6in KC above main deck, 4in and 3in KC between lower and main deck.
GUNSHIELDS: 9in KC front, 9in KC forward side plates, 7in KC rear side plates, 11in rear, 4.25in KNC roof.
FORECASTLE DECK: 0.75–1in HT.
UPPER DECK: 1in HT forward and abreast 'X' barbette.
MAIN DECK: 0.75in HT flat, 1in HT slope (2in HT over magazines).
LOWER DECK: 1in HT forward, 1in–1.5in HT aft. (3in over steering gear).
TORPEDO BULKHEADS: 1.5in–1in HT.
FUNNEL UPTAKES: 0.75in sides (forecastle to shelter deck).

Furious as *Courageous* class except:
GUNSHIELDS: 9in KC front and sides, 11in rear, 5in KNC roof.

Hood
MAIN BELT: 12in KC amidships, 6in and 5in KC forward, 6in KC aft.
MIDDLE BELT: 7in KC amidships, 5in KC forward.
UPPER BELT: 5in KC amidships.
LOWER BELT: 3in KNC abreast boiler rooms, 0.75in HT abreast magazines and engine rooms.
BULKHEADS: 5in KC fore and aft (4in KC at aft end of upper belt).
BARBETTES: 12in and 10in KC outside citadel, 6in and 5in KC inside citadel.
GUNHOUSES: 15in KC front, 12in KC (front) and 11in KC (rear) side plates, 11in KC back, 5in KNC roof.
FORWARD CT: 11in, 10in, 9in and 7in KC walls, 5in KNC roof, 2in KNC floors, 6in NC and 3in KC base, 3in KNC communication tube, 10in, 6in and 5in GCT, 6in–3in cast steel director hood.
TORPEDO CT: 3in sides, 3in roof, 2in floor, 4in–3in cast steel hood, 0.75in HT communication tube.
FORECASTLE DECK: 1.75in–2in HT.
UPPER DECK: 0.75in–2in HT.
MAIN DECK: 1in–3in HT (plus 2in slope).
LOWER DECK: 1in–3in HT.
TORPEDO BULKHEADS: 1.5in–1.75in HT.
SPLINTER BULKHEADS: 1in–2in HT.

Note: All the battlecruisers up to and including *Tiger* had additional 1in plating fitted to the magazine crowns and turret roofs after Jutland. These alterations were carried out in the later ships before completion and are reflected in the above tables.

Conclusion

Judging Fisher's battlecruiser concept is difficult, as he never clearly defined his ultimate intentions for the type. The original vessels of the *Invincible* and *Indefatigable* classes were simply armoured cruisers armed with 12in guns, a combination which can only be regarded as valid so long as they only had armoured cruisers of the older type to face. Their value would, and did, diminish dramatically on the production of a similar type by a foreign power. Unfortunately for the British, the German approach was more along the lines of a fast Second Class battleship than a big-gun armoured cruiser. All the 12in gun British ships were seriously outclassed by their German rivals, which were better protected and, more importantly in relation to Fisher's ideas, faster. It actually seems likely that after the first battlecruisers were laid down the officers of the Admiralty, with the sole exception of Fisher, began to doubt the whole concept – hence the lack of any further ships of this type in the Naval Estimates of the following two years and the proposed return to the 9.2in gun when the armoured cruiser did eventually come up for discussion. However, as soon as Germany began to build such vessels the British had little choice but to follow and in so doing made the initial mistake, with *Indefatigable*, of assuming these would be similar to the *Invincible*s. In the following 13.5in gun ships the respective speeds of the rival battlecruisers, with the exception of *Tiger*, were fairly closely matched, with a possible slight advantage on the British side but this is by no means certain. At the Dogger Bank, although the British managed to overhaul the German ships, the latter were not running at maximum speed during the time the opposing forces were engaged, because they were held back in support of the slower *Blücher*. At Jutland again the German ships were seldom steaming at full speed which, on the Run to the North, allowed Beatty to get far enough ahead to turn the German battlecruisers away from the approaching Grand Fleet, thus preventing them carrying out their function of scouting ahead of the main fleet. In fact the value of speed seems to have been largely demonstrated by the British – in pursuit of a fleeing enemy, as at the Dogger Bank, and in fleeing from a pursuing enemy, as in the Run to the North at Jutland. Its value in general action, given the closely-matched speeds of the opposing forces seems to have been minimal.

All the German battlecruisers had vertical armour which was both substantially thicker than that of their British equivalents and covered a larger proportion of the hull – in particular the belt retained its full thickness throughout the length of the citadel and was not thinned abreast the forward and after barbettes. This enhancement over the protection provided in British ships was made possible by the weight savings gained from small-tube boilers and the use of lighter-calibre (but higher-velocity) guns and the fact that German designs were more compact, making greater use of the available

Indomitable in 1918. (Imperial War Museum: S1796)

Princess Royal in 1918. (Author's collection)

space at the expense of habitability and convenience. (This is not a point of detail: habitability was of considerable importance to the British, who expected their ships to be able to serve in all climates from the tropics to the North Sea without excessive strain on the general health and well-being of the crew.) Like the British, the Germans thinned their barbette armour where it fell behind the side armour and their deck protection was not appreciably better than that in British ships, so that in respect of shells falling at steep angles of descent they were almost as vulnerable. It is also worth noting that the battleships of the fleet were little better in this respect and it is not therefore entirely valid to see this fault as peculiar to the battlecruisers.

The loss of the three battlecruisers at Jutland came as a great shock to the British who, while accepting that losses would take place, expected at the very least equivalent losses to the enemy. Nor was the catastrophic nature of these losses, with such heavy casualties, expected – at least not on such a grand scale. One magazine explosion might have been set aside as bad luck but three had to be recognised as the sign of a much more fundamental problem. Although the post-Jutland committees investigated all the aspects related to the losses of these ships, the area that seems to have received the primary blame was their scale of protection, particularly that provided to the decks and turret roofs. However, a question arises as to whether this is an entirely valid conclusion when the primary cause of loss was the ready inclination of their ammunition to explode, which in turn raises questions as to the quality of both the magazine safety systems and of the ammunition itself. Given the circumstances of the time it was not reasonable to expect the protection to provide complete immunity. This had after all been deliberately sacrificed for speed, and to provide for both would have required an increase in size that was politically unacceptable pre-war. Absolute immunity was not something that could be either provided or guaranteed. Apart from the obvious requirement to stay afloat, the pre-war philosophy required that protection serve to limit damage and improve the chances of survivability for the machinery and armament. Of the two, machinery was seen as the more critical, hence the greater thickness of belt armour provided abreast the engine and boiler rooms, which is perfectly understandable when one considers that a ship might, and often did, continue in action with part of its main armament out of action, but was unlikely to be able to do so with its speed diminished. At the best, damage to the machinery would lead to the need to retire from action and at the worst would leave a ship at the mercy of a pursuing enemy, as was the case with *Lion* and *Blücher* respectively at the Battle of the Dogger Bank.

Although the explosion of a magazine was not regarded as an impossibility, prior to the events of Jutland it was regarded as being fairly unlikely – except possibly as a result of a mine or torpedo explosion in the immediate vicinity of the magazine. The general opinion of the time was expressed by Admiral Tupper in the following passage referring to trials in the old battleship *Colossus* in the Solent in 1907:

> we tried the effect of exploding some cases of cordite in a filled magazine, specially fitted to evacuate gas above a certain pressure. Everybody thought the magazine would explode, but it did not, and I am still at a loss to know just how it was that the *Queen Mary* and *Invincible* blew up at Jutland. Personally, I felt quite sure that even if flames got into the magazine it would not explode, while since this opinion had been strengthened by the result of the *Colossus* experiments we had taken additional precautions to prevent it.[1]

These and other trials, although linked to the possible dangers from enemy action, were primarily concerned with magazine safety in relation to the dangers inherent in the deterioration of cordite. It was known that cordite would deteriorate over time and that this deterioration would be accelerated by high temperatures and contamination – the latter most likely during manufacture. The *Invincible* class ships were originally intended to have their 12in cordite charges stowed in air-tight lockers containing a large number of charges. In 1907, when it was realised that the spontaneous ignition of one charge in such a locker could lead to a major explosion, small cylindrical brass cases, each containing two quarter charges, were substituted instead. These cases were fixed in the magazine racks, with an air space between them and were intended to limit the spread of a fire if one charge was to spontaneously ignite. The cases had a lid at one end which, in later versions, was weakened so that it would readily yield to internal pressure to avoid the possibility of the case itself exploding, rather than just burning out, and damaging adjacent cases.

The problem relating to high temperatures was solved by fitting magazine cooling machinery to ensure the temperature did not rise above 70° F and instituting regular checks of magazine temperatures (this also provided for an improved regulation of ballistics as the muzzle velocity of a gun would vary with the initial temperature of the cordite charge).

It was also critical to ensure that the pressure, in the event of a cordite fire, did not rise to a level that would cause an explosion and in 1908 (following on the *Colossus* trials) it was decided to fit all magazines with venting arrangements. These consisted of openings at the top of the bulkheads between the magazines and handing rooms, covered with thin plates that would yield to internal pressure but resist external pressure. It is worth noting that, according to the DNC at the time, Philip Watts, the division between magazine and handing room was only provided 'for the more rapid flooding of the magazines and the support of the structure overhead and not as necessary for the general subdivision of the ship',[2] which implies it was not fitted for safety purposes either. Since ammunition could only be passed from the magazine to the handing room with the door open there would always be at least some periods of time when a fire in the handing room could be communicated to the magazine and in many ships, particularly the battlecruisers, the doors were, understandably, kept permanently open during action to help maintain a steady rate of supply for rapid fire.

A magazine explosion as a result of enemy action was seen as unlikely because the brass cases that enclosed the charges were expected to limit the spread of a fire. In addition, pressure was not expected to rise to a dangerous level because, with a limited number of charges involved, it was assumed that the burning cordite, in its search for air, would vent itself through the ship's structure – principally upward through the gun mounting and the ventilation system. The difference between expectations and reality were clearly demonstrated during the Battle of Jutland, the more important events of which, in relation to the battlecruisers were as follows:

Indefatigable: Engaged with the *Von der Tann* for about 15 minutes when shortly after 1600 she was hit by two (or, less likely, three) shells from a single salvo on the upper deck abreast 'X' turret. There was an explosion and the ship swung out of line to starboard, apparently sinking by the stern. Shortly after this she was straddled by a second salvo, one shell being observed to hit 'A' turret and another the forecastle. After a brief interval the forward magazines blew up and the ship sank very rapidly. Judging by the lack of smoke from the first explosion it would seem that the hit aft resulted in a partial magazine explosion which holed the ship's bottom and destroyed the control shafts between the steering engines (in the engine room) and the steering gear aft. There were only two survivors (both picked up by German destroyers) from her crew of 1024 (including five civilians).

Queen Mary: Shortly after 1620 while under fire from both *Derfflinger* and *Seydlitz* a shell hit 'Q' turret and disabled the right gun. About four minutes later her forward magazines blew up, the ship breaking apart from an area forward of the foremast. The ship was rapidly enveloped in a large cloud of smoke but the after end of the ship was observed with the stern high out of the water and the propellers still revolving, shortly before she rolled over and sank. Several eyewitnesses thought that the midships magazine had blown up but as there were survivors from 'Q' turret this obviously did not occur. However, these survivors did report a cordite fire in the working chamber and it seems likely that 'Q' barbette may have been hit and holed by a shell from the same salvo that destroyed the fore part of the ship. There were nine survivors from her crew of 1275 (those killed included assistant constructor K Stephens of the DNC's Department).

Lion: Was heavily hit during the early phase of the battle but only one of these caused major damage. This was at 1600 when a 12in shell from *Lützow* struck 'Q' turret at the joint between the roof plate and front plate, adjacent to the left gun port. The shell penetrated, detonated over the left gun and blew the front roof plate and the centre front plate off the turret. All the gunhouse and working chamber crews were killed or wounded. A fire started in the gunhouse but this was thought to have been extinguished by a fire party that played hoses into the mounting through the damaged roof. However, there was still something smouldering in the gunhouse (later conjectured to be the insulation on electric cables) which, about 30 minutes after the initial explosion, ignited the charges at the top of the loading system. This quickly communicated itself down through the charges in the working chamber, central cages and magazine hoppers, sending a sheet of flame high into the air through the open roof and killing most of the magazine and shell room crews who were still in the lower part of the mounting. Fortunately, the magazine doors had been closed and the compartment flooded. The officer of the turret, Major Harvey, RMA, received a posthumous Victoria Cross for giving the orders for the latter despite his serious wounds, but in a memorandum on the event issued by Jellicoe on 16 June 1916 it only says that 'Sergeant-Major was sent by Officer of Quarter (Harvey) to bridge with a message to say turret was out of action.'[3] At the same time it mentions that the Chief Gunner visited 'Q' magazine shortly after the hit and was made aware of the situation by a member of the working chamber crew, who had come down the turret trunk. It was, according to this version, that orders were then given to close the magazine doors and it was not until later that orders came from the bridge for the magazine to be flooded. It is of course possible that the man from the working chamber was

Lion as she appeared during July–September 1916 with 'Q' turret removed for repair. (Imperial War Museum: SP1039)

sent down by Major Harvey and it seems likely that a broad interpretation was put on his actions as initiating the train of events that resulted in the magazines being secured. There is, however, another version of events given by Private Willons, RMLI, who said that while he was standing by the magazine door he heard the officer of the turret give the order that they should be closed.[4]

Invincible: During her engagement with the German battlecruisers she was fired on by both *Derfflinger* and *Lützow*. Shortly after 1830 a shell, generally credited to the latter vessel, penetrated the front of 'Q' turret and detonated inside, blowing the roof off. Almost immediately there was a heavy explosion from the midships magazines, which blew the ship in half. It is also possible that the explosion spread fore and aft and ignited 'X' (and possibly 'A') magazine. Film of the ship's wreck shows no roof on 'X' turret and it seems unlikely that this could have been removed by any other means than an internal explosion.

In contrast to these events the propellant charges used by the German Navy, while not immune from ignition, showed no instance of magazine explosions. The most dramatic occurrence of this nature took place aboard *Seydlitz* during the Battle of the Dogger Bank when the 9in armour of her aftermost barbette was holed (although the shell did not enter the barbette) by a 13.5in shell from *Lion*. The detonation of the shell sent splinters into the turret's working chamber and started a fire among some waiting charges that rapidly spread upwards into the gunhouse and down the supply trunk to the magazine loading chamber. In an attempt to escape, the loading chamber crew opened a communicating door to the loading chamber of 'X' mounting, allowing the fire to spread forward and both the after mountings were burnt out with heavy loss of life Under similar circumstances a British ship would certainly have been lost. There were also propellant fires in *Blücher* at the Dogger Bank and in *Derfflinger* (in two turrets), *Seydlitz* and *Lützow* at Jutland. In the last three ships these were caused by hits on the turret or barbette armour but only in the case of *Derfflinger* did the shell actually pass through the armour as opposed to just holing it.

Of the events in the British ships those in *Lion* are the most enlightening, as there is a clear record of what occurred. In all only eight full charges were involved (2344lbs cordite) but the fire was violent enough to buckle and force inward the magazine bulkhead despite the fact that this was supported by the water in the magazine. It was also found that flash had penetrated past the edges of the vent plates at the top of the magazine bulkhead without, fortunately, doing harm to the contents (it would seem that the compartment was not fully flooded at this time). In contrast, the fire in *Seydlitz* at the Dogger Bank involved sixty-two full charges (14,322lbs) which with British propellant was more than enough to cause an explosion.

After Jutland a very broad range of measures was introduced to reduce the risks from cordite fires, which were briefly as follows:

(a) Improved flash protection to gun mountings.
(b) Fitting flash-tight scuttles to magazine doors – the doors themselves being kept closed at all times while in action.
(c) The sealing-off of all vent plates to magazines.
(d) Modifying magazine doors (where necessary) to open outwards into handing room.

The forecastle and 'A' turret of *Australia*, 1917. Note the additional 1in plating bolted to the roof of the turret. (Imperial War Museum: Q18717)

(e) All ventilator, magazine cooling trunks, hatches etc, into magazine to be kept closed during action as long as air remained fit to breathe.
(f) Charges were not to be removed from cases in the magazine until required, and lids were not to be removed from cases until absolutely necessary. This was particularly relevant to the Battlecruiser Fleet where, during the period between the Dogger Bank and Jutland, great emphasis had been placed on the maintenance of high rates of fire. This had led to the practice of removing cordite charges from their cases well before they were required and a consequent heavy build-up of bare charges in the handing rooms and magazines.
(g) Fitting sprayers in magazines to drench exposed charges.
(h) Fitting additional 1in plating to magazine crowns and the roofs of turrets.

These improvements were introduced over an extended period and were not finally complete until the early 1920s. The first changes were to a large extent temporary measures by the ships' staff, subsequent alterations becoming steadily more permanent and more carefully considered. All these changes, with the exception of the added protective plating, were aimed at limiting the spread of a cordite fire and did not address the basic problem of why such fires would spread so rapidly and so violently in British ships. The more obvious conclusions were that the German charges were slower to ignite and slower in burning, thus retarding the process sufficiently to prevent a rapid rise in pressure. Several reasons were advanced for this namely that:

(a) German charges were enclosed in thin brass cases, which slowed the transfer of a fire from one charge to another and could, if the lid was still in place, prevent the ignition of the charge completely.
(b) British charges had a gunpowder igniter sown into the end of each half charge, which assisted in the transference of fire from one charge to another, gunpowder being much more susceptible to ignition by flash than the charge itself.
(c) German charges were inherently more stable as a result of better methods of manufacture and more careful control of the purity of the explosive during manufacture.
(d) The age deterioration of British charges made them steadily more liable to ignition and more rapid and violent burning, particularly if any impurities were present in the cordite.

Of these the most serious was the last and by April 1917 the control of cordite production had been considerably improved and work had begun on replacing all the old cordite in the fleet. In addition, experimental work was started which was largely aimed at following German practice, and included the investigation of new coverings (including metal envelopes), abolition of igniters and improved methods of manufacture, of which only the last actually produced any concrete results. The British eventually concluded that although they had introduced measures that

Tiger at Rosyth in 1918 with a US battleship in the distance. (Imperial War Museum: SP2181)

would prevent the spread of a cordite fire through a mounting and its loading system, it would be impossible to provide any guarantee for the safety of the magazine itself if it were directly penetrated by a projectile or splinter. Under these circumstances, therefore, it was seen as essential that these compartments should be armoured on a scale that would give them immunity at expected battle ranges. However, the evidence from Jutland implies that in the majority, if not all, cases the explosion of magazines was most likely to follow from damage to the turret or barbette. Most German shells that penetrated 6in armour or less detonated between 5ft and 20ft beyond the plate (one in *Princess Royal* did reach 54ft) and it was found that it was rare for splinters from these shells to penetrate the protective deck. (This did occur in *New Zealand*, which was hit only once – on 'X' turret – splinters from which penetrated the main deck but without causing serious damage.) However, it was possible for a shell at a steep angle of descent to go over the top of the belt armour and detonate near the base of a barbette where splinters might just have penetrated the magazine crown. This was particularly the case with the battlecruisers, where the magazines were immediately below the main deck (except for 'Q' mounting in all the 13.5in gun ships), whereas in contemporary battleships they were positioned one deck lower.

It may be concluded from this that given less volatile ammunition and improved flash protection the British battlecruiser would have emerged from the First World War with a much better reputation, which would have given support to the justification of their construction. Even under these ideal circumstances, however, it seems doubtful that they actually filled any need. It cannot be said that they served any function that an armoured cruiser armed with 9.2in guns could not have fulfilled, except for the more severe punishment that they might have inflicted on the enemy battle line in support of their own battleships. They did not require heavy guns to fight other armoured cruisers, to operate in the trade protection role or to scout for the fleet. To begin with, of course, with only armoured cruisers to face, they had a distinct advantage but called upon to face ships of their own kind the normal balance of opposing forces was restored and the power to overwhelm the enemy, which Fisher was consistently striving to obtain, evaporated very rapidly. Fisher in effect generated a hybrid type with excellent short-term prospects but dubious long-term value. The Falkland Islands battle demonstrated clearly that they could be very successful when called upon to fulfil the role envisaged for them in 1905. However, while operating in support of the Grand Fleet they invariably found themselves facing the opposing battlecruiser squadron over which, variations in the design criteria of British and German ships excepted, they did not have the same excess of gun-power as that available when engaging armoured cruisers. On this basis it is difficult to see what had been gained in escalating the armoured cruiser into a more expensive big-gun type.

The pre-war Navy was overconfident in its abilities, ships and equipment, in particular in believing that its heavier guns and advanced fire-control equipment would give the advantage of 'hitting first and hitting hard'. This thinking certainly seems to have affected Fisher's judgement of requirements and caused him to undervalue armour to an excessive degree. He does, moreover, seem to have held a constant view in this respect, judging by the fact that the scale and arrangement of armour in *Renown* and *Repulse* varied little from that of the *Invincible* class. The question that must remain open is that if technology had moved forward sufficiently to allow the production of a true fast battleship, as it did in the 1930s, would Fisher have accepted the resulting ship as an ideal or would he still have wanted a reduction in the armour of such a ship in favour of even higher speeds and greater gun power? It seems to this author, at least, that the latter is the more likely.

To some extent the Navy was justified in its belief in its hitting power: the larger shells and more powerful bursting charges of British ships did do much more damage to German ships than the smaller German shells did to British ships (magazine explosions omitted). After Jutland the surviving British battlecruisers returned to base with extensive, but for the most part superficial, damage – the most serious being that to *Lion*'s 'Q' turret. On the other hand, the *Lützow*, *Seydlitz* and *Derfflinger* suffered heavy structural damage, particularly forward, which led to extensive flooding. In *Lützow* this became so severe that she had to be abandoned and sunk on the way home, while *Seydlitz* reached base only with considerable difficulty. Repairs to *Derfflinger* lasted until mid-October while those to *Seydlitz* lasted until 16 September. In contrast, the repairs to *Tiger*, *Princess Royal* and *Lion* were completed on 1, 15 and 28 July respectively, although in the case of *Lion* this was without 'Q' turret, which was removed (it was replaced in September).

It is clear from this that had the British ships been provided with ammunition of equivalent quality to that in German ships and if they had had more secure arrangements of magazine isolation they would certainly not have suffered the losses that they did – probably none at all. The critical point here is that it was not so much the design of the ships that was at fault as their ammunition and the security of its supply to the gun-house. Add to this the fact that British projectiles were also inferior in design (something corrected post-Jutland) to those of the Germans and it is not difficult to see that much of the advantage, in offensive qualities, possessed by the British ships was lost through inadequate development prior to the war when spending money on ships, which had high visibility for the taxpayer, was far easier than gaining finance for extensive experimental work. Given the problems with poor quality APC shells, the lack of time fuses and the fact that the Battlecruiser Fleet's gunnery was inferior to

Lion in 1919 showing her final appearance. She has the late wartime additions of a clinker screen on the fore funnel (the only battlecruiser so fitted), a rangefinder tower added to the fore end of the CT roof (the original rangefinder hood having been replaced by a lookout position) and a rangefinder tower at the after end of the superstructure similar to that in *Princess Royal*. (Author's collection)

Renown at Auckland, New Zealand on 24 April 1920. (Author's collection)

that of the main fleet, it is not surprising that the balance of advantage shifted towards the Germans. One cannot help but conclude that on balance the path chosen by the British, without benefit of war experience, was the correct one but that the overall policy was seriously let down at a detail level. To a large extent this is of course academic in that it is written with the benefit of hindsight but it should be clear that in essence the pre-war battlecruiser was not of inherently flawed design. The Department of Naval Construction produced ships which met the design requirements set by the Admiralty so it would be unreasonable to blame the design department for any inherent failings resulting from a concept for which they were not responsible. Nor were they responsible for the supply of ammunition, although they must, at least in part, be held responsible for the weaker features of armour distribution. In essence, it is this author's opinion that it was simply the concept that *was* inherently flawed for the reasons explained above. The decision to fit heavy guns in an armoured cruiser could only be justified by the requirement to support the battlefleet when acting as a fast wing. This function became invalid as soon as Germany began to build ships of similar type given that the opposing battlecruisers would and did end up engaging each other rather than providing gun support to their battle squadrons. If the British battlecruisers had not been built then neither would those of Germany and the normal evolution of warship design would have provided armoured cruisers with a uniform armament and possibly the initial step towards the production of fast battleships. There is, of course, no reason to believe that the naval war in the North Sea would then have progressed any differently but this in itself says much about the true value of the battlecruiser.

Summary of Service

Invincible
8 Sep 1908: Captain Mark E F Kerr appointed.
26 Sep 1908: Undocked.
21 Oct 1908: Sailed from Tyne for Spithead.
23 Oct 1908: Arrived Portsmouth.
3–11 Nov 1908: Trials in English Channel.
23 Jan–6 Mar 1909: Docked at Hebburn-on-Tyne.
16 Mar 1909: Completed.
17 Mar 1909: Sailed for Portsmouth from Tyne.
20 Mar 1909: Commissioned at Portsmouth for 1st CS, 1st Division Home Fleet.
12 Jun 1909: Imperial Conference Review, Spithead.
20 Jul 1909: Fleet Review off Southend.
31 Jul 1909: Review of Fleet off Cowes by King Edward VII during visit of Tsar of Russia.
13 Aug–29 Dec 1909: Under refit at Portsmouth (docked 16 Aug–2 Sep).
23–27 Jun 1910: Docked at Portsmouth.
3 Aug–27 Oct 1910: Refitting at Portsmouth (docked 23 Aug–14 Sep).
15 Feb –2 Jun 1911: Portsmouth (reduced to nucleus crew). Refitting 13 Mar–2 Jun (docked 1– 2 May and 8 –22 May).
28 Mar 1911: Captain R P F Purefoy appointed.
16 May 1911: Recommissioned at Portsmouth for 1st CS.
24 Jun 1911: Coronation Review for King George V at Spithead.
15 Dec 1911–11 Jan 1912: Under refit at Portsmouth.
9 Jan 1912: Captain H J L Clarke appointed.
16 Apr–4 May 1912: Under refit at Portsmouth (docked 19–30 Apr).
1 May 1912: Captain M Culme-Seymour appointed.
9 Jul 1912: Parliamentary Review of Home Fleet at Spithead.
5 –26 Sep 1912: Baltic cruise.
1–28 Nov 1912: Under refit at Portsmouth (docked 6 –14 Nov).
1 Jan 1913: 1st CS became 1st BCS.
17 Mar 1913: Submarine *C34* collided with *Invincible* while she was at anchor in Stokes Bay, no damage, blame attributed to submarine.
Aug 1913: Transferred to 2nd BCS, Mediterranean Fleet, Captain H B Pelly appointed.
30 Oct–5 Nov 1913: Under refit at Malta (docked 30 Oct–4 Nov).
7 Dec 1913: Sailed from Malta to return to UK for major refit.
31 Dec 1913: Paid-off into Dockyard Control at Portsmouth, reduced to nucleus crew, Captain Pelly remaining in charge.
Jan–Jul 1914: Refitting at Portsmouth (conversion of electric power mountings to hydraulic – docked 23 Apr–?).
1 Aug 1914: Captain C M de Bartolome appointed.
3 Aug 1914: Commissioned for 2nd BCS.
12 Aug 1914: Hoisted flag of Rear Admiral Sir A G H W Moore, commanding 2nd BCS.
16 Aug 1914: Sailed from Portsmouth.
17–19 Aug 1914: Milford Haven.
19 Aug 1914: Sailed for the Humber, via Deal (21–22 Aug).
22–27 Aug 1914: Off Grimsby. Joined by *New Zealand* on 23rd the two ships temporarily being designated Force K.
27–30 Aug 1914: At sea with *New Zealand* to provide distant support for a destroyer raid on the patrols in the Heligoland Bight. During the subsequent Action off Heligoland on 28th she briefly engaged the cruiser *Cöln*.
12 Sep 1914: With *Inflexible* re-designated as 2nd BCS.
22–27 Oct 1914: At sea with *Inflexible* to provide distant cover for the air raid on the Cuxhaven Zeppelin Sheds that took place on 25th.
31 Oct 1914: Captain P T H Beamish appointed.
5 Nov 1914: Detached from Grand Fleet for service in South Atlantic. Flag of Rear Admiral Sir A G H W Moore transferred to *New Zealand*.
8–11 Nov 1914: At Devonport for docking and repairs (docked 8–10 Nov). Hoisted flag of Rear Admiral Sturdee on 9 Nov, flag captain Captain P T H Beamish replacing Captain Bartolome.
11 Nov 1914: Sailed for South Atlantic, via St Vincent (17–18 Nov) and Abrolhos Rocks (26–28 Nov) and arrived Port Stanley, Falkland Islands on 7 Dec.
8 Dec 1914: Battle of Falkland Islands.
16 Dec 1914: Sailed for UK after searching for *Dresden*. En route called at Montevideo (20 Dec), Abrolhos Rocks (26–27 Dec), Pernambuco (29 Dec) and St Vincent (4–6 Jan).
11 Jan–13 Feb 1915: Refit and repair at Gibraltar (docked 11 Jan–?).
19 Feb 1915: Arrived Scapa Flow. Captain A T Cay appointed.
4 Mar 1915: Joined 3rd BCS at Rosyth.
25 Apr–12 May 1915: Under refit on the Tyne.
26 May 1915: Became flagship of Rear Admiral H Hood, commanding 3rd BCS.
30 Sep –6 Oct 1915: Refitting Belfast (docked 30 Sep–6 Oct)
25 Apr 1916: Collided with the patrol yacht *Goissa* while returning to Rosyth, following an abortive attempt by the Battlecruiser Fleet to intercept the German battlecruisers that bombarded Lowestoft earlier the same day.
27 Apr–22 May: Docked for repairs at Rosyth.
23–30 May: At Scapa Flow with 3rd BCS for gunnery and torpedo practices.
31 May 1916: Sunk in action at Battle of Jutland.
3 Jun 1916: Officially paid off.

Inflexible
1 Jun 1908: Captain Henry H Torlesse appointed.
20 Oct 1908: Commissioned at Chatham for Nore Division, Home Fleet.
20 Oct 1908– 9 Jan 1909: Under refit and repair at Chatham following damage caused during gun trials.
15 Jan 1909: Sailed from Sheerness for Bantry Bay.
15 –21 Jan 1909: Bantry Bay.
21 Jan 1909: Sailed for Mediterranean. Gibraltar (24–27 Jan), Aranci Bay (30 Jan–15 Mar), Malta (16–25 Mar), Gibraltar (28–29 Mar), arrived Sheerness 2 Apr.
Mar 1909: Transferred to 1st CS, Home Fleet on its formation.
2 Apr 1909: Returned to Sheerness.
12 Jun 1909: Imperial Conference Review, Spithead.
20 Jul 1909: Fleet Review off Southend.
31 Jul 1909: Review of Fleet off Cowes by King Edward VII during visit of Tsar of Russia.
27 Aug–16 Sep 1909: Refitting at Portsmouth (docked 28 Aug–2 Sep).
16 Sep 1909: Hoisted flag of Admiral-of-the-Fleet Sir F H Seymour for visit to New York on occasion of the Hudson-Fulton celebrations. Sailed same day.
24 Sep–9 Oct 1909: New York.
18 Oct 1909: Returned UK.
14 Dec 1909: Captain C L Napier appointed.
7–22 Jun 1910: Refitting at Chatham (docked 8–22 Jun).
12 Oct 1910: Recommissioned at Chatham (same service).
26 May 1911: In collision with *Bellerophon* off Portland. Bows damaged. Blame attributed to *Bellerophon*.
29 May–14 Jun 1911: Under repair at Portsmouth (docked 29 May–2 Jun).
6 Oct–25 Nov 1911: Under refit at Chatham (docked 3–17 Nov).
21 Nov 1911: Captain R F Phillimore appointed.
18 Nov 1911–8 May 1912: Temporary flagship of 1st CS, Rear Admiral Bayly, during absence of *Indomitable* for refit (relieved as flagship by *Lion* on 8 May).
28 May–14 Jun 1911: Refitting at Portsmouth (docked 29 May–12 Jun).
24 Jun 1911: Coronation Review for King George V at Spithead.
8 May 1912: Captain R S Phipps-Hornby appointed.
9 Jul 1912: Parliamentary Review of Home Fleet at Spithead.
5 –26 Sep 1912: Baltic cruise.
10 Oct–11 Nov 1912: Refitting at Chatham (docked 31 Oct–4 Nov).
5 Nov 1912: Recommissioned by Captain A N Loxley at Chatham as flagship of Admiral Sir A Berkeley-Milne, C-in-C Mediterranean Fleet.
15 Nov 1912: Sailed from Sheerness to join Mediterranean Fleet.
22 Nov 1912: Arrived Malta.
7–19 Aug 1913: Refitting at Malta (docked 7–12 Aug).
9 Dec 1913–31 Jan 1914: Refitting at Malta (docked 7–16 Jan).
Aug 1914: Involved in unsuccessful search for *Goeben* and *Breslau*.
18 Aug 1914: Sailed from Malta for Devonport via Gibraltar (21 Aug), arrived on 24 Aug.
28 Aug 1914: Captain R F Phillimore appointed.
29 Aug 1914: Joined Grand Fleet at Scapa Flow (temporarily attached to 1st BCS 30 Aug–5 Sep).
5–12 Sep 1914: Force K with *Invincible*.
12 Sep 1914: With *Invincible* reformed as 2nd BCS.
22–27 Oct 1914: At sea with *Invincible* to provide distant cover for the air raid on the Cuxhaven Zeppelin Sheds that took place on 25th.
5 Nov 1914: Detached from Grand Fleet for service in South Atlantic.
8–11 Nov 1914: Devonport.
11 Nov 1914: Sailed for South Atlantic, via St Vincent (17–18 Nov) and Abrolhos Rocks (26–28 Nov) and arrived Port Stanley, Falkland Islands on 7 Dec.
8 Dec 1914: Battle of Falkland Islands.
13 Dec 1914: Sailed for Gibraltar after searching for *Dresden*. En route called at Port William (23–24 Dec), Abrolhos Rocks (31 Dec) and the Cape St Vincent (7– 8 Jan).
13–18 Jan 1915: Gibraltar.
24 Jan 1915: Arrived Dardanelles to replace *Indefatigable* as flagship of Admiral Carden, C-in-C Mediterranean Fleet.
19 Feb–18 March 1915: Dardanelles.
18 Mar 1915: Mined during assault on Dardanelles.
10–21 Apr 1915: Under temporary repair at Malta (docked 11–20 Apr).
13 Apr 1915; Captain H F Heaton-Ellis appointed.
24 Apr–15 Jun: Refit and repair at Gibraltar (docked 1 May–2 Jun).
15 Jun 1915: Sailed for Scapa Flow arriving on 20 Jun.
28 June 1915: Arrived Rosyth and joined 3rd BCS.
early Oct 1915: Briefly flagship of 3rd BCS (Admiral H Hood) during absence of *Invincible* for refit.
22 Dec 1915–11 Jan 1916: Refitting at Newcastle (docked 22 Dec–4 Jan).
31 May 1916: Battle of Jutland.
5 Jun 1916: Transferred to 2nd BCS.
21–31 Jul 1916: Docked at Rosyth.
29 Nov 1916: Captain A A M Duff appointed.
10 Feb–13 Mar 1917: Refitting at Rosyth (docked 9–13 Mar).
2 Jul–25 Aug 1917: Refitting at Newcastle (docked 14–25 Aug).
21 Aug 1917: Captain B S Thesiger appointed.
Nov 1917: Captain J R P Hawksley appointed.
1 Feb 1918: Collided with submarine *K22* off May Island – no significant damage.
14 May–1 Jun 1918: Refitting at Rosyth (docked 18–31 May).
21 Nov 1918: Present at surrender of High Sea Fleet.
15 Mar 1919: Captain E W Denison appointed.
27 Mar 1919: Joined Nore Reserve Fleet as flagship (Rear Admiral H L Mawbey).
5 Nov 1919: Recommissioned at Chatham (same service).
31 Mar 1920: Paid off.
1 Dec 1921: Sold to Stanlee, Dover for breaking-up.
8 Apr 1922: Left Devonport for Dover under tow, resold and broken-up in Germany.

Indomitable
20 Jun 1908: Commissioned at Portsmouth by Captain H G King-Hall for detached service to convey Prince George to Canada for Quebec Tercentenary celebration. Sailed, with cruiser *Minotaur* 15 July, at Quebec 22–29 Jul and returned 3 Aug.
10 Aug 1908: Arrived Chatham and handed over to contractors for completion.
28 Oct 1908: Transferred from contractors and joined Nore Division of Home Fleet.
21 Nov 1908: Sailed from Spithead for Mediterranean. Gibraltar (24–26 Nov), Aranci Bay (29 Nov–16 Jan), Gibraltar (18–19 Jan). Returned Sheerness 24 Jan 1909.
Mar 1909: 1st CS, Home Fleet.
25 Mar–12 Apr: Refitting at Chatham.
12 Jun 1909: Imperial Conference Review, Spithead.
20 Jul 1909: Fleet Review off Southend.
26 Jul 1909: Became flagship of Rear Admiral S Colville, commanding 1st CS, and Captain C M de Bartolome appointed.
31 Jul 1909: Review of Fleet off Cowes by King Edward VII during visit of Tsar of Russia.
24 Dec 1909–2 Mar 1910: Refitting at Chatham (docked 8 25 Feb).
4–20 Aug 1910: Refitting at Chatham (docked 4–17 Aug).
9 Aug 1910: Recommissioned at Chatham (same service).
3 Jan 1911: Captain A A M Duff appointed.
11 Feb–3 Apr 1911: Refitting at Chatham (docked 13–27 Feb, and 18–31 Mar).
24 Feb 1911: Became flagship of Rear Admiral Lewis Bayly (same service).
24 Jun 1911: Coronation Review for King George V at Spithead.
25 Nov 1911: Reduced to nucleus crew for refit, flag transferred to *Inflexible*.
18 Nov 1911–22 Feb 1912: Refitting at Chatham.
21 Feb 1912: Recommissioned as flagship of Rear Admiral Sir George Warrender, commanding 2nd CS, and Captain G H Baird appointed.
9 Jul 1912: Parliamentary Review of Home Fleet at Spithead.
23 Sep–14 Oct 1912: Baltic Cruise.
11 Dec 1912: Temporarily transferred to 1st CS (1st BCS from Jan 1913), Home Fleet, Captain F W Kennedy appointed.
28 Jan–26 Feb 1913: Refitting at Chatham (docked 13–21 Feb).
27 Aug 1913: Transferred to 2nd BCS, Mediterranean and sailed for Gibraltar following day.
23 Feb–2 Mar 1914: Refitting at Malta (docked 24 Feb–1 Mar).
24 Jul–2 Aug 1914: Refitting at Malta (docked 28–30 Jul).
Aug 1914: Involved in search for *Goeben* and *Breslau*.
Sep–Nov 1914: Dardanelles (bombarded outer defences 3 Nov).
23 Nov–15 Dec 1914: Refitting at Malta (docked 26 Nov–4 Dec).
15 Dec 1914: Sailed for UK. Joined Battlecruiser Force in North Sea on 26 Dec and arrived Rosyth on the following day. Temporarily attached to 1st BCS
15 Jan 1915: Transferred to 2nd BCS.
24 Jan 1915: Battle of Dogger Bank.
26 Jan 1915: At Rosyth. Fire in starboard engine room required extensive re-wiring of electrical installation. Work carried out by Rosyth Dockyard and completed on 26 Feb.
Feb 1915: Transferred to 3rd BCS.
15–27 Jun 1915: Refitting Invergordon (docked 18–22 Jun).
17–25 Jan 1916: Refitting, Tyne Floating Dock
31 May 1916: Battle of Jutland.
5 Jun 1916: Transferred to 2nd BCS.
7 Jun 1916: Captain M H Hodges appointed.
1–22 Aug 1916: Refitting at Rosyth (docked 1–11 Aug).
10 May–21 Jun 1917: Refitting at Newcastle.
13 Aug 1917: Captain E K Loring appointed.
8 Apr–13 May 1918: Refitting at Rosyth (docked 12–30 Apr).
21 Nov 1918: Present at surrender of High Sea Fleet.
16 Jan 1919: Captain L P Heard appointed.
27 Jan 1919: Arrived Sheerness to join Nore Reserve Fleet.
31 Mar 1920: Paid off for disposal.
1 Dec 1921: Sold to Stanlee, Dover.
30 Aug 1922: Towed to Dover for breaking-up.

Indefatigable
17 Jan 1911: Captain A C Leveson appointed.
24 Feb 1911: Commissioned at Devonport for 1st CS, Home Fleet.
19 Jul–1 Aug 1911: Refitting at Devonport (docked 19–29 Jul).
Jan 1913: 1st CS became 1st BCS.

SUMMARY OF SERVICE | 123

24 Feb 1913: Captain C F Sowerby appointed.
17 Jun 1913: Recommissioned at Devonport (same service).
24 Jun 1911: Coronation Review for King George V at Spithead.
29 Feb–2 May 1912: Refitting at Devonport (docked 7–25 Mar).
5–26 Sep 1912: Baltic cruise.
4 Dec 1912– 1 Feb 1913: Refitting Devonport (docked 4–27 Jan).
10–14 Jul 1913: Refitting Devonport (docked 12 Jul).
1 Jan 1914: Sailed from Devonport to join 2nd BCS, Mediterranean Fleet. Arrived Malta 10 Jan.
20 Apr–22 Jun 1914: Refitting Malta (docked 10 May–11 Jun)
Aug 1914: Involved in search for *Goeben* and *Breslau*.
20 Sep 1914: Became flagship of Vice Admiral S H Carden, C-in-C, Mediterranean Fleet.
Nov 14–Jan 1915: Dardanelles.
25 Jan 1915: Proceeded Malta for refit.
27 Jan–14 Feb 1915: Refitting Malta (docked 27 Jan–5 Feb).
14 Feb 1915: Sailed from Malta for UK, arrived Scapa Flow 24 Feb.
4 Mar 1915: Joined 2nd BCS at Rosyth.
2–12 Jul 1915: Refitting at Invergordon (docked 3 – 11 Jul).
14–23 Feb 1916: Refitting at Newcastle (docked 14–22 Feb).
23 Apr–8 May 1916: Temporary flagship of 2nd BCS in absence of *Australia*.
31 May 1916: Sunk during Battle of Jutland.

New Zealand
21 Sep 1912: Captain Lionel Halsey appointed.
19 Nov 1912: Commissioned with nucleus crew at Govan.
23 Nov 1912: Completed to full crew at Devonport for 1st CS, Home Fleet.
6 Feb 1913: Sailed from Portsmouth for world cruise and visit to New Zealand. Out via Cape of Good Hope, home via Pacific and Panama Canal.
8 Dec 1913: Returned Devonport.
1 Jan–1 Feb 1914: Refitting at Devonport then joined 1st BCS, Home Fleet.
10–18 Feb: Visit to Brest with 1st BCS.
12 Jun–2 Jul 1914: Baltic cruise.
22 Aug–5 Sep: Detached to Force 'K'.
28 Aug 1914: Heligoland Bight action.
5 Sep 1914: Rejoined 1st BCS.
25 Oct–3 Nov 1914: Refitting Invergordon (docked 26–31 Oct).
5 Nov–2 Dec 1914: Flagship of Rear Admiral Sir A G H W Moore, 2nd in command 1st BCS.
15 Jan 1915: Transferred to 2nd BCS.
17 Jan 1915: Flagship of Rear Admiral Sir A G H W Moore, commanding 2nd BCS.
24 Jan 1915: Battle of Dogger Bank.
8 Jun 1915: Captain J E F Green appointed.
7 Mar 1915: Flag 2nd BCS transferred to *Australia*.
22–27 May 1915: Refitting Invergordon (docked 22–27 May).
Mid Jul 1915: Temporary Flag 2nd BCS while *Australia* refitting.
6–17 Nov 1915: Refitting Devonport (docked 6–15 Nov).
Late Jan–early Feb 1916: Temporary Flag 2nd BCS while *Australia* refitting.
22 Apr 1916: Collided with *Australia*.
23 Apr– 4 May 1916: Under repair and refit at Rosyth (docked 23 Apr–4 May).
8 May–9 Jun 1916: Temporary flag of 2nd BCS in absence of *Australia*.
31 May 1916: Battle of Jutland.
5 Jun 1916: Transferred to 1st BCS but continued to operate with the 2nd BCS during Jun–Jul until the completion of repairs to the battlecruisers damaged at Jutland.
14–27 Nov 1916: Refitting Rosyth (docked 14–27 Nov).
Nov 1916: Transferred to 2nd BCS.
5 Dec 1916–10 Jan 1917: Temporary flagship Rear Admiral A Leveson, commanding 2nd BCS.
30 Dec 1916–13 Jan 1917: Refitting at Rosyth.
21 Jun–9 Jul: Refitting at Rosyth (docked 21 Jun–3 Jul).
1 Oct 1917: Captain R Webb appointed (from Dec 1917 to Jan 1918 Commander E Kennedy served as commanding officer during the absence of Webb).
1–18 Jun 1918: Refitting at Rosyth (docked 1–14 Jun).
29 Sep 1918: Captain A B Donaldson appointed.
21 Oct–14 Nov 1918: Temporary flagship Rear Admiral L Halsey, commanding 2nd BCS.
21 Nov 1918: Present at surrender of High Sea Fleet.
31 Dec 1918–21 Feb 1919: Refitting at Devonport (docked 24–31 Jan).
11 Feb 1919: Captain L E Leggett appointed.
21 Feb 1919: Sailed from Devonport as flagship Admiral Sir John Jellicoe for Dominion Tour.
2 Feb 1920. Returned to Portsmouth.
15 Mar 1920: Paid off into reserve at Rosyth.
1 Jul 1921: Became flagship of Rear Admiral C B Miller commanding the Reserve Fleet at Rosyth.
Oct 1921: Reduced to C and M.
19 Apr 1922: Paid off
19 Dec 1922: Sold to Rosyth SB Co for breaking-up

Australia
17 May 1913: Captain S H Radcliffe appointed.
21 Jun 1913: Commissioned at Portsmouth as Flagship of the Royal Australian Navy.
23 Jun 1913: Hoisted flag Rear Admiral G E Patey (Vice Admiral from 14 Sep 1914).
Jul 1913: Sailed from Portsmouth for Australia with cruiser *Sydney*.
26–28 Aug 1913: Simonstown Dockyard.
4 Oct 1913: Arrived Sydney.
May 1914: Refitting Cockatoo Dockyard (docked).
Aug–Nov 1914: Involved in unsuccessful search for warships of German East Asiatic Squadron and provided escort for transports and cover for the occupations of Samoa, Rabaul and German New Guinea.
8 Nov 1914: On news of the Battle of Coronel, sailed from Fiji for South America.
26 Nov–10 Dec: Searched along coast of South America until news arrived of the Battle of the Falkland Islands.
14 Dec 1914: Sailed from Gulf of Panama for Jamaica via Straits of Magellan to become flagship of West Indies Station.
2–5 Jan 1915: Port Stanley, Falkland Islands. Undergoing temporary repairs at Port Stanley following propeller damage received during passage of Straits of Magellan.
6 Jan 1915: En route to Jamaica intercepted and sank the German liner SS *Eleonore Woermann*.
11 Jan 1915: While on passage to Jamaica, ordered to divert to Gibraltar but on arrival at St Vincent she was ordered instead to Plymouth.
28 Jan–12 Feb 1915: Paid off at Devonport for docking and refit.
17 Feb 1915: Joined 2nd BCS at Rosyth.
22 Feb 1915: Became flagship of 2nd BCS (Vice Admiral G E Patey).
7 Mar 1915: Vice Admiral Patey relieved by Rear Admiral W C Pakenham.
13–22 Jul 1915: Refitting at Invergordon (docked 13–20 Jul).
31 Jan–9 Feb 1916: Refitting at Newcastle (docked).
22 Apr 1916: In collision with *New Zealand*.
23 Apr– 1 May 1916: Under temporary repair in floating dock on Tyne.
4–31 May 1916: Under repair at Devonport (docked).
9/10 Jun 1916: Rejoined 2nd BCS at Rosyth.
28 Nov–19 Dec 1916: Refitting at Rosyth (docked 28 Nov–6 Dec).
5 Dec 1916: Rear Admiral Pakenham relieved by Rear Admiral A C Leveson but flag temporarily in *New Zealand* until 10 Jan 1917.
16 Dec 1916: Captain O Backhouse appointed.
Sep 1917: Refitting at Rosyth (docked 9–23 Sep).
12 Dec 1917: In collision with *Repulse*.
13 Nov–6 Dec 1917: Docked at Rosyth for repairs.
1 Sep 1918: Captain T N James appointed.
4 Sep 1918: Rear Admiral Leveson relieved by Rear Admiral L Halsey.
28 Oct–12 Nov 1918: Refitting at Rosyth (docked 29 Oct–12 Nov).
21 Nov 1918: Present at surrender of High Sea Fleet.
Jan–Apr 1919: Refitting at Portsmouth.
22 Mar 1919: Captain J S Dumaresq appointed as Commodore commanding Australian Fleet, (Dumaresq was promoted Rear Admiral in Jun 1921).
9 Apr 1919: Captain C L Cumberlege appointed.
23 Apr 1919: Sailed from Portsmouth for Australia via Suez Canal, Aden and Colombo.
28 May–1 Jun 1919: Freemantle.
15 Jun 1919: Arrived Sydney.
2 Sep 1919: Recommissioned at Sydney.
21 Sep 1920: Captain S R Miller appointed.
12 Dec 1921: Paid off into Reserve at Sydney.
12 Apr 1924: Scuttled 24 miles east of the entrance to Sydney Harbour.

Lion
Nov 1911: Captain A A M Duff appointed.
Jan 1912: First steam trials.
Jan–May 1912: Under reconstruction at Devonport.
4 Jun 1912: Commissioned at Devonport as flagship of Rear Admiral Lewis Bayly, 1st CS, Home Fleet.
5–26 Sep 1912: Cruise to Norway and Denmark.
27 Sep 4 Oct 1912: Refitting at Sheerness (docked in Medway Floating Dock 2–3 Oct).
1 Jan 1913: 1st CS became 1st BCS.
1 Mar 1913: Captain A E M Chatfield appointed and became flagship of Rear Admiral David Beatty (acting Vice Admiral 9 Apr 1915, promoted Vice Admiral 9 Aug 1915). Served as flagship of Grand Fleet battlecruisers throughout 1914–18 War.
9–25 Sep 1913: Refitting at Devonport.
27 Nov 1913–29 Jan 1914. Refitting at Devonport.
10–18 Feb: Visit to Brest with 1st BCS.
13 Jun–8 Jul 1914: Baltic cruise.
12–15 Jul 1914: Refitting at Devonport (docked 14–15 Jul).
28 Aug 1914: Heligoland Bight action.
24 Jan 1915: Battle of Dogger Bank.
26 Jan–8 Feb 1915: Under temporary repair at Rosyth.
9 Feb–28 Mar 1915: Under repair on the Tyne.
28 Mar–7 Apr: Refitting at Invergordon (docked 29 Mar–5 Apr).
7 Apr 1915: Rejoined Battlecruiser Fleet at Rosyth.
24 Nov–1 Dec: Refitting at Jarrow (docked 24 Nov–1 Dec).
31 May–1 June 1916: Battle of Jutland.
2–27 Jun 1916: Under repair at Rosyth.
27 Jun–8 Jul 1916: Under repair at Newcastle.
8 –19 Jul 1916: Refit and repair at Rosyth (docked 8–19 Jul).
19 Jul 1916: Rejoined Battlecruiser Fleet at Rosyth, less 'Q' turret.
6–23 Sep 1916: Refitting at Newcastle, 'Q' turret replaced.
16 Nov 1916: Captain R R C Backhouse appointed.
29 Nov 1916: Became flagship of Vice Admiral W C Pakenham, commanding Battlecruiser Force, on Beatty becoming C-in-C Grand Fleet.
13–21 Mar 1917: Refitting at Rosyth (docked 13–21 Mar)
May 1918: Captain A J Davies appointed.
13 Sep–15 Oct 1918: Refitting at Rosyth (docked 20 Sep–6 Oct).
21 Nov 1918: Present at surrender of High Sea Fleet.
28 Feb 1919: Pakenham superseded by Vice Admiral Sir H Oliver as commander of BCF, Grand Fleet.
21 Mar 1919: Oliver superseded by Rear Admiral R J B Keyes as commander BCF, Grand Fleet.
7 Apr 1919: Flagship BCS, Atlantic Fleet.
2–16 May 1919: Refitting at Rosyth (docked 6–8 May).
8 Oct–16 Nov 1919: Refitting at Rosyth.
1 Jan 1920: Captain A P Addison appointed.
31 Mar 1920: Reduced to reserve at Rosyth.
3 May 1921: Became flagship Rear Admiral C B Miller, commanding Reserve Fleet, Rosyth.
30 May 1922: Paid off.
31 Jan 1924: Sold for breaking-up.

Princess Royal
1 Aug 1912: Captain O de B Brock appointed.
14 Nov 1912: Commissioned at Devonport for 1st BCS.
5 Mar–28 Apr 1913: Refitting at Portsmouth (docked 8–18 Apr).
4 Nov–30 Dec 1913: Refitting at Portsmouth (docked 29 Nov–16 Dec).
11–17 Feb 1914: Visiting Brest with 1st BCS.
12 Jun–7 Jul. Baltic Cruise.
28 Aug 1914: Heligoland Bight Action.
3 Oct 1914: Sailed from Scapa Flow to meet and escort Canadian troop convoy to UK.
10 Oct 1914: Met troop convoy in mid N Atlantic.
18 Oct 1914: Rejoined 1st BCS at Loch Na Keal.
12 Nov 1914: Sailed from Cromarty for service in Atlantic as part of search for Admiral Von Spee's Squadron.
21 Nov 1914: Arrived Halifax then operated off New York before moving to Caribbean to watch the Panama Canal.
19 Dec 1914: Sailed from Kingston, Jamaica for UK via Halifax (23–25 Dec).
2 Jan 1915: Arrived Scapa Flow.
6 Jan 1915: Rejoined 1st BCS at Rosyth.
24 Jan 1915: Battle of Dogger Bank.
24 Jan–9 Apr 1915: Temporary flagship acting Vice Admiral Sir D Beatty during absence of *Lion*.
17 Feb 1915: Captain W Cowan appointed but did not take up is appointment until 9 April when Brock was promoted to command of the 1st BCS.
9 April 1915: Flagship Commodore (promoted Rear Admiral 5 Mar 1915) O de B Brock, commanding 1st BCS.
3–13 May 1915: Refitting Invergordon (docked 5–11 May).
2–9 Dec 1915: Docked in Jarrow Floating Dock.
31 May–1 Jun 1916: Battle of Jutland.
2–10 Jun 1916: Rosyth dockyard.
13 Jun–17 July 1916: Under refit and repair at Portsmouth (docked 13 Jun–10 Jul).
21 Jul 1916: Rejoined 1st BCS at Rosyth.
9–31 Oct 1916: Refitting at Rosyth (docked [illegible]–28 Oct).
29 Mar–18 May: Rosyth. Repairs to stripped turbine carried out by dockyard 30 Apr–9 May.
Nov 1916: Rear Admiral R F Phillimore superseded Rear Admiral Brock but did not assume command until 23 Dec 1916. Flag transferred to *Renown* 15 Jan 1917.
15 Jan–23 Mar 1917: Rosyth. Refitting from Jan–Feb (docked 29 Jan–8 Feb).
Mar 1917: Temporary flag Rear Admiral W C Pakenham while *Lion* refitting
9 Jul 1917: Captain J D Kelly appointed.
Oct–Dec 1917: Captain S R Drury-Low in temporary command during absence of Captain Kelly.
17 Nov 1917: 2nd Heligoland Bight Action.
24 Mar–11 Apr 1918: Refitting at Rosyth (docked 26 Mar–11 Apr).
15–19 Aug 1918: Refitting at Rosyth (docked 15 –19 Aug).
21 Nov 1918: Present at Surrender of High Sea Fleet.
Apr– 31 May 1919: BCS, Atlantic Fleet.
31 May 1919: Paid off
13 Feb 1920: Reduced to Reserve complement, Rosyth.
2 Nov 1921: Recommissioned at Rosyth with reserve complement as tender to *New Zealand*.
1 May 1922: Paid off at Rosyth.
19 Dec 1922: Sold to A J Purvis and then resold to Rosyth Ship Breaking Co.
13 Aug 1923: Arrived at ship breakers.

Queen Mary
1 Jul 1913: Captain W R Hall appointed.
4 Sep 1913: Commissioned at Portsmouth for 1st BCS, Home Fleet.
12 Jun–7 Jul 1914: Baltic Cruise.
13 Oct 1914: Captain C I Prowse appointed.
28 Aug 1914: Heligoland Bight action.
17–24 Jan 1915: Refitting at Portsmouth (docked 17–23 Jan).
19–29 Jul 1915: Refitting Invergordon (docked 21–28 Jul).
25 Feb–3 Mar 1916: Refitting at Jarrow (docked 25 Feb–3 Mar).
31 May 1916: Sunk in action at Battle of Jutland.

Tiger
3 Aug 1913: Captain H B Pelly appointed.
3 Oct 1914: Commissioned at Clydebank for 1st BCS, Grand Fleet.
6 Nov 1914: Joined 1st BCS at Scapa Flow.
24 Jan 1915: Battle of Dogger Bank.
26–31 Jan 1915: Rosyth, repairing boiler defects.
1–8 Feb 1915: Refit and repair at Newcastle.
31 May–11 Jun: Refitting at Invergordon (docked 1 Jun)
13–21 Dec 1915: Refitting at Newcastle (docked 13–21 Dec).
31 May 1916: Battle of Jutland.
2 Jun–5 Aug 1916: Under repair at Rosyth (docked 3 Jun–2 Jul).
29 Jun 1916: Captain R W Bentinck appointed.
2 Jul 1916: Rejoined Fleet.
21 Dec–29 Jan 1917: Refitting at Rosyth (docked 2–28 Jan).
7 Apr–12 May 1917: Refitting at Rosyth.
14 Aug 1917: Captain A M Duff appointed.
Oct 1917: Refitting at Rosyth (docked 7–21 Oct).
17 Nov 1917: 2nd Heligoland Bight Action.
17–22 Dec 1917: Refitting at Rosyth.
3–18 Jul 1918: Refitting at Rosyth (docked 3–18 Jul).
21 Nov 1918: Present at Surrender of High Sea Fleet.
29 Mar 1919: Captain W H D Boyle appointed.
Apr 1919: Joined BCS, Atlantic Fleet.

5 Aug–27 Oct 1919: Refitting at Rosyth (docked 14 Aug–17 Oct).
3 Aug–3 Sep 1920: Refitting at Devonport (docked 16–27 Aug).
Late Nov 1920: In collision with battleship *Royal Sovereign* at Portland.
6 Dec 1920–13 Jan 1921: Repair and refit at Devonport (docked 23 Dec–12 Jan).
29 Mar 1921: Captain J E Cameron appointed.
22 Aug 1921: Paid off into reserve.
17 Oct 1921: Reduced to 3/5th complement.
7 Apr 1922: Paid off at Rosyth for extensive refit.
15 Feb 1924: Recommissioned with special complement at Portsmouth for service as gunnery training and trials ship.
1926: Rejoined BCS, Atlantic Fleet following her replacement as gunnery training ship by the *Iron Duke*.
17 May 1929: Recommissioned at Portsmouth (same service).
15 May 1931: Paid off at Rosyth.
Feb 1932: Sold to T W Ward for breaking-up.

Renown
Aug 1916: Captain H F P Sinclair appointed.
12 Sep 1916: Commissioned at Fairfield's Yard for service in 1st BCS.
18 Sep 1916: Left Fairfield's.
19 Sep 1916: Gun trials.
20 Sep 1916: Steam trials then sailed to Portsmouth for docking.
22 Sep–4 Nov 1916: Portsmouth (docked 25 Sep–14 Oct and 23 Oct–4 Nov).
9 Jan 1917: Joined 1st BCS at Rosyth.
15–29 Jan 1917: Temporary flagship Rear Admiral R F Phillimore commanding 1st BCS.
29 Jan–1 Apr 1917: Refitting at Rosyth (docked 30 Jan–24 Feb and 15–31 Mar).
Aug 1917: Captain M H Hodges appointed.
17 Apr 1918: Captain A W Craig appointed.
30 Aug–13 Sep 1918: Refitting at Rosyth (docked 30 Aug–13 Sep).
17 Nov 1917: 2nd Heligoland Bight Action.
Dec 1918–7 Apr 1919: Flagship Rear Admiral H F Oliver commanding 1st BCS.
21 Nov 1918: Present at surrender of High Sea Fleet.
14 Jan 1919: Captain E A Taylor appointed.
7 Apr 1919: BCS, Atlantic Fleet.
5 Aug–1 Dec 1919: Detached from BCS to carry Prince of Wales on Royal tour of Canada and the West Indies, together with visits to Rio de Janeiro and New York.
16 Mar–10 Oct 1920: Detached from BCS to carry Prince of Wales on Royal tour of the Pacific, Australia, New Zealand and West Indies.
1 Nov 1920–15 Sep 1921: Paid off into Reserve at Portsmouth.
18 Oct 1921–18 Jun 1922: Detached to carry Prince of Wales on Royal tour to Middle East, India, Far East and Japan.
28 Jul 1922: Paid off into Reserve.
May 1923–July 1926: Extensive refit at Portsmouth Dockyard.
Aug 1948: Sold for breaking-up.

Repulse
2 Aug 1916: Captain C T M Fuller appointed.
15 Aug 1916: Steam trials in Firth of Clyde.
18 Aug 1916: Gun trials en route to Portsmouth for completion.
20 Aug–12 Sep 1916: Portsmouth (docked 22 Aug–8 Sep).
15 Sep 1916: Steam trials at Arran while on passage north to join fleet.
21 Sep 1916: Arrived Scapa Flow to work up prior to joining 1st BCS.
10 Nov 1916–6 Jan 1917: Refit and repair at Rosyth (docked 20 Nov–6 Jan).
6 Jan 1917: On leaving dockyard *Repulse* fouled the ram of *Queen Elizabeth* while passing across her bow. Starboard side damaged abreast bridge.
7–29 Jan: Damage repairs at Rosyth (docked 7–28 Jan).
29 Jan 1917: Hoisted flag Rear Admiral R F Phillimore, commanding 1st BCS.
21 Oct–5 Nov 1917: Refitting at Rosyth (docked 21 Oct–5 Nov).
6 Nov 1917: Capt W H D Boyle appointed.
17 Nov 1917: 2nd Heligoland Bight action.
14 Mar 1918: Rear Admiral Sir H F Oliver superseded Phillimore as commander 1st BCS. Flag transferred to *Renown* cNov 1918.
1–15 Aug 1918: Refitting at Rosyth (docked 1–15 Aug).
21 Nov 1918: Present at surrender of High Sea Fleet.
17 Dec 1918–13 Jan 1921: Paid off at Portsmouth for long refit.
10 Dec 1941: Sunk by Japanese aircraft off Malaya.

Glorious
27 Aug 1916: Captain B Miller appointed.
23 Oct 1916: Commissioned for trials.
Jan 1917: Commissioned as flagship 3rd LCS, Grand Fleet.
8 Aug 1917: 1st CS, Grand Fleet.
17 Nov 1917: 2nd Heligoland Bight action.
31 Jan–22 Mar 1918: Refitting at Devonport (docked 31 Jan–16 Mar).
13–20 Jun 1918: Refitting at Rosyth.
21 Nov 1918: Present at surrender of High Seas Fleet.
31 Dec 1918–30 Jan 1919: Refitting at Rosyth (docked 2–21 Jan).
1 Feb 1919: Placed in reserve at Rosyth.
May 1920: Transferred to Devonport Reserve.
Jun–Jul 1920: Refitting at Devonport.
Jul 1920: Turret drill ship, Devonport.
1921–22: Flagship of Rear Admiral Reserve Fleet, Devonport.
Sep 1923: In reserve, Portsmouth.
14 Feb 1924: Paid off at Rosyth for reconstruction as an aircraft carrier.
8 June 1940: Sunk by *Scharnhorst* and *Gneisenau* during Norwegian Campaign.

Courageous
8 Sep 1916: Captain A Bromley appointed.
15 Nov 1916–4 Jan 1917: Under repair (stripped astern–turbines) at Rosyth.
Jan 1917: 3rd LCS, Grand Fleet.
6 Feb–19 Apr 1917: Refitting at Portsmouth (docked 8 Feb–5 Apr).
30 Jul 1917: Flag acting Vice Admiral T D W Napier Commanding 1st CS.
8 Aug 1917: 1st CS, Grand Fleet.
17 Nov 1917: 2nd Heligoland Bight action.
19 Dec 1917–18 Jan 1918: Refitting at Rosyth (docked 19 Dec–18 Jan).
14 Jun–18 Aug 1918: Refitting at Rosyth (docked 18–31 Jun).
21 Nov 1918: Present at surrender of High Sea Fleet.
1 Feb–Apr 1919: Flag Vice Admiral Napier commanding Reserve Fleet Rosyth.
1 May–Dec 1919: Flag Rear Admiral C F Corbett commanding Reserve Fleet Rosyth.
4 Dec 1919: Recommissioned at Rosyth.
Dec 1919–May 1924: Flagship of Reserve Fleet and turret drill ship at Portsmouth.
29 June 1924: Taken in hand at Devonport for conversion into an aircraft carrier.
17 Sept 1939: Torpedoed and sunk by *U29*.

Furious
20 Mar 1917: Captain W S Nicholson appointed.
4 Jul 1917: Joined Grand Fleet at Scapa Flow.
14 Nov 1917–17 Mar 18: After 18in Gun mounting removed and converted to full aircraft carrier at Armstrong Naval Yard, Walker-on-Tyne (docked in Jarrow floating dock 7–17 Mar 1918).
15 Mar 1918–May 1919: Flag Rear Admiral Sir F R Phillimore commanding Flying Squadron.
21 Nov 1918: Present at surrender of High Seas Fleet.
14 Mar–30 Apr 1919: Refitting at Rosyth (docked 14 Mar–2 Apr).
Apr–Nov 1919: Flying Squadron, Atlantic Fleet.
6–8 Sep 1919: Visiting Copenhagen.
21 Nov 1919: Reduced to reserve at Rosyth.
1922–25: Under major reconstruction.
15 Mar 1948: Sold for breaking-up.

Sources

Published
Admiralty, *Narrative of the Battle of Jutland* (HMSO, 1924).
Admiralty, *Battle of Jutland, Official Despatches* (HMSO, undated).
Bacon, Admiral Sir R H, *The Life of John Rushworth Earl Jellicoe* (Cassell, 1936).
Bacon, Admiral Sir R H, *Lord Fisher, Admiral of the Fleet*, 2 vols (Hodder and Stoughton, 1929).
–, *A Naval Scrap-Book* (Hutchinson, 1940).
–, *From 1900 Onwards* (Hutchinson, 1940).
Brooks, J, *Dreadnought Gunnery and the Battle of Jutland* (Routledge, 2005).
Burt, R A, *British Battleships of World War One* (Arms and Armour Press, 1986; new edition Seaforth Publishing, 2012).
Campbell, N J M, *Battlecruisers* (Warship Special 1) (Conway Maritime Press, 1978).
Campbell, N J M, *Jutland: An Analysis of the Fighting* (Conway Maritime Press, 1986).
Corbett, Sir J S, *Naval Operations* Vols I–III (Longmans, 1920-23).
D'Eyncourt, Sir E H W T, *A Shipbuilder's Yarn* (Hutchinson, undated c1947).
Fisher, Admiral of the Fleet Lord, *Memories* (Hodder and Stoughton, 1919).
Fisher, Admiral of the Fleet Lord, *Records* (Hodder and Stoughton, 1919).
Henderson, W H (ed), *The Naval Review Vol V* (The Naval Society, c1920).
Jose, A W, *Official History of Australia in the War of 1914–18*, Vol IX: *The Royal Australian Navy* (Angus and Robinson, 1928).
Kemp, Lt-Com P K (ed), *The Papers of Admiral Sir John Fisher*, 2 vols (The Navy Records Society, 1960 & 1964).
Mackay, R F, *Fisher of Kilverstone* (Clarendon Press, 1973).
Marder, A J, *The Anatomy of British Sea Power* (Frank Cass, 1964 [originally published 1940]).
–, *Fear God and Dread Nought*, Vol 1 and 2 Jonathan Cape, 1952 and 1956).
–, *From the Dreadnought to Scapa Flow*, 5 vols (Oxford University Press, 1961–70; reprinted Seaforth Publishing, 2013–14).
The Naval Annual, various editions 1900–1914 (Griffin, 1900–1914).
Northcott, Maurice, *Ensign Special: Hood – Design and Construction* (Bivouac Books, 1975).
Northcott, Maurice, *Ensign 8: Renown and Repulse* (Battle of Britain Prints International Ltd, 1978).
Parkes, Dr Oscar, *British Battleships* (Seeley Service, 1966).
Patterson, A T (ed), *The Jellicoe Papers*, 2 vols (The Navy Records Society, 1966 & 1968).
Ranft, B (ed), *The Beatty Papers*, Vol 1: 1902–1918 (The Navy Records Society, 1989).
Raven, A and Roberts, J, *British Battleships of World War Two* (Arms and Armour Press, 1976).
Richardson, Alex, 'The Evolution of the Parsons Steam Turbine', *Engineering* (1911).
Ropp, Theodore (ed S Roberts), *The Development of a Modern Navy: French Naval Policy 1871-1904* (Naval Institute Press, 1987).
Sumida, Jon Tetsuro, *In Defence of Naval Supremacy: Finance, Technology and British Naval Policy, 1889–1914* (Unwin Hyman 1989).
Tupper, Admiral Sir R, *Reminiscences* (Jarrolds, undated c1923).
Usborne, Vice Admiral C V, *Blast and Counterblast* (Murray, 1935).

Unpublished
Extracts from Confidential Papers. Mediterranean Fleet 1899–1902 (Admiralty).
Manual of Gunnery for HM Fleet, Vol I, 1915 (Admiralty).
Addenda to Manual of Hydraulics – 12in BL Mountings B VIII (Vickers) 1907 (Admiralty).

Ship's Covers (held by National Maritime Museum)
Invincible class, ADM138/2 84 and 285.
Bellerophon class, ADM138/250 and 251.
Battlecruiser 'E' and Battleship 'F', ADM138/3 19.
St Vincent class, ADM138/265.
Indefatigable class, ADM138/324 and 325.
Neptune, ADM13 8/2 64.
Hercules and *Colossus*, ADM138/320.
Orion class, ADM138/346 and 347.
Lion and *Princess Royal*, ADM138/348 and 349.
King George V class, ADM138/338 and 339.
Queen Mary, ADM138/378.
Tiger, ADM138/420.
Queen Elizabeth class, ADM138/340 and 341.
Royal Sovereign class, ADM138/417 and 418.
Renown, *Repulse* and *Resistance* [battleships 1914–15 Prog], ADM138/416.
Renown and *Repulse* [battlecruisers], ADM138/463 and 464.
Courageous class, ADM138/453 and 454.
Hood class, ADM138/449-452. 'G3' battlecruisers, ADM138/623 and 624.

The National Archives, Kew. (Formerly Public Record Office). (Admiralty Documents)
Notes on Tactical Exercises – ADM1/7597.
Effect on Gunnery Technique of New Developments in Fleet Tactics, 1910 – ADM1/8051.
Design of 12in A* gun – ADM1/8064.
Changes to Battle Practice Regulations – ADM1/8065.
Battlecruiser Design, 1916 – ADM1/9209.
Hood class, armour, 1916 – ADM1/9210.
HM Ships, Designs, 1909 – ADM116/1013A.
Report of Fire Control Committee, 1921 – ADM116/2068.
Protection of Magazines – ADM116/2348.
Armaments of HM Ships, Improvements – ADM116/4041.
Pamphlet on the Use of the Dreyer Fire Table – ADM137/466.
Reports of Post Jutland Committees – ADM137/2028.
Various reports on Dogger Bank and Jutland – ADM137/2134.
Addenda to Hydraulic Manual, 13.5in BL Mountings MkII and II* – ADM186/190.
Progress in Gunnery Material, 1920 – ADM186/244.
Progress in Naval Gunnery 1914–18 – ADM186/238.
Steamships of England – ADM186/837.
Armaments of HM Ships – ADM1 86/865.
Principle Questions dealt with by DNO, 1900–1911 – ADM256/36-44.
Director Handbook, 1917 – ADM 186/227.
Battlecruiser Ship's Logs – ADM 53.

Admiralty Library.
Fire Control in H.M. Ships. Technical History and Index, TH23 (Admiralty, 1919).
Handbook of Captain F C Dreyer's Fire Control Tables (Admiralty, 1918).

Notes

Origins

1. *A Naval Scrap Book*, p255. Bacon expanded these comments in *From 1900 Onward*, p24: 'He was a living winnowing machine. He welcomed suggestions from all who possessed ideas. These he assimilated, separating the wheat from the chaff. The majority of our Admirals never consulted any officer under the rank of Post Captain; and few even unbent to this extent. Fisher was just the opposite; rank and age to him had no meaning so far as gathering information was concerned. All grist was welcome at his mill. Moreover, he always gave full credit to those who helped him; he never pretended that all his schemes originated in his own brain; he was most magnanimous in acknowledging assistance.'
2. *Extracts from Confidential Papers, Mediterranean Fleet 1899–1902* {hereafter cited as *Med Papers*}, pp75–6. The quoted passage was written in the summer of 1902 and was to reappear in modified or shortened form in various papers, including *Naval Necessities* and in the preliminary reports of the Committee of Designs of 1905. Fisher was advancing similar arguments at least as early as 1900.
3. Fisher to Lord Selborne, *Fear God and Dread Nought*, Vol 1, pp177–8.
4. These French battleships were the *République* class (two ships) and *Liberté* class (four ships) laid down in 1901–3 as part of the fleet expansion programme of 1900.
5. *Med Papers*, pp10–11.
6. A design for a high-velocity 10in/50cal gun was called for by the Admiralty in 1901 and a design by the EOC was recommended by the Ordnance Committee. It was eventually approved by the Board of Admiralty but none were ever ordered. This may have been at Fisher's suggestion, although there is no documentary evidence to support the idea. However, Fisher's close ties with Sir Andrew Noble had certainly made him aware of its existence as he referred on several occasions to the 10in gun that was available from Armstrong's.
7. *The Development of a Modern Navy*, p301.
8. *Med Papers*, p31.
9. Ibid, p3. The reference to '3000 yards if pursuing' relates to the combined closing speeds of the torpedo and target.
10. *A Naval Scrap-Book*, pp241–4 and *From 1900 Onward*, pp31–2. Bacon does not actually give a date but this was during his time as Commander of the *Empress of India* in the Mediterranean Fleet, which he left on promotion to Captain in June 1900. Bacon claims he proved his point several times on the tactical board without fail.
11. *Med Papers*, p90.
12. The US Navy had recent experience of naval combat as a result of the Spanish–American War of 1898. Following upon this conflict US design policy changed from one of providing a fleet for the defence of the American coast to one of building a blue-water navy. In providing the larger, more seaworthy battleships required for this change they followed their standard pattern of heavy secondary batteries and heavy armour.
13. Although originally intended for the 1903–4 Programme the *Lord Nelson* and *Agamemnon* were delayed for a year and were not laid down until 1905.
14. These were the *Connecticut* class (16,000 tons load, 17,600 tons deep, 4 x 12in, 8 x 5in, 12 x 7in guns, 11in belt armour, 18kts) and the *Tennessee* class (14,500 tons load, 15,700 tons deep, 4 x 10in, 16 x 6in guns, 5in belt, 22kts). Both designs were approved in December 1901 and authorised by Congress in July 1902. The first pair of each class was laid down in 1903 and completed in 1906.
15. *Tactical Value of Speed, as Compared with Extra Armour and Guns, for a Battleship in a Decisive Battle*, ADM1/7597. Although written in February the printed version of this report did not appear until May 1902. (It is worth noting that Bacon was on the War Course in the previous year.)
16. Ibid. Custance did not care for Fisher or his proposals and was to become a leading member of the group opposed to Fisher's reforms. Fortunately for Fisher, Custance's successor was Prince Louis of Battenberg, another of Fisher's close associates, who took over as DNI in November 1902.
17. *Notes by Captain H J May, of Tactical Exercises and Problems carried out at the Royal Naval College, Greenwich*, ADM1/7597.
18. Bacon, *Life of Lord Fisher*, Vol 1, p248.
19. The other members of this group eventually included Captains Jellicoe, Madden and Jackson, Commander W Henderson and A Gracie. Fisher referred to this unofficial committee collectively as 'the seven brains'.
20. *Life of Lord Fisher*, Vol 1, p256.
21. The full membership of the Committee was: *Naval:* Rear Admiral Prince Louis of Battenberg (DNI); Engineer Rear Admiral Sir John Durston (E-in-C); Rear Admiral Alfred L Winsloe (Commander of Torpedo and Submarine Craft Flotillas); Captain Henry B Jackson (about to become Third Sea Lord and Controller); Captain John R Jellicoe (about to become DNO); Captain Charles E Madden (about to become Naval Assistant to the Controller); Captain Reginald H S Bacon (Naval Assistant to First Sea Lord). *Civilian*: Phillip Watts (DNC); Lord Kelvin (physicist and mathematician); Professor J H Biles (Professor of Naval Architecture, Glasgow University); Sir John Thornycroft (Thornycroft Shipbuilding Co); Alexander Gracie (Fairfield Shipbuilding Co); R E Froude (Superintendent of the Admiralty Experiment Works, Haslar); W H Gard (Chief Constructor Portsmouth Dockyard and about to become Assistant DNC). In addition Commander Wilfred Henderson served as secretary and Assistant Constructor E H Mitchell as assistant secretary.
22. These details came from the Committee's First Progress Report, (*Fisher Papers*, Vol 1, p215) of February 1905 but there is evidence that these had been modified slightly from their original form as the stated 25kt speed was in fact set at 25.5kt when the Committee first sat.
23. In many respects these conclusions could be contested but to go into this adequately would occupy too much space. See D K Brown RCNC, 'The Russo-Japanese War: Technical lessons as perceived by the Royal Navy', *Warship 1996* (London 1996), p66.
24. *Life of Lord Fisher*, Vol 1, p251.
25. Given the lateness of the decision to fit the armoured cruiser with 12in guns it seems likely that it was not considered worthwhile for Gard to re-work his 9.2in gun design. Unfortunately little is known of what occurred in the development of the designs during October–December 1904. In particular, Fisher originally limited both the battleship and armoured cruiser to 16,000 tons but with one exception (armoured cruiser design 'C' which only had six 12in guns) all those examined by the Committee exceeded this rather optimistic figure – in the case of some of the battleship designs by a considerable margin.
26. *Invincible* class, Ship's Cover (ADM138/284).

Design and Construction 1905–14

1. Machinery weight had increased to 3430 tons and hull weight to 6225 tons. At the same time general equipment reduced to 665 tons and armour to 3360 tons.
2. The class name should be *Indomitable* (the first to be launched and completed), which was that normally used at the time, but I have followed the modern convention of using *Invincible.*
3. It is not unusual for sketch designs to be missing from a sequence. It does not necessarily follow that these missing designs were submitted to the Board for examination. Designs could be rejected by the DNC or the Controller before reaching higher levels
4. Prof J T Sumida, *In Defence of Naval Supremacy*, p60.
5. Note that 200ft is insufficient to cover more than the engine rooms, midships magazines and some of the boiler rooms.
6. The sketch designs for the battleship of the 1907–8 Programme were produced in parallel with those for the battlecruiser. The design approved in December ('F') was identical in layout to design 'E' but employed triple 12in/50cal mountings in the wing positions.
7. A revised list of weights was produced for design 'E' on 5 June 1907 in which the displacement had increased to 22,000 tons (general equipment 720 tons, armament 2960 tons, machinery 4190 tons, coal 1000 tons, armour 5470 tons, hull 7560 tons, margin 100 tons). As late as April 1908, R E Froude, Superintendent of the AEW, was asking if further experiments were required for designs 'E' and 'E*' (the latter either a further modification of the design or a variation on hull form) – the answer was no.
8. Mackay, *Fisher of Kilverstone*, p386.
9. Marder, *Fear God and Dread Nought*, Vol 2, p195.
10. Ibid, p229. Cruiser 'H' was the German battlecruiser *Goeben* of the 1909 Programme. Her sister ship, *Moltke*, was cruiser 'G', *Von Der Tann* was 'F' and *Blücher* was 'E'. The designations are those given to the ships by the Germans before they were named.
11. Ibid, p239.
12. Board Minutes of 12 May 1909 (ADM167/43). The German ships (the *Kaiser* class) were 31,000shp ships but their designed speed was only 21kts. No doubt Fisher would have been more upset if he had known that the German ships were of practically the same displacement as the 23kt design, and some 2000 tons more than that chosen for the *Orions*.
13. *Lion* class, Ship's Cover (ADM138/348).
14. Ibid.
15. *Tiger*, Ship's Cover (ADM138/420).
16. W S Churchill, *The World Crisis 1911–18* (1930).
17. *Tiger*, Ship's Cover (ADM138/420).

Battlecruiser Revival

1. Marder, *Fear God and Dread Nought Vol 2*, p451.
2. The full 1914–15 battleship programme consisted of three *Royal Sovereign* class ships – *Resistance*, *Renown* and *Repulse* – and one *Queen Elizabeth* class ship, the *Agincourt*. Two, *Resistance* and *Agincourt*, were to have been built at Devonport and Portsmouth Dockyards respectively. The dockyard ships were cancelled on 26 August 1914 and the work on the two contract ships was suspended on the same day. The re-allocation of the twin 15in gun turrets from the contract ships proved somewhat involved. The eight turrets under construction were the slightly modified MkI* as opposed to the MkI of earlier ships. In early 1915 three each were earmarked for the *Renown* and *Repulse* and one each to *Courageous* and *Glorious*, leaving a shortfall of two turrets for the latter pair. There were also two more required for the monitors *Marshal Ney* and *Marshal Soult*. The deficit was covered by an order for four twin MkI* in March 1915 (two to Armstrong and two to Vickers). However, the necessity to give construction priority to the new ships soon generated changes in the allocation of the turrets being manufactured by Armstrong. Two of the MkI* turrets intended for *Repulse* were re-allocated to *Courageous* and replaced with two MkI turrets from the battleship *Royal Oak*. The *Royal Oak* outfit was restored with two turrets from her sister *Resolution* which in turn received the two MkI* turrets ordered from Armstrong in March 1915. The single MkI* turret originally allocated to *Courageous* was transferred to the monitor *Erebus*. The *Glorious* was completed with the two MkI* turrets ordered from Vickers in March 1915 – the mountings of the single MkI* turret (under manufacture by the Coventry Ordnance Works) originally allocated to her being completed as reserves. Oddly, *Marshal Ney* and *Marshal Soult* were allocated MkI mountings (manufactured by Vickers) which had registered numbers implying new construction (*ie* the numbers post-date those already under construction for the 1913–14 Programme battleships and their reserves). However, given that they were required to complete within a year it would be surprising if they were not actually built utilising a substantial amount of the material transferred from the earlier orders for MkI mountings, regardless of the registered number (Vickers also had the orders for the eight turrets of the battleships *Revenge* and *Ramillies*). In addition 'Alteration in the armament of H.M. Ships During the War' (Vol 4 of 'The Technical History and Index') states that the mounting in *Erebus* was taken from the 'alternative armament which had been ordered for *Furious*'. This refers to a possible substitution of two 15in for the single 18in in her turrets if the latter gun proved unsatisfactory. However, there appears to be no evidence to support this ever being done, given that all the registered numbers for the 15in mountings, including reserves, can be accounted for without the inclusion of *Furious*. However, since *Marshal Ney* and *Marshal Soult* were actually supplied with MkI mountings it may have been originally intended to employ two of the MkI* mountings ordered in March 1915, this subsequently being overtaken by the general re-allocations mentioned above. It should be added that intentions with regard to re-allocations can often confuse the actual sequence of events. The final dispositions of the mountings as indicated above are those of the completed ships. It should be noted that the registered number of the 'mounting' applied to the individual gun mountings (two per turret).
3. It is probable that the change from two to three twin 15in turrets resulted from Fisher fully utilising all six of the turrets he intended to employ in three ships following the Cabinet decision to approve only two ships.
4. *The Jellicoe Papers*, p115.
5. D'Eyncourt, *A Shipbuilder's Yarn*, pp69–70.
6. Ibid, pp65–6.
7. Fisher, *Records*, pp208–9.

Machinery

1. Parsons had begun developing his turbine design for marine use in 1891 and three years later founded the Marine Steam Turbine Co. He built the *Turbinia*, a 44-ton steel launch that eventually achieved 34.5kts at full power. It was demonstrated (with permission) at Queen Victoria's Jubilee Fleet Review at Spithead in 1897 and made a considerable impression. The Admiralty ordered a turbine driven destroyer, the *Viper*, in the following year and also purchased a private venture turbine destroyer under construction by Armstrong Whitworth (*Cobra*) but both vessels were lost in 1901 before their machinery could be fully evaluated. In 1902 the Admiralty decided that the destroyer *Eden* of the 'River' class and the Third Class cruiser *Amethyst* of the 'Gem' class should be constructed with turbine machinery for comparative trials against their

sister ships. The trials with *Eden* began in early 1904 but *Amethyst* was not ready until after the Committee on Design had begun its deliberations. The only other turbine warship available to the Admiralty was the destroyer *Velox* ordered from Parsons in 1902 and completed in 1904. There were also some small turbine-driven passenger ferries in existence and by 1904 plans were in train for the construction of turbine-driven ocean liners.

2. The weights given are for the machinery without engineer's stores. The weights for the final version of sketch design 'E' with reciprocating engines were adjusted upward by Whiting at the end of January to 3800 tons for machinery and 6300 tons for the hull, giving a total load displacement of 17,850 tons. On this basis the overall saving would have been 600 tons. The weight anticipated in the original request for a turbine installation design (28 December 1904) was 2300 tons!

3. Froude's conclusions were reported to the Committee in an interim report on 21 January and a final report on 27 January. The most important was that power was independent of propeller size and increased proportionally with the speed. If, however, the propeller ran fast enough to draw in air from the surface it would begin to race and lose its efficiency so its depth of immersion was important.

4. *Indefatigable*, Ship's Cover (ADM138/324).

5. It should be emphasised that comparison on the basis of boiler room length, while giving a valid overall picture, is simplistic. The overall balance of a design is affected by a number of factors and all savings in weight tend to multiply in their effects on other areas of the design. There are also other factors, like the broader beam of German ships, which would have required a relatively higher machinery power than an equivalent British ship for the same speed and hence greater weight, which again will have a multiplying effect on other areas of the design. A full comparison is impossible without detailed particulars. A more valid idea can be gained from the comparison of those British ships with large-tube and small-tube boilers, although again this is not simple as the latter vessels also had geared turbines, which effected the boiler power required.

6. *Hood*, Ship's Cover (ADM138/449).

7. The propeller coefficient was a measure of the difference between a 'perfect' performance and that actually achieved. For example, if a propeller had a pitch of 10ft then ideally it would move the ship 10ft for one revolution. There is, however, a high level of slippage and if the actual movement was 5ft the propeller coefficient would be 50 per cent.

8. *Lion* class, Ship's Cover (ADM138/349).

9. Ibid.

Armament

1. Principal Questions dealt with by DNO, 1907. ADM256/43.

2. Admiral Sir Reginald Tupper, *Reminiscences*, p184.

3. I originally thought that the modified shell handling arrangements was the reason for the addition of the star to the mark number. However, *Royal Oak* also had this modification in all four of her turrets as did 'A' and 'B' turrets of *Repulse* and all these were designated as MkI. In addition, both the MkI turrets in *Repulse* had the curved gunhouse shield, while the two MkI* turrets in *Resolution* had the faceted form. No solution to this anomaly has come to light.

4. *Lion* and *Princess Royal*, Ships' Cover (ADM138/349).

5. Pollen also produced a plotter for use in conjunction with the Argo Clock but this was a separate item and not an 'integral' part of the clock. The battleship *Orion* was the only ship of the trial group to install the Argo rate-plotter as well as the Argo Clock, these two, plus a further five Argo Clocks and forty-five stabilised (for bearing) rangefinder mountings being the only items supplied by the Argo Company to be adopted by the service.

6. To be fair it has to be pointed out that, subsequent to the Admiralty trial, Pollen introduced the more advanced Argo Clock MkV with a gyro compass input. However, in the next version of the Dreyer Table electric motors set the clock rates automatically – at this point (1914) both these versions of the Argo Clock and Dreyer Table ran automatically.

7. The MkII Table in *Hercules* was removed in the latter half of 1916 and replaced with a MkI Table. The MkII designation was then re-allocated to the Argo Clock/ Dreyer Plotter combination – by then only applicable to battleships *Centurion*, *Ajax* and *Conqueror* since the *Queen Mary* was lost at Jutland and the only other ship so fitted (*Audacious*) was lost in 1914. Note that *Orion* also used the MkIII* designation for her plotter but with the qualification 'improvised'. She later adopted the MkII designation like the other ships with Argo Clocks but it is unclear if her installation remained as first fitted or if her plotter had been replaced with the Dreyer version. The MkIII* designation previously applied to the Dreyer Plotter was later employed for the modified MkIII tables fitted in the *Carlisle* class and Repeat 'D' class light cruisers. There is no record of any Table being fitted in *Indomitable*, she being missing from all the available lists up to and including that in the 1918 Dreyer Table Handbook. There is no mention of the 'Local Turret Table' in *Queen Mary* in any 1916 list and it therefore seems likely that this equipment was either removed from that ship or, being the prototype and only fitted in one turret, was not considered worthy of mention. (It was of different design to those installed in later ships.) Note that the April 1916 list states that it applies to ships for which Dreyer Tables are 'installed or on order'. While it seems likely that the latter qualification applies to a number of those ships still under construction, it is also possible that it applies to some of the MkI tables – in particular that of *Invincible*.
Primary sources: lists in AWO/972 of March 1914 (TNA, ADM182/5), Pamphlet on the Use of the Dreyer Fire Control Table, April 1916 (TNA, ADM137/466) and CB1456, Handbook of Captain F C Dreyer's Fire Control Tables, 1918 (Admiralty Library).

8. This seems to have been initiated by *Lion's* Flag Captain (Chatfield) who made this and other observations in his post action report (*Beatty Papers*, p232). It appears in similar form in Grand Fleet Gunnery and Torpedo Order No34 of Sep 1915 (ADM137/2006) which states that '..."overs" are entirely wasted' but does not mention 'long range' or Chatfield's suggestion of creeping up to the target with small 'ups', something that was regarded as bad practice pre-war.

9. ADM137/2134.

10. Ibid. No evidence has yet come to light to prove that the German Navy did employ a ladder system at this time. In fact most available evidence appears to show that the German system was much the same as the British bracket system. On the other hand Lt Com Smith's observations appear to support the idea that they did (three rapid salvoes spread for range does not accord with rapid fire which would not be spread for range – at least not beyond any correction for inclination). Unfortunately, Smith did not make clear if this was a single or multiple observation. It is of course possible that he was misreading what was actually occurring – perhaps, for example, the fall of shot from more than one ship or the occasional use by the German squadron of their secondary 5.9in guns at the same time as the main armament. It is also possible that the Imperial Navy allowed some latitude in the methods adopted by their gunnery officers and one ship at least was attempting to employ a form of ladder. An example that the systems employed by the German Navy were not entirely rigid is provided by *Lützow*, which at Jutland fired alternate salvos from her forward and after turrets rather than from the left and right guns like the other ships in her squadron.

11. *The Naval Review*, Vol V, pp158–9.

12. *Queen Mary*, Ship's Cover (ADM138/378).

13. These sixteen 5.5in guns and mountings are something of a mystery. They were ordered by Greece but were not those of *Birkenhead* and *Chester* and were not numbered among the twenty-two for the battleships. They could of course have been spares, although the number seems excessive; they may have been intended for other ships, although none which specified this gun calibre, other than the three previously mentioned, are known to have been ordered; or they may have been intended for shore fortifications.

Armour

1. The curve of the shell from the point to the full diameter measured in multiples of the shell's calibre. Thus a 4crh 12in shell had a radius of curvature of 48in.

2. *Fisher Papers*, Vol 1, p220.

Conclusion

1. Admiral Sir Reginald Tupper, *Reminiscences*, p186.

2. *St Vincent* class, Ship's Cover (ADM138/265).

3. ADM137/2134.

4. *The Beatty Papers*, p354.

Index

Page references in italics denote photographs/diagrams

Agamemnon 17
Anson 58, 60-1
APC (capped armour-piercing) shells 100, 101-3
Argo Clock 93
armament
    9.2in guns 19, 28, 114
    10in guns 12-13, 18-19
    12in guns 12-13, 18-19, 21, 26-7, 80-1, 82, 84-5, 95, 114
    13.5in guns 27, 32, 33, 36, 85-8, 85-9, 95, 114
    15in guns 59, 89-90, 89-90
    and armoured cruisers 14-17
    ATB guns 18, 19, 97-9
    blast 21, 91
    and Committee on Designs 19-21, 25, 91
    director firing systems 91, 92, 93-4
    fire control 13, 18, 34, 37, 52, 57, 91-7
    German comparisons 114, 120-1
    high-velocity guns 82, 89, 97, 100
    hydraulic power 84, 85, 90-1
    long-range gunnery 8-9, 13, 16, 17, 21, 82, 95, 97
    MD (Modified) cordite 82
    quick-firing guns 12-13, 14, 16, 18
    range-finding 94-7
    and Senior Officers' War Course 17, 18
    torpedoes 7, 13, 36, 48, 61, 92, 97
    uniform-calibre armament 18, 26
    see also under individual ships and classes
armour 100-109
    and armoured cruisers 15-16, 114
    and Committee on Designs 22-3, 25
    German comparisons 114-15, 120-1
    magazine protection 22, 59, 61, 109-10, 115-19, 120
    torpedo protection 13, 27, 53, 109-11
    turrets 109
    see also under individual ships and classes
armoured cruisers 7-8, 14-22, 24, 25, 26, 28, 37, 65-6, 114, 119, 121
ATB (anti-torpedo-boat) guns 18, 19, 97-9
Australia 30, 85, 104, 118
    armament 84, 85, 92, 93
    armour 104, 112
    design/construction 7, 29, 31, 41
    dimensions 43
    displacement 44
    machinery 72, 74, 78
    speed 78
    summary of service 123

Bacon, Admiral Sir Reginald 10, 13-14, 18, 19, 21, 86, 91, 101
Baltic Project 50-3
Battenberg, Admiral Prince Louis of 37, 46
Beatty, Admiral David 8, 9, 47, 57, 59-60, 96, 114
Bellerophon class 27
Beresford, Admiral Lord Charles 28
Birkenhead 99
Blücher 8, 8, 26, 32, 39, 114, 115
boilers 10, 21-2, 34, 36-8, 40, 56-7, 65, 68-70, 71, 74, 114, 115
Bridgeman, Admiral Sir Francis 37, 85
Briggs, Rear Admiral Charles 34-5, 37, 38, 75

Champion 68
Chatfield, Captain 9
Chester 99
Churchill, Winston 37, 46-8, 51
Cochrane 15

Colossus 32, 34, 88, 115, 116
Committee on Designs 19-23, 24-5, 26, 65, 66, 91, 109-10
Courageous 51, 90, 95, 96, 110
    armament 54, 90, 93, 95, 96
    armour 54, 110
    design/construction 8, 47, 50, 53-5
    dimensions 54, 63
    displacement 54, 64
    machinery 70, 77, 79
    speed 54, 77, 79
    summary of service 124
Courageous class 63, 74, 83, 113
CPC (common pointed capped) shells 101, 102
Cressy class 14
Croxford, C H 21-2
CT (conning tower) 91-2, 94
Custance, Captain R 17-18

D'Eyncourt, Sir Eustace T 46, 47-8, 51-2, 53, 69-70
Dardanelles Campaign 51
Davis, W T 73, 75
Derfflinger 8-9, 39, 116, 117, 120
Devonshire class 14
Dewar, Vice Admiral K G B 10
director firing systems 91, 92, 93-4
Dogger Bank, Battle of (1915) 8-9, 95-7, 114, 115, 117, 118
Drake class 14
Dreadnought 10, 19, 21, 25, 26, 31, 34, 47, 48, 70, 84
'Dreadnought Revolution' 7, 65
Dreyer Table 93
Dreyer, Admiral F C 93
Duff, Captain, A A M 34
Duke of Edinburgh class 15
Durston, J 65-6

Egerton, Vice Admiral Sir G le C 37
Essex 14

Falkland Islands, Battle of (1914) 8, 47, 119
fire control 13, 18, 34, 37, 52, 57, 82, 86, 91-7, 120
Fisher, Admiral Sir John 7-9
    and armament 12-17, 18-19, 32, 33, 82, 98, 99
    and Baltic Project 50-3
    and Committee on Designs 19, 26, 109-10
    emphasis on speed 8, 10, 11-12, 13, 15-17, 18, 31, 32, 33, 37, 46, 47, 51-2, 114
    and reform of Royal Navy 10
    and Senior Officers' War Course 18
    and turbines 10, 65
    verdict on battlecruiser concept 114, 119-20
    war construction programme 46-9, 51-4
    warship design/construction 26, 28-9, 31-3, 37, 40
    warship origins/design 10-17, 18-19
Froude, R E 19
Furious 53, 54, 55
    armament 52, 54, 83, 93, 99
    armour 54, 113
    design/construction 50, 52-3, 54
    dimensions 54, 63
    displacement 53, 54, 64
    machinery 68, 74, 77
    speed 54, 77
    summary of service 124

Gard, Constructor W H 10, 16, 18-19, 21
Glorious 52
    armament 90, 93

    armour 54
    design/construction 47, 50, 53-5
    dimensions 63
    displacement 54, 64
    machinery 77, 79
    speed 54, 77, 79
    summary of service 124
Gneisenau 8
Goeben 39, 69

Harvey, Major 116-17
HE (high explosive) shells 101, 102-3
Hercules 32, 34, 88, 93
Hero 91
Hindenburg 39, 60
Hipper, Admiral 9
Hood 58, 60, 61, 77, 90, 108, 111
    armament 59, 61, 82, 83, 90, 91, 94, 97, 99
    armour 58, 59-60, 61-2, 108, 109, 111, 113
    design/construction 8, 56-62
    dimensions 63
    displacement 58-9, 61, 64
    machinery 68-9, 70, 74, 77, 79
    speed 59, 62, 77, 79
Hood, Admiral H L A 9
Howe 58, 60-1
hydraulic power 84, 85, 90-1

Indefatigable 28, 103
    armament 84, 91-2, 97
    armour 103-4, 112, 116
    design/construction 7, 29, 31, 41-2
    dimensions 43
    displacement 44
    in action 9, 116
    machinery 69, 72, 74, 78
    speed 72, 78
    summary of service 122-3
Indefatigable class
    armament 28, 29, 82, 83, 84, 98
    armour 29, 31
    design/construction 7, 28-9, 31
    dimensions 29, 43
    displacement 29, 31
    machinery 29, 31, 67, 70
Indomitable 7, 23, 24, 72, 114
    armament 84, 94
    design/construction 7, 25, 41
    dimensions 43
    displacement 44
    in action 8, 9
    machinery 69, 70, 78
    speed 70, 78
    summary of service 122
Inflexible 23, 25, 28, 82, 98, 99
    armament 84, 93, 94, 98, 99
    design/construction 7, 25, 41
    dimensions 43
    displacement 44
    in action 8, 9
    machinery 78
    speed 78
    summary of service 122
Invincible 23, 27, 66-7
    armament 84-5, 91, 93, 94, 95
    armour 103, 117
    design/construction 7, 41-2
    dimensions 43
    displacement 44
    in action 8, 9, 117
    machinery 66-7, 74, 78
    speed 78
    summary of service 122
Invincible class 100
    armament 24, 25-6, 27, 83, 91-2, 97-8

    armour 24, 27, 100-101, 103, 104, 110, 112, 116
    and Committee on Designs 20, 21
    design/construction 7, 10, 24, 25-7
    dimensions 24, 43
    displacement 24, 44
    machinery 24, 67, 70, 74
    speed 70
Iron Duke 95
Iron Duke class 53

Jackson, Rear Admiral Henry 10, 27, 28
Jellicoe, Admiral Sir John 8, 10, 33, 34, 47, 51, 56-7, 58, 59, 66, 69, 84, 85-6, 101, 116
Jutland, Battle of (1916) 9, 58, 59, 62, 94-6, 114, 115, 116-17, 118, 119

Kelvin, Lord 19, 26

'ladder' system 95, 96
Lion 9, 32, 34, 65, 71, 73, 87, 105, 106, 117, 120
    armament 87, 88-9, 91, 92-3, 97, 98
    armour 103-4, 105, 106, 116-17, 120
    design/construction 7, 32, 34-5, 41-2
    dimensions 43
    displacement 44
    in action 8-9, 96, 97, 115, 116-17
    machinery 67, 69, 71, 73, 74, 75, 78
    speed 73, 75, 78
    summary of service 123
Lion class
    armament 32, 33, 83
    armour 33, 34, 112
    design/construction 31-5
    dimensions 33, 43
    displacement 33, 34, 44
    machinery 33, 70, 74
    speed 33
long-range gunnery 8-9, 13, 16, 17, 21, 82, 95, 97
Lord Nelson 17, 18
Lord Nelson class 84
Lützow 9, 39, 116, 117, 120
Lyddite shells 101-2

machinery
    boilers 10, 21-2, 34, 36-8, 40, 56-7, 65, 68-70, 71, 74, 114, 115
    and Committee on Designs 19-22, 25, 65, 66
    reciprocating engines 20-2, 65-6
    and speed 65-7, 68, 70, 72-5, 76-9
    steam trials 70, 72-3, 75-9
    turbines 10, 20-2, 25, 65-6, 67-9, 70, 74
    see also under individual ships and classes
Mackensen class 60
Madden, Captain Charles 10, 37, 66
magazine protection 22, 59, 61, 109-10, 115-19, 120
May, Admiral Sir W H 17, 28, 97
May, Captain H J 17, 18
McKenna, Lord 31-2, 37
Minotaur 19, 21
Minotaur class 15
Moltke 8, 9, 39, 39, 68, 69
Monmouth class 14
Moore, Rear Admiral A G H W 9, 75
MPI (mean point of impact) 95

Nelson 91
New Zealand 30, 70-1, 104
    armament 84, 92, 93, 96-7
    armour 104, 112
    design/construction 7, 29, 31, 41
    dimensions 43
    in action 8-9, 96-7

machinery 70-1, 72, 74, 78
speed 78
summary of service 123
Noble, Sir Andrew 10, 18, 109-10

Oram, H J 69-70, 75
Orion 32, 34
Orion class 32, 33

Pakenham, Rear Admiral 37, 96
Parsons, Sir Charles 22, 66
Perfection 16
Pollen, A H 93
Powerful 11
Prince of Wales 93
Princess Royal 9, 35, 40, 65, 71, 75, 88, 105, 115
    armament 88-9, 91, 92-3, 97, 98
    armour 105
    design/construction 7, 35, 41
    dimensions 43
    displacement 45
    in action 8, 9
    machinery 67, 71, 74, 75-6, 78
    speed 75-6, 78
    summary of service 123

QF (quick-firing) guns 12-13, 14, 16, 18
Queen Elizabeth class 40, 53, 59, 62, 67, 89
Queen Mary 36, 80-1, 86, 105, 108
    armament 35-6, 83, 86, 88-9, 91, 92-3, 97, 98

    armour 35-6, 103, 104, 105, 108, 112, 116
    design/construction 7, 35-6, 41-2
    dimensions 36, 43
    displacement 35-6, 45
    in action 9, 116
    machinery 36, 67, 70, 74, 79
    speed 76, 79
    summary of service 123

range-finding 94-7
reciprocating engines 20-2, 65-6
Renown 16, 46, 49, 50, 63, 76, 107, 121
    armament 16, 48, 90, 93
    armour 16, 48, 50, 53-4, 104, 107, 110, 111, 113
    design/construction 8, 46-50, 57, 62
    dimensions 48, 63
    displacement 16, 48, 49, 62, 64
    machinery 67, 68, 69, 70, 77, 79
    origins/design of 15, 16
    speed 16, 48, 49, 77, 79
    summary of service 124
Renown class 48, 63, 74, 83
Repulse 50, 89, 107
    armament 48, 89, 90, 93
    armour 48, 50, 53-4, 104, 107, 110, 111, 113
    design/construction 8, 46-50, 57, 62
    dimensions 48, 63
    displacement 48, 49, 62
    machinery 67, 68, 69, 70, 74, 77, 79

    speed 48, 49, 77, 79
    summary of service 124
'*Rhadamanthus*' 46, 47
Rodney 58, 60-1, 91
Royal Sovereign class 46, 47, 89

Scharnhorst 8
Selborne, Lord 17, 19, 26
Seydlitz 8-9, 39, 69, 116, 117, 120
Skate 97
Smith, Engineer Captain Edgar C 65
Smith, Lieutenant-Commander 96
speed 19, 21, 22-3, 26, 27
    Fisher's emphasis on 8, 10, 11-12, 13, 15-17, 18, 31, 32, 33, 37, 46, 47, 51-2, 114
    German comparisons 114
    and machinery 65-7, 68, 70, 72-3, 76-9
    and Senior Officers' War Course 17-18
    see also under individual ships and classes
steam trials 70, 72-3, 75-9
Superb 88
Swiftsure 12

Terrible 11
Tiger 9, 38, 65, 68, 92, 94, 102, 106, 109, 119
    armament 36-7, 40, 83, 88-9, 91, 92, 93-4, 97, 98
    armour 40, 102, 104, 106, 109, 110, 112-13
    design/construction 7, 36-8, 40, 41-2
    dimensions 43

    displacement 38, 45
    in action 8-9
    machinery 38, 67, 68, 70, 74, 76-7, 79
    speed 38, 40, 76, 79
    summary of service 123-4
torpedoes 7, 13, 36, 48, 61, 92, 97
    torpedo protection 13, 27, 53, 57, 59, 70, 97-9, 109-11
Triumph 12
TSs (transmitting stations) 91-2
Tupper, Admiral Reginald 84-5, 115
turbines 10, 20-2, 25, 65-6, 67-9, 70, 74
Tweedmouth, Lord 28, 31

Unapproachable 18-19
uniform-calibre armament 18, 26
Usborne, Vice Admiral C V 82
Vanguard 93
Von der Tann 9, 26, 29, 29, 39, 116

Warrior 18
Warrior class 15
Watts, Sir Philip 10, 15, 17, 18, 31, 36, 38, 65, 116
White, Sir William 14-15
Whiting, W H 21, 65-6
Willons, Private 117
Wilson, Admiral Sir A K 37
Winsloe, Rear Admiral A 28, 66